AFRICAN GROWTH AND OPPORTUNITY ACT: AN IMPLEMENTATION GUIDE

AFRICAN GROWTH AND OPPORTUNITY ACT: AN IMPLEMENTATION GUIDE

OFFICE OF THE UNITED STATES
TRADE REPRESENTATIVE

Nova Science Publishers, Inc.
New York

For permission to use material from this book please contact us:
Telephone 631-231-7269; Fax 631-231-8175
Web Site: http://www.novapublishers.com

Library of Congress Cataloging-in-Publication Data

African Growth and Opportunity Act : an implementation guide / Office of the United States Trade Representative.
p. cm.
Includes bibliographical references and index.
ISBN 13: 978-1-60021-389-2
ISBN 10: 1-60021-389-8 (alk. paper)
1. United States--Commerce--Africa, Sub-Saharan. 2. Africa, Sub-Saharan--Commerce--United States. 3. Foreign trade regulation--United States. 4. Foreign trade regulation--Africa, Sub-Saharan. 5. United States. African Growth and Opportunity Act. I. United States. Office of the U.S. Trade Representative.
HF3132.A37
382'.097306--dc22 2006024361

Published by Nova Science Publishers, Inc. ✣New York

CONTENTS

PREFACE

On May 18, 2000 President Clinton signed into law the historic Trade and Development Act of 2000, containing the African Growth and Opportunity Act (AGOA). The Act provides unprecedented opportunities and aims to promote increased trade and investment between the United States and sub-Saharan African countries by providing eligible African countries with unprecedented liberal access to the U.S. market. Essentially all products of these eligible countries will have quota free/duty free access to the almost 10 trillion dollar United States market. It also promotes economic development and reform in sub-Saharan Africa, moving across a wide range of industries, granting tangible benefits to entrepreneurs, farmers, and families. This development increases access and opportunities for U.S. investors and businesses in sub-Saharan Africa.

The African Growth and Opportunity Act offers a wide variety of benefits to businesses, workers, manufacturers, and farmers in eligible countries. It is important to remember that the Act can only offer opportunities. African countries are encouraged to seize the opportunities provided in the Act and to create enabling environments to strengthen prospects for expanded trade and investment. This new book focuses on the Act's trade preference benefits. The Guide is divided into 10 Chapters. Chapter 2 provides answers to frequently asked questions such as "how can I determine whether the products I manufacture and want to export could benefit from the Act?" Other chapters contain information on the specific trade benefits available and on the eligibility criteria that must be met for a country to receive these benefits. Chapter 8 provides a brief summary of other provisions of the Act and Chapter 10 provides a time line of key dates. Information on general U.S. agricultural market access is provided in Chapter 9.

Chapter 1

INTRODUCTION

On May 18, 2000 President Clinton signed into law the historic Trade and Development Act of 2000, containing the African Growth and Opportunity Act (AGOA). (The text of the Act is available at the AGOA website, www.agoa.gov and at the USTR website www.ustr.gov). The Act provides unprecedented opportunities and aims to:

- Promote increased trade and investment between the United States and sub-Saharan African countries by providing eligible African countries with unprecedented liberal access to the U.S. market. Essentially all products of these eligible countries will have quota free/duty free access to the almost 10 trillion dollar United States market.
- Promote economic development and reform in sub-Saharan Africa, moving across a wide range of industries, granting tangible benefits to entrepreneurs, farmers, and families.
- Promote increased access and opportunities for U.S. investors and businesses in sub-Saharan Africa.

The African Growth and Opportunity Act offers a wide variety of benefits to businesses, workers, manufacturers, and farmers in eligible countries. It is important to remember that the Act can only offer opportunities! African countries are encouraged to seize the opportunities provided in the Act and to create enabling environments to strengthen prospects for expanded trade and investment.

Although the Act provides a variety of benefits, this guide focuses on the Act's trade preference benefits. The Guide is divided into 10 Chapters. Chapter 2 provides answers to frequently asked questions such as "how can I determine whether the products I manufacture and want to export could benefit from the Act?" Other chapters contain information on the specific trade benefits available and on the eligibility criteria that must be met for a country to receive these benefits. Chapter 8 provides a brief summary of other provisions of the Act and Chapter 10 provides a time line of key dates. Information on general U.S. agricultural market access is provided in Chapter 9.

Chapter 2

SUMMARY OF THE AFRICAN GROWTH AND OPPORTUNITY ACT

The African Growth and Opportunity Act/Trade and Development Act of 2000 authorizes a new U.S. trade and investment policy toward Africa. It promotes increased trade and economic cooperation between the United States and eligible sub-Saharan African countries. This legislation represents a solid, meaningful and significant opportunity, which could result in billions of dollars in new trade and investment flows between the U.S. and Africa.

KEY ELEMENTS OF THE ACT AND BENEFITS FOR AFRICA

General Trade Benefits

The Act:

- Institutionalizes a process for strengthening U.S. relations with African countries and provides incentives for African countries to achieve political and economic reform and growth.
- Offers beneficiary sub-Saharan African countries duty-free and quota-free U.S. market access for essentially all products through the Generalized System of Preferences (GSP) program.
- Provides additional security for investors and traders in African countries by ensuring GSP benefits for eight years.
- Eliminates the GSP competitive need limitation for African countries.
- Establishes a U.S.-sub-Saharan Africa Trade and Economic Cooperation Forum to facilitate regular trade and investment policy discussions.
- Promotes the use of technical assistance to strengthen economic reforms and development, including assistance to strengthen relationships between U.S. firms and firms in sub-Saharan Africa.

Apparel and Textile Preferences

The Act:

- Lifts all existing quotas on textiles and apparel products from sub-Saharan Africa (within 30-days of a U.S. Government determination that Kenya and Mauritius have adopted effective visa systems).
- Extends duty/quota free U.S. market access for sub-Saharan African apparel made from yarns and fabrics not available in the United States.
- Extends duty/quota free treatment for apparel made in Africa from U.S. yarn and fabric and for knit-to-shape sweaters made in Africa from cashmere and some merino wools as well as apparel produced in Africa from silk, velvet, linen, and other fabrics not produced in commercial quantities in the United States.
- Extends duty free and quota free U.S. market access for apparel made in Africa with African/regional fabric and yarn. Such imports, however, are subject to a cap (limit) ranging from 1.5 to 3.5% of the multibillion dollar U.S. apparel import market over an 8 year period. African apparel imports made with African fabric/yarns currently total about $250 million. Normal MFN duties would be levied on apparel (regional fabric) imports over the cap.
- Provides an average 17.5% duty advantage on apparel imports in the U.S. market and promotes economic development and diversification in Africa's poorest countries through a special provision in the cap which allows African countries with an annual GNP of under $1,500 ("lesser developed beneficiary countries") to use third country fabric inputs for four years. This special investment incentive for the poorest African countries is aimed at providing a market stimulus to economic development for areas with little existing industry.

Chapter 3

FREQUENTLY-ASKED QUESTIONS

The following questions and answers are provided to briefly clarify some of the provisions of AGOA. More detailed descriptions of the law's provisions are provided in subsequent chapters of this guide.

What is an "Eligible Sub-Saharan African (SSA) Country"?

The eligibility requirements contained in the African Growth and Opportunity Act (AGOA) were developed in consultation with African countries. The criteria reflect an understanding that the trade benefits and market access accorded in the Act will only generate sustainable economic growth and development if countries have appropriate domestic policies. The criteria constitute "best practice" policies that will ultimately attract trade and investment and foster widely-shared prosperity. They include: establishment of market-based economies; development of political pluralism and the rule of law; elimination of barriers to U.S. trade and investment; protection of intellectual property; efforts to combat corruption; policies to reduce poverty and increase availability of health care and educational opportunities; protection of human rights and worker rights, and elimination of certain practices of child labor. AGOA states that eligible sub-Saharan African countries must implement their obligations to combat the worst forms of child labor. The phrases "eligible sub-Saharan African country" and "beneficiary sub-Saharan African country" are used in this Guide interchangeably.

The first list of eligible countries was published in the *Federal Register* on October 4, 2000 and is provided at Annex 1. A second list of additional countries may be published at the beginning of 2001.

What Products are Eligible for Duty-Free Treatment?

Essentially all products will be eligible, as long as they meet AGOA's rule of origin requirements and are imported directly from a beneficiary sub-Saharan African country. Exceptions include fabrics and yarns not imported as part of a finished apparel product, and products determined by the U.S. Government to be import sensitive. A listing of products currently eligible for GSP is provided at Annex 3. A listing of additional products that are potentially eligible for duty-free treatment under AGOA is provided at Annex 2. A final list of additional products that will be eligible for duty-free treatment under AGOA will be published in the *Federal Register* by the end of 2000 and will be available at the Internet web site www.agoa.gov. The African Growth and Opportunity Act also permits duty-free entry for certain apparel products. Further details on apparel benefits are provided in Chapter 5.

How do I Tell if the Products I Want to Export are Eligible for Duty-Free Access to the U.S. Market?

There are three basic means by which a product may have duty-free access to the U.S. market. For many products, the U.S. has already set the tariff at zero for all countries' exports of that product. In addition, many products are already eligible for duty-free treatment under the U.S. Generalized System of Preferences (GSP) Program. Under the African Growth and Opportunity Act, many more products will be eligible for duty-free access to the U.S., providing duty-free and quota-free U.S. market access for essentially all products from eligible sub-Saharan African countries.

The first step in determining the United States' tariff rate for a product is to determine what the U.S. Harmonized Tariff Schedule (HTSUS) number is for the product(s). An electronic version of the HTSUS is available on the Internet at http://www.usitc.gov/taffairs.htm. An alphabetized index and listing of articles, is located at the back of the HTSUS.

Once the product HTSUS number is known, you may determine the U.S. tariff rate by consulting the HTSUS (or the International Trade Commission's U.S. Tariff and Import Database (under the Links button of the www.agoa.gov Internet site). Alternatively, you may use this Guide to determine if your product is eligible for duty-free treatment under GSP (see Annex 3 which lists all GSP eligible products (for all GSP countries) and Annex 2 which includes within the list those products that are eligible for GSP only for countries that are GSP "least developed beneficiary countries") or is potentially eligible for duty-free treatment under the African Growth and Opportunity Act (see Annex 2 with a list of products that are potentially eligible for duty-free treatment under AGOA). A determination on what products will be eligible for duty-free treatment under AGOA is expected by the end of 2000. It is important to note that if a product is not listed as eligible for duty-free treatment under GSP or under AGOA it may be because the tariff is already zero for all countries.

In order to receive duty-free market access for a product under the GSP program or under AGOA, the product must be produced or manufactured in a GSP or AGOA beneficiary country and must meet the GSP or AGOA rules of origin requirements. A list of GSP beneficiary countries is provided at Annex 1. A list of designated sub-Saharan African beneficiary countries is provided in Annex 1.

What are the Main Benefits Available to Exporters from Eligible Sub-Saharan African Countries?

First, as detailed above, zero duties apply to U.S. imports of eligible products from eligible countries in sub-Saharan Africa. "Eligible products" are those currently receiving duty-free treatment under the U.S. GSP program, plus an expanded list of products (excluding textiles and apparel) not otherwise eligible for duty-free treatment under GSP. A detailed list of these products is found in Annex 3 of this Guide.

Second, a guarantee of GSP benefits for eligible sub-Saharan African countries through September 30, 2008 (the GSP program is scheduled to expire for non-sub-Saharan African countries on September 30, 2001 and must be renewed by Congress if duty-free treatment is to resume). In addition, the GSP program's "competitive needs" limitation which prohibits the importation of GSP-eligible products above a certain level is waived for eligible sub-Saharan countries under the AGOA.

Third, duty-free treatment for imports of sub-Saharan African apparel, some of which may be made with sub-Saharan African textiles and yarn. This benefit will give exporters in eligible Sub-Saharan Africa countries a decided advantage in exporting apparel to the United States. While sub-Saharan African apparel that meets AGOA's criteria will continue to be duty-free through September 30, 2008, U.S. imports of apparel from all other suppliers with which the United States does not have free trade agreements will continue to be assessed regular tariff duties, which average 17.5% of the value of the apparel product. However, apparel products made with sub-Saharan African fabrics or yarns or third-country fabrics or yarns may lose duty-free benefits if the U.S. Secretary of Commerce determines that imports into the United States of those products are "surging" -- in other words, being imported in such increased quantities as to cause the U.S. industry producing the same or a similar product serious damage or threat thereof.

Fourth, establishment of an U.S.-sub-Saharan Africa Trade and Economic Cooperation Forum which institutionalizes a Presidential and Cabinet-level dialogue between the U.S. and the countries of sub-Saharan Africa.

Fifth, expanded support from the Overseas Private Investment Corporation and the U.S. Export-Import Bank that will increase the interest of American exporters and investors in undertaking projects in sub-Saharan Africa.

Can a Country Lose AGOA Benefits?

Yes. The President must conduct an annual review of each sub-Saharan African country's progress towards meeting the AGOA eligibility criteria. The President must terminate the designation of any beneficiary sub-Saharan African country if he determines that the country is not making continual progress towards meeting the eligibility criteria.

What Specific Requirements Must Be Met to Import Merchandise under AGOA?

The imported merchandise must be eligible for AGOA benefits; produced in a designated beneficiary sub-Saharan Africa country; meet the value-added requirements for non-textile/apparel products, and the various specific requirements for different apparel products; be imported directly into the United States from a beneficiary sub-Saharan Africa country; be accompanied by import documentation that claims AGOA benefits on the appropriate shipping documents.

What are the Rule of Origin Requirements for Qualifying AGOA Apparel Products?

The rules vary with the product. The U.S. Customs Service has issued interim Customs Regulations on the African Growth and Opportunity Act. These interim regulations are available at www.agoa.gov. General information on apparel rules of origin is included at Annex 4. In general, apparel qualifying for duty-free benefits may be made with U.S. fabric in turn made with U.S. yarn, sub-Saharan African fabric in turn made with sub-Saharan African yarn (subject to quantitative limit) or, in the case of least developed sub- Saharan Africa countries, third-country fabric (subject to quantitative limits). Certain third country fabrics and yarns may also be used by sub-Saharan African apparel producers provided such fabrics are on a short supply list - maintained by the Department of Commerce (contained in Annex 5 to this Guide). Third-country yarn and fiber may also be used to produce cashmere or certain wool knit-to-shape sweaters.

What are the Rule of Origin Requirements for Other Products?

The item must be the growth, product, or manufacture of a beneficiary developing country and the sum of (a) the cost or value of materials produced in a one or more beneficiary countries plus (b) the direct cost of processing performed in those countries may not be less than 35 percent of the appraised value of the product when it enters the United States. Up to 15 percentage points of that 35 percent may be derived from U.S. parts or materials used to produce the product in a beneficiary sub-Saharan Africa country or countries for new products designated for GSP benefits for AGOA beneficiaries. Their products also enjoy cumulation benefits. Questions regarding rule of origin requirements for specific products and/or classification of products may be directed to the U.S. Customs Service by writing to: Director, National Commodity Specialist Division, U.S. Customs Service, 6 World Trade Center, New York, New York 10048.

What is Meant by the Requirement that the Article be "Imported Directly"?

The article must be shipped directly from the beneficiary country to the United States without passing through the territory of any other country. Or, if shipped through the territory of any other country, the merchandise must not have entered the commerce of that country while in route to the United States. In all cases, the invoices, bills of lading and other documents connected with the shipment must show that the United States is the final destination of the imported article. (See 19 CFR 10.175(d) for the U.S. Customs Service definition of "imported directly.")

How Can the Correct HTSUS Classification of a Product be Determined?

Questions about a specific product HTSUS number should be referred to the U.S. Customs Service by writing to: Director, National Commodity Specialist Division, U.S. Customs Service, 6 World Trade Center, New York, New York 10048. General information from U.S. Customs including information on classification and rules of origin can be found at www.customs.gov

Who Makes the Determinations Regarding AGOA Product and Country Eligibility?

The apparel and textile benefits provided under AGOA are generally specified in the African Growth and Opportunity Act. The GSP Subcommittee of the Trade Policy Staff Committee, chaired by the Office of the United States Trade Representative, reviews non-apparel/textile product coverage. All Executive Branch Agencies directly involved in trade participate in the inter-agency review of GSP eligibility modifications including expansion of GSP product coverage for eligible sub-Saharan African countries through AGOA. The U.S. Customs Service determines the classification of products and whether or not they meet the requirements specified in the Act.

Country eligibility decisions are made through an inter-agency process involving all relevant Executive Branch Agencies and chaired by the Office of the United States Trade Representative. Recommendations on product coverage and country eligibility are provided to the President whose final decisions are printed in the *Federal Register*.

How Can an Exporter in an AGOA Beneficiary Country Know the Value at Which the U.S. Customs Authorities Will Appraise an Article?

In most cases, U.S. Customs will appraise the merchandise at the transaction value, that is, the price actually paid or payable for the merchandise when sold for export to the United States. This value would include the following elements:

1. The packing costs incurred by the buyer
2. The selling commission incurred by the buyer
3. The value of any assistance provided to the producer free of charge by the buyer
4. The royalty or license fee that the buyer is required to pay as a condition of the sale
5. The proceeds accruing to the seller of any subsequent resale, disposal, or use of the imported merchandise

In general, shipping and other costs related to transporting the GSP articles from the port of export to the United States are included neither in the value of the article nor in the value-added calculation.

What Costs may be Included in the Direct Costs of Processing?

The direct costs of processing include all costs, whether directly incurred in, or those that can be reasonably allocated to the growth, production, manufacture, or assembly of the merchandise in question. These include the following:

- Actual labor costs involved in producing the goods, fringe benefits, and on-the-job training costs
- Engineering, supervisory, quality control, and similar personnel costs
- Dies, molds, and tooling costs, as well as depreciation on machinery and equipment
- Research, development, design, blueprints and engineering, and inspection and testing costs

What Costs may not be Included in the Direct Costs of Processing?

The costs that may not be included in the direct costs of processing are those that are not directly attributable to the merchandise being considered or are not "costs" of manufacturing. These costs include profit and general expenses and business overhead such as administrative salaries, casualty and liability insurance, advertising, and sales representative's salaries, commissions, or expenses.

What is an "Effective Visa System," Related to Apparel/Textile Shipments?

An effective visa system, applicable to the textile and apparel products that claim benefits under AGOA, is a government-industry process that demonstrates that the goods for which benefits are claimed were in fact produced in a sub-Saharan Africa country or countries according to the rules of origin required to claim those benefits. The U.S. Government has provided countries with guidance on what the United States believes is required by an effective visa system. This includes the requirement that each shipment by covered by an original visa stamped on an original invoice. The visa must contain certain information such as the date of the visa, the quantity of goods being shipped, the preference grouping the goods qualify under, and a country code. In addition, governments must agree to cooperate with the U.S. Customs Service to prevent unlawful transshipment and use of counterfeit documentation, must agree to permit verification visits to factories, producers, exporters, and/or manufacturers, and must require factories, producers, exporters, and manufacturers to retain proper records relating to the production of goods for a period of five years.

What are the Apparel/Textile Preference Groupings?

The following are general descriptions of the preference groups. Articles under preference group "I" must be determined through bilateral consultations between the United States and sub-Saharan African countries.

A: Apparel assembled from U.S.-formed and cut fabric from U.S. yarn. [19 CFR 10.213(a)(1)]

B: Apparel assembled and further processed from U.S.-formed and cut fabric from U.S. yarn. [19 CFR 10.213(a)(2)]

C: Apparel cut and assembled from U.S. fabric from U.S. yarn and thread. [19 CFR 10.213(a)(3)]

D: Apparel assembled from regional fabric from yarn originating in the U.S. or one or more beneficiary countries. [19 CFR 10.213(a)(4)]

E: Apparel assembled in one or more lesser developed beneficiary countries. [19 CFR 10.213(a)(5)].

F: Sweaters knit to shape in chief weight of cashmere. [19 CFR 10.2 13(a)(6)]

G: Sweaters knit to shape with 50 percent or more by weight of fine wool. [19 CFR 10.2 13(a)(7)]

H: Apparel cut and assembled in one or more beneficiary countries from fabrics or yarn not formed in the United States or a beneficiary country (as identified in NAFTA) or designated as not available in commercial quantities in the United States. [19 CFR 10.21 3(a)(8) or (a)(9)]

I: Handloomed, handmade or folklore articles.[19 CFR 10.213(a)(10)]

Do the Apparel Products that are Eligible for Duty-Free and Quota-Free Benefits Under the AGOA Have to Satisfy the 35% Value-Added Requirement of the GSP Program?

No. Apparel products eligible for benefits under the AGOA must meet the preference grouping requirements set forth in the AGOA apparel provisions. These requirements do not include the 35% value-added requirement. The 35% value-content requirement applies to those products currently eligible for GSP treatment (which do not include most textile and apparel products), as well as additional products (again excluding textiles and apparel) that may be designated as eligible for duty-free treatment under the expansion of the GSP program for AGOA beneficiary countries.

Which Countries are Considered to be "Lesser Developed Beneficiary" Countries under the AGOA?

The majority of countries in sub-Saharan Africa would be considered lesser developed countries under the AGOA. The criterion requires that a country's per capita GNP as measured by the World Bank in 1998 be under $1,500. Annex 1 includes a list of lesser-developed AGOA beneficiary countries.

How will Apparel Exports from Sub-Saharan Africa be Counted Against the Cap on Imports of Apparel Made with Regional or Third-Country Fabric?

On a "first-come, first-served" basis. This means that eligible imports from any eligible country will be counted against the cap as they are imported. Once the cap is filled, products may still be imported; however, the prevailing normal trade relations tariff rate will be assessed. For the first year, two-thirds of the cap was made available on October 2, 2000. The remaining one-third of the cap, plus any quantity remaining unfilled from the earlier two-thirds of the cap, will be made available on January 1, 2001. The yearly cap period begins on October 1 of each year and runs through September 30 of the next year.

What is "Transshipment"?

AGOA describes transshipment as a claim for a textile or apparel article for duty-free benefits that is - false with respect to country of origin, manufacture, processing or assembly of the article or any of its parts.

If transshipment is found, the United States will deny all benefits for future textile or apparel shipments from the transshipping sub-Saharan African exporter for five years.

For Apparel/Textiles, What Types of Records Must be Kept and By Whom?

Exporters, producers, or manufacturers are required to keep proper records relating to the production of goods, including materials used in production, information relating to the place of production, the number and identification of the types of machinery used in production, and the number of workers employed in production. These records should be retained for five years. If the U.S. Customs Service visits the facility of a producer or exporter in a beneficiary country, it may also expect to see inventory records, documentation for payments for raw material purchases, export/shipping records, contracts with subcontractors, payroll records, cutting records, assembly records, letters of credit and out-processing records.

Chapter 4

TRADE BENEFITS (NON-APPAREL/TEXTILE)

AGOA builds on existing U.S. programs designed to increase trade and investment between the United States and developing countries. AGOA expands benefits available under the Generalized System of Preferences (GSP) program. GSP offers duty-free treatment to imports of selected products from specific beneficiary countries. Duty-free treatment for a broader range of products is provided for imports from least developed beneficiary developing countries. The GSP program must be renewed by Congress each time it expires; it is currently scheduled to expire September 30, 2001. Detailed information about the program, including the products and countries eligible for duty-free benefits, can be found on the Internet at: http://www.ustr.gov/reports/gsp/index.html, or under the Links button on the www.agoa.gov Internet site.

DUTY-FREE TREATMENT FOR PRODUCTS

U.S. imports from most sub-Saharan Africa countries are already eligible to receive duty-free access for some 4,650 products under the U.S. GSP program. Another 1,783 products imported from least-developed sub-Saharan African countries are also eligible to receive duty-free treatment. A list of products currently eligible for GSP is contained in Annex 2. However, the GSP program excludes from this extensive list of products duty-free treatment for textiles, apparel, watches, footwear, handbags, luggage, flat goods, work gloves and leather wearing apparel, and certain electronic, steel and glass products as well as other products that are deemed import-sensitive. In addition, under GSP, benefits may be lost when imports from a beneficiary country reach prescribed thresholds. Finally, GSP benefits for all products imported from all beneficiary countries expire on September 30, 2001 unless renewed by Congress.

AGOA provides three important benefits to eligible sub-Saharan African exporters. First, it extends the duty-free treatment under the GSP program for eligible sub-Saharan African countries through September 30, 2008. Second, the AGOA eliminates most of the limitations of the GSP program for eligible sub-Saharan African countries. Third, AGOA expands the product coverage of the GSP program but only for products of sub-Saharan Africa.

AGOA permits the President to extend duty-free treatment to imports of essentially all products, except textiles and apparel, if they are the "growth, product or manufacture" of a beneficiary sub-Saharan Africa country, meet a value-added requirement, and the President determines that the products are not import-sensitive in the context of imports from beneficiary sub-Saharan Africa countries. Annex 3 provides a full list of the products under review. Textile and apparel benefits are treated separately from GSP under AGOA. The U.S. GSP Subcommittee is currently conducting a review of these products and it is expected that the President will announce the final list of products eligible for duty-free treatment under AGOA before the end of the year 2000. The list will be published in the U.S. *Federal Register* and will be made available on the Internet at www.agoa.gov.

This provision of AGOA gives sub-Saharan African suppliers a competitive edge over suppliers in other countries with which the United States does not have a free trade agreement. The tariff rates on many of these products can be quite high, and reducing them to zero for sub-Saharan

Africa exporters in eligible sub-Saharan African countries will enable those suppliers to compete more effectively with suppliers elsewhere.

More Certainty for Duty-Free Benefits

Regular and expanded GSP duty-free benefits will remain in place for sub-Saharan African exporters through September 30, 2008, irrespective of whether or not the GSP program applicable to other developing countries is extended past September 30, 2001. This benefit provides more certainty for both sub-Saharan African exporters and their U.S. customers, each of whom will likely incorporate sub-Saharan African suppliers more securely into their international sourcing plans as a result of the assurance that duty-free treatment will not lapse for some time.

End of Competitive Need Limits for Sub-Saharan Africa

AGOA also exempts eligible sub-Saharan African countries from normal GSP program limitations on value and percentage of trade in a specific product, known as "competitive need limitations." Normally, a GSP participant loses benefits for a certain product if imports of that product into the United States account for more than 50 percent of total U.S. imports of that product, or if imports reach a certain value ($90 million in 1999). AGOA amends the GSP statute to exempt sub-Saharan Africa beneficiary countries from these competitive need limitations. This benefit will also contribute to a more secure long-term sourcing relationship between sub-Saharan African exporters and U.S. customers.

GSP RULE OF ORIGIN FOR IMPORTS FROM SUB-SAHARAN AFRICA

A product must meet the GSP program rules of origin to qualify for duty-free access to the U.S. *under the GSP program.* The GSP rules of origin require that a product be the "growth, product or manufacture" of a beneficiary sub-Saharan African country and that:

- The article must be imported directly from the beneficiary country into the United States; and
- The sum of the cost or value of materials produced in the beneficiary country plus the direct processing costs must equal at least 35 percent of the appraised value of the product at the time of entry into the United States.

Imported materials may be counted toward the 35 percent but only if the materials are "substantially transformed" into new and different constituent materials of which the eligible article is composed. If an imported article has been produced in part in several countries that are members of an association of countries contributing to the regional economic integration of its members, the articles will be accorded duty-free entry if the value of their collective production of the article accounts for at least 35 percent of the appraised value of the article. The level of value added is the same as would be required for a product imported from a single country. The U.S. Customs Service is charged with determining whether an article meets the GSP rule-of-origin requirements. Members of the West African Economic and Monetary Union (WAEMU), the Southern African Development Community (SADC), and the Tripartite Commission on East African Cooperation (EAC) are potentially eligible for this cumulation benefit. The President has delegated to the U.S. Trade

Representative the responsibility for determining which members of these organizations qualify for the cumulation benefit under the GSP program.

AGOA RULE OF ORIGIN FOR IMPORTS FROM SUB-SAHARAN AFRICA

A product must meet the AGOA program rules of origin to qualify for duty-free access to the U.S. *under AGOA*. The AGOA rules of origin require that a product be the "growth, product or manufacture" of a beneficiary sub-Saharan Africa country and that:

- The article must be imported directly from the beneficiary country into the United States; and
- The sum of (a) the cost or value of materials produced in a one or more beneficiary countries plus (b) the direct cost of processing performed in those countries is not less than 35 percent of the appraised value of the product when it enters the United States. Up to 15 percentage points of that 35 percent may be derived from U.S. parts or materials used to produce the product in a beneficiary Sub-Saharan Africa country or countries.

General Rule of Origin Guidelines

In most cases, U.S. Customs will appraise the merchandise at the transaction value, that is, the price actually paid or payable for the merchandise when sold for export to the United States. This value would include the following elements:

1. The packing costs incurred by the buyer
2. The selling commission incurred by the buyer
3. The value of any assistance provided to the producer free of charge by the buyer
4. The royalty or license fee that the buyer is required to pay as a condition of the sale
5. The proceeds accruing to the seller of any subsequent resale, disposal, or use of the imported merchandise

In general, shipping and other costs related to transporting the GSP articles from the port of export to the United States are included neither in the value of the article nor in the value-added calculation.

The direct costs of processing include all costs, whether directly incurred in or those that can be reasonably allocated to the growth, production, manufacture, or assembly of the merchandise in question. These include the following:

- Actual labor, fringe benefits, and on-the-job training costs
- Engineering, supervisory, quality control, and similar personnel costs
- Dies, molds, and tooling costs, as well as depreciation on machinery and equipment
- Research, development, design, blueprints and engineering, and inspection and testing costs

The costs that may not be included in the direct costs of processing are those that are not directly attributable to the merchandise being considered or are not "costs" of manufacturing. These costs include profit and general expenses and business overhead such as administrative salaries, casualty and liability insurance, advertising, and sales representative's salaries, commissions, or expenses.

Questions regarding rule of origin requirements for specific products may be directed to: Director, National Commodity Specialist Division, U.S. Customs Service, 6 World Trade Center, New York, New York 10048.

Chapter 5

TRADE BENEFITS FOR TEXTILES AND APPAREL

AGOA extends duty-free and quota-free benefits to imports of a number of apparel items, and textile products used to make those goods, produced in eligible sub-Saharan African countries. In most instances, these benefits are available without limits on the total volume of apparel exported from eligible sub-Saharan African countries to the United States. In two specific instances, however, the volume of U.S. imports of particular types of apparel exported from eligible Sub-Saharan Africa countries is subject to a cap.

In order for apparel/textile products of a country to be eligible for duty-free treatment, the AGOA beneficiary country must be designated as eligible for apparel/textile benefits. Such a designation requires that the United States determine that the country has an effective visa system to prevent the unlawful transshipment of apparel/textile articles and the use of counterfeit documents relating to the importation of the articles into the United States. USTR will publish a Federal Register notice when it designates a country(ies) as eligible for AGOA apparel/textile benefits. This information will be available at www.ustr.gov and at www.agoa.gov

DUTY-FREE, QUOTA-FREE TREATMENT

AGOA provides that the following five types of textile and apparel products imported from eligible sub- Saharan African countries can enter the United States duty-free and quota-free. It should be recognized that many complicated factors may be involved in customs issues and that this information is for general information purposes only. Customs regulations pertaining to AGOA are available at www.agoa.gov under product eligibility. For answers to specific questions or to request a ruling, direct enquiries to: Director, National Commodity Specialist Division, U.S. Customs Service, 6 World Trade Center, New York, New York 10048.

- Apparel assembled in sub-Saharan Africa from fabrics wholly formed and cut in the United States, from yarns wholly formed in the United States.

- Apparel cut and assembled in sub-Saharan Africa, using U.S. thread, from fabrics wholly formed in the United States from yarns wholly formed in the United States.
- Sweaters knit to shape from cashmere or certain wool. The sweaters must be in chief weight of cashmere, or 50 percent or more by weight of merino wool measuring 18.5 microns in diameter. Fiber and yarn can come from any country, including countries outside sub-Saharan Africa.
- Apparel cut or knit to shape and assembled in sub-Saharan Africa from third-country yarn or fabric in short supply. The yarns and fabrics considered in "short supply" is derived from the North American Free Trade Agreement (see Annex 401 of the NAFTA). Briefly, they currently include, among others, silk, linen, fine-count cotton circular knit fabrics for certain apparel, cotton velveteen, fine wale cotton corduroy, Harris Tweed, batiste fabrics, and nine types of lightweight high-thread count broadwoven fabrics for men's and boy's shirts. (A list of "short supply" yarns and fabrics is provided at Annex 5. Additional yarns and fabrics may be added in the future through procedures detailed in the AGOA).
- Handloomed, handmade and folklore articles. Products covered under this category will be determined through U.S. consultations with the beneficiary country (or countries) and must also be certified by the competent authority of the beneficiary country (or countries) as a handloomed, handmade, or folklore article.
- Certain other apparel products will be duty-free and quota-free up to a specified cap (aggregate level of imports of these products from all beneficiary sub-Saharan African countries) that is based on U.S. total apparel imports in a previous 12-month period. The specific products covered under the cap are:
- Apparel assembled in sub-Saharan Africa from fabric wholly formed in sub-Saharan Africa from U.S. or sub-Saharan African yarn.
- Apparel assembled in sub-Saharan Africa from non-U.S., non-sub-Saharan African fabric ("third country" fabric). Only lesser-developed sub-Saharan African countries, defined as those with a per capita gross national product of less than $1,500 a year in 1998 as measured by the World Bank, may export apparel wholly assembled in their countries, regardless of the origin of the fabric, through September 30, 2004. According to the World Bank's 1999/2000 World Development Report, which gives 1998 data, all sub-Saharan African countries except Botswana, Equatorial Guinea, Gabon, Mauritius, Namibia, Seychelles, and South Africa fall below this per capita threshold and are eligible to use third-country fabric in their duty-free apparel exports to the United States through September 30, 2004.

The single cap on preferential treatment for these two categories of apparel is as follows:

The duty-free cap is not allocated among countries. It will be filled on a "first-come, first-served" basis. In any year that the cap is met, subject apparel products from sub-Saharan Africa may still enter the United States; however, they will be assessed the prevailing normal trade relations duty rate (Column 1 rates detailed in the Harmonized Tariff System of the United States) at the time of entry. For the first year, two-thirds of the cap was made available on October 2, 2000. The remaining one-third of the cap, plus any quantity remaining unfilled from the earlier two-thirds of the cap, will be made available on January 1, 2001.

Share of Total U.S. Apparel Imports, Measured In Square Meter Equivalents, In Previous 12-Month Period for Which Data Are Available

October 1,	2000	– September 30,	2001	1.50%
October 1,	2001	– September 30,	2002	1.78%
October 1,	2002	– September 30,	2003	2.06%
October 1,	2003	– September 30,	2004	2.34%
October 1,	2004	– September 30,	2005	2.62%
October 1,	2005	– September 30,	2006	2.90%
October 1,	2006	– September 30,	2007	3.18%
October 1,	2007	– September 30,	2008	3.50%

In addition to the cap on these imports, AGOA includes protection for U.S. industries from surges in apparel imports wholly assembled in sub-Saharan Africa countries from regional and third-country fabric and yarn. The Secretary of Commerce will monitor these apparel imports on a monthly basis. If the Secretary determines that there has been a surge of imports in such increased quantities as to cause serious damage, or threat thereof, to U.S. producers, then the President must suspend benefits for that particular product from the sub-Saharan African country or countries that are exporting it. The Secretary will only make a determination after a notice has been published in the *Federal Register* and a thorough investigation has been concluded.

Quotas on Imports from Kenya and Mauritius

Existing U.S. quotas on textile and apparel products imported into the United States from Kenya and Mauritius will be terminated within 30 days after the U.S.Government has determined that each country has adopted an effective visa system to prevent the transshipment of textile and apparel articles and the use of counterfeit importation documents.

Findings and Trimmings

An apparel article is eligible for benefits even if the article contains findings or trimmings of foreign origin, if the value of such findings and trimmings does not exceed 25 percent of the cost of the components of the assembled article. Examples of findings and trimmings include sewing thread (except when used to assemble in sub-Saharan Africa U.S.-cut fabric), hooks and eyes, snaps, buttons, "bow buds," decorative lace trims, elastic strips, and zippers. Elastic strips are considered findings or trimmings only if they are each less than 1 inch in width and used in the production of brassieres.

Certain Interlinings

Certain interlinings are eligible for duty-free treatment as findings and trimmings. The interlinings permitted include only a chest type plate, a "hymo" piece, or "sleeve header" made of woven or weft-inserted warp knit construction, and made of coarse animal hair or man-made filaments. This benefit will terminate if the President determines such interlinings are made in the United States in commercial quantities.

De Minimis Rule

Apparel products assembled in sub-Saharan Africa which would otherwise be considered eligible for AGOA benefits but for the presence of some fibers or yarns not wholly formed in the United States or the beneficiary sub-Saharan African country will still be eligible for benefits as long as the total weight of all such fibers and yarns is not more than 7 percent of the total weight of the article.

Chapter 6

CUSTOMS-RELATED REQUIREMENTS FOR APPAREL BENEFITS: PROTECTION AGAINST TRANSSHIPMENT

Preferential treatment for textile and apparel articles under AGOA is conditioned on the enforcement of measures to prevent transshipment. Transshipment is defined as the use of false information in claiming the country of origin, manufacture, processing, or assembly of an article or any of its components. This false information is used to export an article duty-free to the United States when it otherwise would be deemed dutiable and/or counted against a quota. When transshipment occurs, the benefits of AGOA accrue to others outside of sub-Saharan Africa, taking away jobs and opportunities from sub-Saharan African countries and people and diminishing the benefits eligible sub-Saharan African countries receive from AGOA. Anti-transshipment measures are aimed at protecting both sub-Saharan African countries and their producers as well as the U.S. market and domestic industry.

In order for an eligible sub-Saharan African country to export qualifying apparel products to the United States duty-free, the United States must determine that the country has met certain customs-related requirements including (the specific provisions are contained in Section 113 of the AGOA):

- adoption of an effective visa system, domestic laws, and enforcement measures to prevent illegal transshipment and the use of counterfeit documents relating to the importation of eligible apparel products into the United States;
- enactment of legislation or issuance of regulations that allow the U.S. Customs Service to thoroughly investigate allegations of transshipment;
- agreement to report total imports and exports of the covered articles in that country;
- agreement to cooperate fully with the United States to address and take action necessary to prevent circumvention;
- agreement to require all producers and exporters of covered articles to maintain complete records of production and all materials used in that production for at least two years after production or export; and
- agreement to provide documentation to the U.S. Customs Service establishing country of origin of covered articles. These documents include production records,

factory information, the number and type of machinery used in production, number of workers employed in production, and certification from both the manufacturer and the exporter.

- implementation of or substantial progress toward implementation of procedures and requirements similar to the relevant procedures and requirements under chapter five of the NAFTA.

The U.S. Customs Service will provide technical assistance to beneficiary sub-Saharan Africa countries in developing and implementing an appropriate visa system, legislation and regulations and in training their officials in anti-transshipment enforcement. Customs will also send production verification teams to at least four beneficiary sub-Saharan African countries each year.

An exporter, any successor of the exporter, and any other entity owned or operated by the principal of the exporter, from a beneficiary sub-Saharan African country that has been determined to have engaged in transshipment of apparel or textiles will lose all apparel and textile duty-free benefits for a period five years. Other penalties may also be applied.

Chapter 7

COUNTRY ELIGIBILITY REQUIREMENTS

The benefits established by AGOA are targeted towards the 48 countries of sub-Saharan Africa. However, sub-Saharan African countries do not automatically receive all of the benefits of AGOA. Certain AGOA trade benefits will be extended only to those countries that meet specific eligibility criteria. These criteria were developed in consultation with sub-Saharan African countries and reflect an understanding that additional U.S. market access provided under AGOA will only generate sustainable economic growth and development if countries have appropriate domestic policies. The criteria constitute "best practice" policies that will ultimately attract trade and investment and foster widely-shared prosperity.

Sub-Saharan African countries designated as eligible or beneficiary countries must undergo an annual review of their status. Countries may be added or withdrawn from the list of eligible or beneficiary countries during this annual review. The President will monitor, review, and report *annually* to Congress each country's progress towards meeting the criteria. The President must terminate the designation of a country as a beneficiary sub-Saharan African country if he determines that the country is no longer making continual progress towards meeting the eligibility criteria. If the President terminates a country's designation, it will be effective January 1 of the year following the year in which the determination is made.

In considering the eligibility of sub-Saharan African countries for AGOA beneficiary status, the AGOA required the President to consider the countries based on the existing criteria under the Generalized System of Preferences program as well as new AGOA criteria and a new GSP criterion. These new criteria include whether these countries have established or are making continual progress toward establishing, a market-based economy, the rule of law, the elimination of barriers to U.S. trade and investment, economic policies to reduce poverty, the protection of internationally recognized worker rights, and a system to combat corruption. Additionally, countries (1) cannot engage in activities that undermine U.S. national security or foreign policy interests, (2) cannot engage in gross violations of internationally-recognized human rights, (3) cannot provide support for acts of international terrorism, and (4) must have implemented their commitments to eliminate the worst forms of child labor.

Eligibility to receive certain benefits under AGOA derives from Section 104(a) of the AGOA, section 502(b) of the Trade Act of 1974, as amended (containing the GSP eligibility criteria), and section 506A of the Trade Act of 1974. Section 104(a) is provided below in its entirety. A summary of relevant parts of Section 502(b) is also included below.

"SEC. 104. ELIGIBILITY REQUIREMENTS

(a) In General.-- The President is authorized to designate a sub-Saharan African country as an eligible sub-Saharan African country if the President determines that the country—

(1) has established, or is making continual progress toward establishing--

(A) a market-based economy that protects private property rights, incorporates an open rules-based trading system, and minimizes government interference in the economy through measures such as price controls, subsidies, and government ownership of economic assets;
(B) the rule of law, political pluralism, and the right to due process, a fair trial, and equal protection under the law;
(C) the elimination of barriers to United States trade and investment, including by—

(i) the provision of national treatment and measures to create an environment conducive to domestic and foreign investment;
(ii) the protection of intellectual property; and
(iii) the resolution of bilateral trade and investment disputes;

(D) economic policies to reduce poverty, increase the availability of health care and educational opportunities, expand physical infrastructure, promote the development of private enterprise, and encourage the formation of capital markets through micro-credit or other programs;
(E) a system to combat corruption and bribery, such as signing and implementing the Convention on Combating Bribery of Foreign Public Officials in International Business Transactions; and
(F) protection of internationally recognized worker rights, including the right of association, the right to organize and bargain collectively, a prohibition on the use of any form of forced or compulsory labor, a minimum age for the employment of children, and acceptable conditions of work with respect to minimum wages, hours of work, and occupational safety and health;

(2) does not engage in activities that undermine United States national security or foreign policy interests; and
(3) does not engage in gross violations of internationally recognized human rights or provide support for acts of international terrorism and cooperates in international efforts to eliminate human rights violations and terrorist activities.

(b) Continuing Compliance: If the President determines that an eligible sub-Saharan African country is not making continual progress in meeting the requirements described in subsection (a)(1), the President shall terminate the designation of the country made pursuant to subsection (a)."

Summary of Section 502(b) of the Trade Act of 1974 as amended.

To be eligible for the GSP benefits, a country must:

1. Not be a Communist country unless its products receives normal trade relations treatment, it is a member of the World Trade Organization and International Monetary Fund or is not dominated or controlled by international communism (Sec. 502(b)(2)(A));
2. Not be a party to an arrangement or participates in any action that withholds or has the effect of withholding vital commodity resources or raises their prices to unreasonable levels, causing serious disruption of the world economy (Sec. 502(b)(2)(B));
3. Not afford preferential treatment to products of a developed country which has or is likely to have a significant adverse effect on U.S. commerce (Sec. 502(b)(2)(C));
4. Not have nationalized, expropriated or otherwise seized property, including trademarks, patents, or copyrights owned by a U.S. citizen without compensation (Sec. 502(b)(2)(D));
5. Recognize or enforce arbitral awards to U.S. citizens or corporations (Sec. 502(b)(2)(E));
6. Not aid or abet, by granting sanctuary from prosecution, any individual or group which has committed international terrorism (Sec. 502(b)(2)(F));
7. Take steps to afford internationally-recognized worker rights, including the right of association, the right to organize and bargain collectively, freedom from compulsory labor, a minimum age for the employment of children, and acceptable conditions of work with respect to minimum wages, hours of work and occupational safety and health (Sec. 502(b)(2)(G)).
8. Implement its commitments to eliminate the worst forms of child labor, as defined by the International Labor Organization's Convention 182 (Sec. 502(b)(2)(H); this provision was added by the Trade and Development Act of 2000 in Section 412). To determine whether a country is complying with this provision, the President should consider (1) whether the country has adequate laws and regulations proscribing the worst forms of child labor; (2) whether the country has adequate laws and regulations for the implementation and enforcement of such measures; (3) whether the country has established formal institutional mechanisms to investigate and address complaints relating to allegations of the worst forms of child labor; (4) whether social programs exist in the country to prevent ht engagement of children in the worst forms of child labor; (5) whether the country has a comprehensive policy for the elimination of the worst forms of child labor and (6) wither the country is making continual progress toward eliminating the worst forms of child labor.

Failure to meet criteria 4 through 7 may not prevent the granting of GSP eligibility if the President determines that such a designation would be in the national economic interest of the United States.

In addition, the President must take into account:

1. A country's expressed desire to be designated a beneficiary country (Sec. 502(c)(1));
2. The country's level of economic development (Sec. 502(c)(2));
3. Whether other major developed countries extend GSP to the country (Sec. 502(c)(3));
4. The extent to which the country provides "equitable and reasonable access" to its markets and basic commodity resources and refrains from unreasonable export practices(Sec. 502(c)(4));
5. The extent to which the country provides adequate and effective protection of intellectual property rights (Sec. 502(c)(5)), and
6. The extent to which the country has taken action to reduce trade-distorting investment practices and policies and reduce or eliminate barriers to trade in services (Sec. 502(c)(6)) and
7. Whether the country has taken or is taking steps to afford internationally-recognized worker rights, as defined above in item 7 (Sec. 502(c)(7)).

Chapter 8

Other AGOA Provisions (Non-Trade Program)

While AGOA primarily focuses on preferential trade programs, it also includes a number of complementary provisions.

AGOA creates a Presidential and Cabinet-level U.S.-Sub-Saharan Africa Trade and Economic Cooperation Forum that will institutionalize America's economic engagement with Africa, and secure, through structured dialogue -- on all levels of government, the private sector, and the non-governmental organization (NGO) community -- practical policies for strengthening trade and investment and building mutually beneficial economic opportunities between the United States and sub-Saharan Africa.

AGOA urges Congress and the President to work together with the international community to make bilateral and multilateral debt relief available to those countries most in need of it.

In addition, AGOA directs the U.S. Overseas Private Investment Corporation to increase loans, guarantees, and insurance that support projects in sub-Saharan Africa, including those undertaken by women entrepreneurs and those that maximize employment opportunities for poor individuals. The United States Export-Import Bank activities in sub-Saharan Africa will also be expanded. These provisions of AGOA will provide greater certainty to U.S. exporters and investors of support in their initiatives in sub-Saharan Africa.

AGOA directs the United States to provide technical assistance to companies and governments in sub-Saharan Africa. This assistance will be used, for example, to liberalize trade and promote exports, facilitate the integration of sub-Saharan African countries into the World Trade Organization, and promote regulatory and fiscal reforms.

Chapter 9

MARKET ACCESS AND REQUIREMENTS FOR AGRICULTURAL PRODUCTS

MARKET ACCESS OF AGRICULTURAL PRODUCTS

Who Initiates the Import Request?

- The national animal and/or plant health authorities of the exporting country
- An importer located in the United States

What Agencies are Responsible for Which Products and Why?

- Aphis restrictions are in effect due to disease and/or pest conditions in a country. Restrictions protect the national animal and plant health of the U.S.
- F&W restrictions are in effect to protect endangered and threatened species
- FSIS restrictions are in effect to ensure meat and poultry are processed under standards equivalent to those of the United States. Restrictions protect human health
- FDA has authority over all meat products not covered by FSIS and all other foods to protect human health

DETERMINE WHICH U.S. AGENCIES HAVE REGULATORY AUTHORITY OVER THE AGRICULTURAL PRODUCT

Animal and Health Inspection Service (APHIS)

- All live animals and animal products
- All live plants and plant products
- APHIS determines enterability of a commodity based on the disease and pest status of the exporting country

Fish and Wildlife Service

- All animals, plants and their products which are CITES listed
- CITES: International agreement which protects endangered and threatened species

Food Safety and Inspection Services (FSIS)

- All meat and poultry processed products containing more than 3% raw meat
- Generally, freedom from disease must be established by APHIS before FSIS works with national authorities to approve meat inspection system

Food and Drug Administration (FDA)

- Jurisdiction over imported foods, fish and meats not covered by FSIS (such as game meat)
- No permit required. Inspection at port of entry.

UNITED STATES DOMESTIC CONTACT INFORMTION

Animal and Plant Health Inspection Service (APHIS) http://www.aphis.usda. gov

Information on import of plants and plant products:

APHIS-PPQ
Unit 133
4700 River Road
Riverdale, Maryland 20737
Tel. 301-734-8261/8262

Information on import of animals and products:

APHIS-VS
Unit 38
4700 River Road
Riverdale, Maryland 20737
Tel. 301-737-3277

Food Safety and Inspection Service (FSIS): http://fsis.usda.gov/oa/programs/import.htm

Information for countries wishing to become eligible to export meat and poultry:

International Policy Division
Food Safety and Inspection Service
U.S. Department of Agriculture
Washington, D.C. 20250
Tel. 202-501-7472/7515

Fish and Wildlife Services (F&W):
http://endangered. fws.gov/contacts.html

Information on CITES:

U.S. Fish and Wildlife Services
Division of Endangered Species
Mail Stop 420ARLSQ
1849 C St., NW
Washington, D.C. 20240
Tel. 703-358-2104 (permit unit)

Foreign Agriculture Service
http://www.fas.gov

Information on Tariffs, Quotas and GSP FAS
1400 Independence Ave. SW
Washington, DC 20250
Tel. 202-720-0762

Food And Drug Administration
http://vm.cfsan.fda.gov/~lrd/import.html

Division of Import
Operations and Policy
15800 Crabbs Branch Way Rockville,
Maryland 20855
Tel. 301-443-6553

Chapter 10

TIME LINE OF IMPORTANT DATES

2000

October 2	Presidential Designation of AGOA Beneficiary Countries
Post - October 2	AGOA Textile and Apparel Benefits go into effect for AGOA Beneficiary Countries that have been Determined to Meet the Customs-Related Requirements**
October 6	The U.S. International Trade Commission Publishes its Advice to the President on the Probable Economic Effect on U.S. Industries of the Elimination of U.S. Import Duties under AGOA for Products that are Potentially Eligible for such Treatment (see *Federal Register* notice of May 25 available on the Internet site www.agoa.gov).
mid-late October	Regional AGOA Seminars for COMESA, IOC, and SADC Countries held in Kenya and Madagascar.
October 20	Deadline for Submissions of Public Comments on U.S. International Trade Commission advice to the President
November	Regional AGOA Seminars for ECOWAS, WAEMU and CEMAC Countries held in Gabon and Nigeria.
November/ December	Presidential Designation of Additional Products Eligible for Duty-Free Treatment Under AGOA

2001

January*	Possible Presidential Designation of Additional AGOA Beneficiary Countries

* Tentative

** The United States will determine which countries meet these requirements through a consultation process with sub-Saharan African countries based on the requirements detailed in Section 113 of the African Growth and Opportunity Act. It is expected that these determinations will be made as the requirements are met and not at any specific date.

Annex 1

COUNTRY LISTS

SUB-SAHARAN AFRICAN COUNTRIES DESIGNATED AS ELIGIBLE FOR THE BENEFITS OF AGOA AS OF OCTOBER 2, 2000

Republic of Benin
Republic of Botswana
Republic of Cape Verde
Republic of Cameroon
Central African Republic
Republic of Chad
Republic of Congo
Republic of Djibouti
State of Eritrea
Ethiopia
Gabonese Republic
Republic of Ghana
Republic of Guinea
Republic of Guinea-Bissau
Republic of Kenya
Kingdom of Lesotho
Republic of Madagascar
Republic of Malawi
Republic of Mali
Islamic Republic of Mauritania
Republic of Mauritius
Republic of Mozambique
Republic of Namibia
Republic of Niger
Federal Republic of Nigeria
Republic of Rwanda
Democratic Republic of Sao Tome and Principe
Republic of Senegal
Republic of Seychelles
Republic of Sierra Leone*
Republic of South Africa
United Republic of Tanzania
Republic of Uganda
Republic of Zambia

Sub-Saharan African Countries Designated as Eligible for the Benefits of AGOA and Considered "Lesser Developed Beneficiary Countries" under AGOA as of October 2, 2000

Republic of Benin
Republic of Cape Verde
Republic of Cameroon
Central African Republic
Republic of Chad
Republic of Congo
Republic of Djibouti
State of Eritrea
Ethiopia
Republic of Ghana
Republic of Guinea
Republic of Guinea-Bissau
Republic of Kenya
Kingdom of Lesotho
Republic of Madagascar
Republic of Malawi
Republic of Mali
Islamic Republic of Mauritania
Republic of Mozambique
Republic of Niger
Federal Republic of Nigeria
Republic of Rwanda
Democratic Republic of Sao Tome and Principe
Republic of Senegal
Republic of Sierra Leone*
United Republic of Tanzania
Republic of Uganda
Republic of Zambia

SUB-SAHARAN AFRICAN COUNTRIES ELIGIBLE FOR GSP

Republic of Angola*
Republic of Benin *
Republic of Botswana Burkina Faso*
Republic of Burundi*
Republic of Cameroon
Republic of Republic of Cape Verde*
Central African Republic*
Republic of Chad*
Federal Islamic Republic of the Comoros*
Democratic Republic of Congo*
Republic of the Congo
Republic of Cote d'Ivoire
Republic of Djibouti*
Republic of Equatorial Guinea*
State of Eritrea*
Ethiopia*
Gabonese Republic
Republic of the Gambia*
Republic of Ghana
Republic of Guinea*
Republic of Guinea-Bissau*
Republic of Kenya
Kingdom of Lesotho*
Republic of Madagascar*
Republic of Malawi*
Republic of Mali*
Islamic Republic of Mauritania*
Republic of Mauritius
Republic of Mozambique*
Republic of Namibia
Republic of Niger*
Federal Republic of Nigeria
Republic of Rwanda*
Democratic Republic of Sao Tome and Principe*
Republic of Senegal
Republic of Seychelles
Republic of Sierra Leone*
Somalia*
Republic of South Africa
Kingdom of Swaziland
United Republic of Tanzania*
Republic of Togo*
Republic of Uganda*
Zambia*
Republic of Zimbabwe

Note: Countries with an "*" are considered "Least-Developed Beneficiary Developing Countries" under GSP.

Annex 2

Products Potentially Eligible for Duty-Free Treatment under AGOA if Imported from Eligible Sub-Saharan Africa Countries

The following is a list of products that are being considered for duty-free treatment, if imported from AGOA beneficiary countries, under AGOA. A determination of what products will be granted duty-free treatment is expected by the end of 2000 and will be published in the Federal Register and available at www.agoa.gov.

These products are arranged by broad product groupings and, within those groupings, classified numerically according to the Harmonized Tariff System (HTS) of the United States. The tariff schedule which details all of the HTS codes applicable to all products imported into the United States may be accessed through the Internet at http://www.usitc.gov/taffairs.htm

Note: If there is an A+ under GSP Status that means that the product is currently duty-free under GSP for countries designated as "least-developed beneficiary developing countries" under GSP. A list of these countries is included at Annex 1.

Products Eligible for Duty-Free Treatment Under AGOA if Exported to the U.S. from an AGOA Beneficiary Country

Product Categories	Product Description	HTS Subheading	Rate of Duty	
			General (if not AGOA or other special category)	GSP Status
Albuminoidal Substances	Animal glue, including casein glue but not including fish glue, not exceeding a net weight of 1 kg, put up for retail sale	3506.10.10	6.50%	A+
Albuminoidal Substances	Egg albumin, dried	3502.11.00	47.6 cents/kg	A+
Albuminoidal Substances	Egg albumin, other than dried	3502.19.00	9.7 cents/kg	A+
Albuminoidal Substances	Inedible gelatin and animal glue valued 88 cents or more per kg	3503.00.40	2.8 cents/kg + 3.8%	A+
Albuminoidal Substances	Inedible gelatin and animal glue valued under 88 cents per kg	3503.00.20	1.2 cents/kg + 3.2%	A+
Aluminum and Aluminum Products	Aluminum (o/than alloy), unwrought, in coils, w/uniform x-section throughout length & w/least cross-sectional dimension n/o 9.5 mm	7601.10.30	2.60%	A+
Aluminum and Aluminum Products	Aluminum alloy, hollow profiles	7604.21.00	1.50%	A+
Aluminum and Aluminum Products	Aluminum alloys, unwrought, in coils, w/uniform x-section throughout length & w/least cross-sectional dimension n/o 9.5 mm	7601.20.30	2.60%	A+
Aluminum and Aluminum Products	Aluminum alloys, w/25% or more by weight of silicon, unwrought nesoi	7601.20.60	2.10%	A+
Aluminum and Aluminum Products	Aluminum, stranded wire, cables & the like w/steel core, not electrically insulated, not fitted with fittings & not made up into articles	7614.10.10	4.90%	A+
Aluminum and Aluminum Products	Aluminum, stranded wire, cables, & the like (o/than elect. conduct or w/steel core), n/elect. insulated, n/fitted w/fittings or articles	7614.90.40	4.90%	A+
Animal Products NESOI	Natural sponges of animal origin	0509.00.00	3%	A+
Animals (Live)	Live asses other than purebred breeding asses	0101.20.20	6.80%	A+
Animals (Live)	Live bovine animals other than purebred or those imported for dairy purposes	0102.90.40	1 cent/kg	A+
Animals (Live)	Live chickens weighing more than 185 g but not not more than 2000 g each	0105.92.00	2 cents/kg	A+
Animals (Live)	Live chickens weighing more than 2000 g each	0105.93.00	2 cents/kg	A+
Animals (Live)	Live chickens weighing not over 185 g each	0105.11.00	0.9 cents each	A+
Animals (Live)	Live ducks, geese and guineas, weighing not more than 185 g each	0105.19.00	0.9 cents each	A+
Animals (Live)	Live ducks, geese, turkeys and guineas, weighing over 185 g each	0105.99.00	2 cents/kg	A+
Animals (Live)	Live foxes	0106.00.30	4.80%	A+
Animals (Live)	Live goats	0104.20.00	68 cents/head	A+
Animals (Live)	Live turkeys weighing not more than over 185 g each	0105.12.00	0.9 cents each	A+
Animals (Live)	Mules and hinnies not imported for immediate slaughter	0101.20.40	4.50%	A+

Products Eligible for Duty-Free Treatment Under AGOA if Exported to the U.S. from an AGOA Beneficiary Country

Arms and Ammunition	Parts and accessories nesoi, for revolvers or pistols of heading 9302	9305.10.20	4.20%	A+
Arms and Ammunition	Revolvers and pistols (o/than of heading 9303 or 9304)	9302.00.00	14 cents each + 3%	A+
Asbestos	Asbestos or mixtures with a basis of asbestos, footwear	6812.50.10	8.30%	
Beverages (non-alcoholic)	Chocolate milk drink	2202.90.10	17%	A+
Beverages (non-alcoholic)	Non-alcoholic milk-based drinks (except chocolate), subject to add US note 10 to Ch. 4, not GN15	2202.90.24	17.50%	A+
Beverages (non-alcoholic)	Non-alcoholic milk-based drinks (except chocolate), subject to gen. note 15 of the HTS	2202.90.22	17.50%	A+
Beverages (non-alcoholic)	Orange juice, fortified with vitamins or minerals, not concentrated and not prepared from concentrate	2202.90.30	4.5 cents/liter	A+
Beverages (non-alcoholic)	Orange juice, fortified with vitamins or minerals, prepared from concentrate	2202.90.35	7.85 cents/liter	A+
Bicycle Equipment	Bicycle speedometers	9029.20.20	6%	A+
Bicycle Equipment	Parts and accessories of bicycle speedometers	9029.90.40	6%	A+
Ceramic Products	Ceramic (o/than porcelain or china) hotel, restaurant or nonhousehold tableware and kitchenware	6912.00.20	30.80%	A+
Ceramic Products	Ceramic (o/than porcelain or china) household tabl/kitch.ware,n/in specif. sets, cups o/$5.25/dz, saucers o/$3/dz, etc.	6912.00.45	4.50%	A+
Ceramic Products	Ceramic (o/than porcelain or china) household table and kitchenware, in sets in which aggregate val. of arts./US note 6(b) o/$38	6912.00.39	4.50%	A+
Ceramic Products	Glazed ceramic flags and paving, hearth or wall tiles; glazed ceramic mosaic cubes and the like, nesoi	6908.90.00	12.70%	
Ceramic Products	Glazed ceramic tiles, cubes & similar arts. w/largest area enclosable in sq. w/sides under 7 cm & n/o 3229 tiles/m2, boundd by straig lines	6908.10.10	14%	
Ceramic Products	Glazed ceramic tiles, cubes & similar arts. w/largest area enclosable in sq. w/sides under 7 cm, nesoi	6908.10.50	12.70%	
Ceramic Products	Porcelain or china (o/than bone china) household tableware & kitchenware, not in specified sets, nesoi	6911.10.80	22.90%	A+
Ceramic Products	Porcelain or china (o/than bone china) hsehld tabl/kit ware n/in specif. sets, cups o/$29/dz, saucers o/$18.75/dz, bowls o/$33/dz, etc.	6911.10.58	6%	A+
Ceramic Products	Porcelain or china (o/than bone china) hsehld tabl/kit.ware n/in specif.sets,cups o/$8 but n/o $29/dz, saucers o/$5.25 but n/o $18.75/dz,etc	6911.10.52	8%	A+
Ceramic Products	Porcelain or china hotel, restaurant & nonhousehold table and kitchenware	6911.10.10	29%	A+
Ceramic Products	Unglazed ceramic flags, paving, hearth or wall tiles, mosaic cubes and the like, nesoi	6907.90.00	14%	
Ceramic Products	Unglazed ceramic tiles, cubes and similar articles with largest area enclosable in a sq. w/sides under 7 cm	6907.10.00	14%	
Cereals	Barley, for malting purposes	1003.00.20	0.1 cents/kg	A+
Cereals	Barley, other than for malting purposes	1003.00.40	0.15 cents/kg	A+
Cereals	Basmati rice, husked	1006.20.20	0.83 cents/kg	A+
Cereals	Broken rice	1006.40.00	0.44 cents/kg	A+
Cereals	Cereals nesi (including wild rice)	1008.90.00	1.10%	A+
Cereals	Durum wheat	1001.10.00	0.65 cents/kg	A+
Cereals	Husked (brown) rice, other than Basmati	1006.20.40	2.1 cents/kg	A+
Cereals	Millet	1008.20.00	0.32 cents/kg	A+
Cereals	Rice in the husk (paddy or rough)	1006.10.00	1.8 cents/kg	A+
Cereals	Rice semi-milled or wholly milled, whether or not polished or glazed, other than parboiled	1006.30.90	1.4 cents/kg	A+

Products Eligible for Duty-Free Treatment Under AGOA if Exported to the U.S. from an AGOA Beneficiary Country

Cereals	Seed of wheat and meslin	1001.90.10	2.80%	A+
Cereals	Wheat & meslin other than durum or seed wheat	1001.90.20	0.35 cents/kg	A+
Cereals (Preparations)	Prep food in airtght cont.,of unroast cereal flake/mixture of unroasted/roasted cereal flake/swelled cereal,no apricot/citrus/peach/pear	1904.20.10	5.60%	A+
Cereals (Preparations)	Prepared foods obtained from unroasted cereal flakes or from mixtures of unroasted and roasted cereal flakes or swelled cereals, nesoi	1904.20.90	14.90%	A+
Cheeses	Blue-veined cheese (except Roquefort or Stilton), grated or powdered, subject to add. US note 17 to Ch.4	0406.20.24	20%	A+
Cheeses	Blue-veined cheese (except Roquefort or Stilton), grated or powdered, subject to gen. note 15 of the HTS	0406.20.22	20%	A+
Cheeses	Blue-veined cheese (except roquefort), processed, not grated or powdered, subject to add. US note 17 to Ch. 4	0406.30.14	20%	A+
Cheeses	Blue-veined cheese (except roquefort), processed, not grated or powdered, subject to gen. note 15 of the HTS	0406.30.12	20%	A+
Cheeses	Blue-veined cheese, nesoi, in original loaves, subject to add. US note 17 to Ch. 4	0406.40.54	15%	A+
Cheeses	Blue-veined cheese, nesoi, in original loaves, subject to gen. note 15 of the HTS	0406.40.51	15%	A+
Cheeses	Blue-veined cheese, nesoi, not in original loaves, subject to add. US note 17 to Ch. 4	0406.40.58	20%	A+
Cheeses	Blue-veined cheese, nesoi, not in original loaves, subject to gen. note 15 of the HTS	0406.40.52	20%	A+
Cheeses	Bryndza cheese, not grated or powdered, not processed	0406.90.05	7.20%	A+
Cheeses	Cheddar cheese, grated or powdered, subject to add. US note 18 to Ch. 4	0406.20.31	16%	A+
Cheeses	Cheddar cheese, grated or powdered, subject to gen. note 15 of the HTS	0406.20.29	16%	A+
Cheeses	Cheddar cheese, neosi, subject to add. US note 18 to Ch. 4	0406.90.08	12%	A+
Cheeses	Cheddar cheese, neosi, subject to gen. note 15 of the & entered pursuant to its provisions	0406.90.06	12%	A+
Cheeses	Cheddar cheese, processed, not grated or powdered, subject to add US note 18 to Ch. 4	0406.30.24	16%	A+
Cheeses	Cheddar cheese, processed, not grated or powdered, subject to gen. note 15 of the HTS	0406.30.22	16%	A+
Cheeses	Cheese (including mixtures) nesoi, grated or powdered, subject to gen. note 15 of the HTS	0406.20.56	10%	A+
Cheeses	Cheese (including mixtures) nesoi, processed, not grated or powdered, subject to gen. note 15 of the HTS	0406.30.56	10%	A+
Cheeses	Cheese (including mixtures), nesoi, n/o 0.5% by wt. of butterfat, grated or powdered, subject to add US note 23 to Ch. 4	0406.20.85	10%	A+
Cheeses	Cheese (including mixtures), nesoi, o/0.5% by wt of butterfat, not containing cow's milk, grated or powdered	0406.20.95	8.50%	A+
Cheeses	Cheese (including mixtures), nesoi, o/0.5% by wt of butterfat, w/cow's milk, grated or powdered, subject to add US note 16 to Ch. 4	0406.20.89	10%	A+
Cheeses	Cheese and substitutes for cheese including mixtures containing/processed from siss/emmentaler/etc, see addl U.S. note 22 (chap 4) & Prov.	0406.90.95	10%	A+
Cheeses	Cheese containing or processed from american-type cheese (except cheddar), grated or powdered, subject to add US note 19 to Ch. 4	0406.20.69	10%	A+
Cheeses	Cheese containing or processed from blue-veined cheese (except roquefort), grated/powdered, subject to add US note 17 to Ch.4	0406.20.61	10%	A+
Cheeses	Cheese containing or processed from bryndza, gjetost, gammelost, nokkelost or roquefort cheeses, grated or powdered	0406.20.57	8.50%	A+

Products Eligible for Duty-Free Treatment Under AGOA if Exported to the U.S. from an AGOA Beneficiary Country

Cheeses	Cheese containing or processed from cheddar cheese, grated or powdered, subject to add US note 18 to Ch. 4	0406.20.65	10%	A+
Cheeses	Cheese containing or processed from edam or gouda cheeses, grated or powdered, subject to add US note 20 to Ch 4	0406.20.73	10%	A+
Cheeses	Cheese containing or processed from italian-type cheeses made from cow's milk, grated or powdered, subject to add US note 21 to Ch. 4	0406.20.77	10%	A+
Cheeses	Cheese containing or processed from swiss, emmentaler or gruyere-process cheeses, grated or powdered, subject to add US nte 22 to Ch.4	0406.20.81	10%	A+
Cheeses	Cheeses & subst. for cheese (incl. mixt.), nesoi, w/ or from Am. cheese except cheddar, subj. to add. US note 19 to Ch.4, not GN15	0406.90.82	10%	A+
Cheeses	Cheeses & subst. for cheese (incl. mixt.), nesoi, w/ or from blue-veined cheese, subj. to add. US note 17 to Ch.4, not GN15	0406.90.72	10%	A+
Cheeses	Cheeses & subst. for cheese (incl. mixt.), nesoi, w/ or from cheddar cheese, subj. to add. US note 18 to Ch.4, not GN15	0406.90.76	10%	A+
Cheeses	Cheeses & subst. for cheese (incl. mixt.), nesoi, w/ or from edam or gouda cheese, subj. to add. US note 20 to Ch.4, not GN15	0406.90.86	10%	A+
Cheeses	Cheeses & subst. for cheese (incl. mixt.), nesoi, w/ or from swiss, emmentaler or gruyere, subj. to add. US note 22 to Ch.4, not GN15	0406.90.90	10%	A+
Cheeses	Cheeses & subst. for cheese (incl. mixt.), nesoi, w/butterfat n/o 0.5% by wt. subject to add. US note 23 to Ch. 4, not GN15	0406.90.93	10%	A+
Cheeses	Cheeses & subst. for cheese (incl. mixt.), nesoi, w/o cows milk, w/butterfat o/0.5% by wt, not GN15	0406.90.99	8.50%	A+
Cheeses	Cheeses & subst. for cheese(incl. mixt.), nesoi, w/romano/reggiano/parmesan/provolone/etc. f/cow milk, subj. Ch4 US note 21, not GN15	0406.90.66	7.50%	A+
Cheeses	Cheeses & substitutes for cheese (incl.mixtures) not cont.romano/reggiano/parmesan/provolone/etc from cows milk, subj. to gen. note 15	0406.90.63	10%	A+
Cheeses	Cheeses & substitutes for cheese (incl.mixtures) w/romano/reggiano/parmesan/provolone/etc from cows milk, subj. to gen. note 15	0406.90.61	7.50%	A+
Cheeses	Cheeses made from sheep's milk, including mixtures of such cheeses, grated or powdered	0406.20.55	9.60%	A+
Cheeses	Cheeses, substitute for cheese (including mixtures of cheeses), nesoi, made from sheep's milk	0406.90.59	9.60%	A+
Cheeses	Colby cheese, grated or powdered, subject to add. US note 19 to Ch. 4	0406.20.36	20%	A+
Cheeses	Colby cheese, grated or powdered, subject to gen. note 15 of the HTS	0406.20.34	20%	A+
Cheeses	Colby cheese, nesoi, subject to add. US note 19 to Ch. 4 and entered pursuant to its provisions	0406.90.52	20%	A+
Cheeses	Colby cheese, nesoi, subject to gen. note 15 of the HTS and entered pursuant to its provisions	0406.90.51	20%	A+
Cheeses	Colby cheese, processed, not grated or powdered, subject to add US note 19 to Ch. 4	0406.30.34	20%	A+
Cheeses	Colby cheese, processed, not grated or powdered, subject to gen. note 15 of the HTS	0406.30.32	20%	A+
Cheeses	Edam and gouda cheese, grated or powdered, subject to add. US note 20 to Ch. 4	0406.20.44	15%	A+
Cheeses	Edam and gouda cheese, grated or powdered, subject to gen. note 15 of the HTS	0406.20.43	15%	A+
Cheeses	Edam and gouda cheese, nesoi, subject to add. US note 20 to Ch. 4	0406.90.16	15%	A+
Cheeses	Edam and gouda cheese, nesoi, subject to gen. note 15 of the HTS	0406.90.14	15%	A+

Products Eligible for Duty-Free Treatment Under AGOA if Exported to the U.S. from an AGOA Beneficiary Country

Cheeses	Edam and gouda cheese, processed, not grated or powdered, subject to add. US note 20 to Ch. 4	0406.30.44	15%	A+
Cheeses	Edam and gouda cheese, processed, not grated or powdered, subject to gen. note 15 of the HTS	0406.30.42	15%	A+
Cheeses	Fresh (unrip./uncured) Swiss/emmentaler cheeses w/o eyes, gruyere-process and cheese cont/proc. from, subj to Ch4 US note 22, not GN15	0406.10.64	10%	A+
Cheeses	Fresh (unripened/uncured) american-type cheese, cheese cont or proc. fr american-type, subj to add. US note 19 to Ch.4, not GN15	0406.10.34	10%	A+
Cheeses	Fresh (unripened/uncured) blue-mold cheese, cheese/subs for cheese cont or procd fr blue-mold cheese, subj to Ch4 US note 17, not GN15	0406.10.14	10%	A+
Cheeses	Fresh (unripened/uncured) cheddar cheese, cheese/subs for cheese cont or proc from cheddar cheese, subj to Ch 4 US note 18, not GN15	0406.10.24	10%	A+
Cheeses	Fresh (unripened/uncured) cheese (ex chongos), incl whey cheese and curd, subj to gen. note 15 of the HTS, not GN15	0406.10.12	10%	A+
Cheeses	Fresh (unripened/uncured) edam and gouda cheeses, cheese/subs for cheese cont or processed therefrom, subj to Ch4 US note 20, not GN15	0406.10.44	10%	A+
Cheeses	Fresh (unripened/uncured) Italian-type cheeses from cow milk, cheese/substitutes cont or proc therefrom, subj to Ch4 US nte 21, not GN15	0406.10.54	10%	A+
Cheeses	Fresh cheese, and substitutes for cheese, cont. cows milk, neosi, o/0.5% by wt. of butterfat, descr in add US note 16 to Ch 4, not GN15	0406.10.84	10%	A+
Cheeses	Fresh cheese, and substitutes for cheese, not cont. cows milk, neosi, o/0.5% by wt. of butterfat	0406.10.95	8.50%	A+
Cheeses	Fresh cheese, and substitutes for cheese,neosi, w/0.5% or less by wt. of butterfat, descr in add US note 23 to Ch 4, not GN15	0406.10.74	10%	A+
Cheeses	Gammelost and nokkelost cheese, nesoi	0406.90.49	5.40%	A+
Cheeses	Gjetost cheese from goat's milk, whey or whey obtained from a mixture of goat's & n/o 20% cow's milk, not grated, powdered or processed	0406.90.20	4.20%	A+
Cheeses	Gjetost cheese, made from goats' milk, whey or whey obtained from a mixture of goats' & n/o 20% cows milk, not grated, powdered or processed	0406.90.25	8.50%	A+
Cheeses	Goya cheese from cow's milk, not in original loaves, nesoi,subject to add. US note 21 to Ch. 4	0406.90.31	25%	A+
Cheeses	Goya cheese not from cow's milk, nesoi, not subject to gen. note 15 or to add. US note 21 to Ch. 4	0406.90.33	21.30%	A+
Cheeses	Goya cheese, nesoi, subject to gen. note 15 of the HTS	0406.90.28	25%	A+
Cheeses	Gruyere-process cheese, processed, not grated or powdered, subject to add. US note 22 to Ch. 4	0406.30.51	6.40%	A+
Cheeses	Gruyere-process cheese, processed, not grated or powdered, subject to gen. note 15 of the HTS	0406.30.49	6.40%	A+
Cheeses	Processed cheese (incl. mixtures), nesoi, n/o 0.5% by wt. butterfat, not grated or powdered, subject to Ch4 US note 23, not GN15	0406.30.85	10%	A+
Cheeses	Processed cheese (incl. mixtures), nesoi, w/cow's milk, not grated or powdered, subject to add US note 16 to Ch. 4, not GN15	0406.30.89	10%	A+
Cheeses	Processed cheese (incl. mixtures), nesoi, w/o cows milk, not grated or powdered, not GN15	0406.30.95	8.50%	A+
Cheeses	Processed cheese cont/procd fr american-type cheese (ex cheddar), not grated/powdered, subject to add US note 19 to Ch. 4, not GN15	0406.30.69	10%	A+
Cheeses	Processed cheese cont/procd fr blue-veined cheese (ex roquefort), not grated/powdered, subject to add US note 17 to Ch. 4, not GN15	0406.30.61	10%	A+

Products Eligible for Duty-Free Treatment Under AGOA if Exported to the U.S. from an AGOA Beneficiary Country

Cheeses	Processed cheese cont/procd fr cheddar cheese, not grated/powdered, subject to add US note 18, not GN15	0406.30.65	10%	A+
Cheeses	Processed cheese cont/procd fr edam or gouda, not grated/powdered, subject to add US note 20 to Ch. 4, not GN15	0406.30.73	10%	A+
Cheeses	Processed cheese cont/procd from italian-type, not grated/powdered, subject to add US note 21 to Ch. 4, not GN15	0406.30.77	10%	A+
Cheeses	Processed cheese cont/procd from swiss, emmentaler or gruyere-process, n/grated/powdered, subject to add US note 22 to Ch. 4, not GN15	0406.30.81	10%	A+
Cheeses	Processed cheese containing or processed from bryndza, gjetost, gammelost, nokkelost or roquefort, not grated or powdered, not GN15	0406.30.57	8.50%	A+
Cheeses	Processed cheeses made from sheep's milk, including mixtures of such cheeses, not grated or powdered	0406.30.55	9.60%	A+
Cheeses	Reggiano, Parmeson, Provolne, and Provoletti cheese, nesoi, not from cow's milk, not subject to gen. note 15	0406.90.43	9.60%	A+
Cheeses	Reggiano, provolone, provoletti, sbrinz and goya cheeses, not made from cow's milk, grated or powdered	0406.20.54	9.60%	A+
Cheeses	Romano (cows milk), reggiano, provolone, provoletti, sbrinz and goya, grated or powdered, subject to gen. note 15 to HTS	0406.20.49	15%	A+
Cheeses	Romano from cows milk, Reggiano, Parmeson, Provolne, and Provoletti cheese, nesoi, subject to gen. note 15 of the HTS	0406.90.39	15%	A+
Cheeses	Romano, Reggiano, Parmeson, Provolne, and Provoletti cheese, nesoi, from cow's milk, subject to add. US note 21 to Ch. 4	0406.90.41	15%	A+
Cheeses	Romano, reggiano, provolone, provoletti, sbrinz and goya, made from cow's milk, grated or powdered, subject to add US note 21 to Ch.4	0406.20.51	15%	A+
Cheeses	Roquefort cheese in original loaves, not grated or powdered, not processed	0406.40.20	2.70%	A+
Cheeses	Roquefort cheese, grated or powdered	0406.20.10	8%	A+
Cheeses	Roquefort cheese, other than in original loaves, not grated or powdered, not processed	0406.40.40	4.50%	A+
Cheeses	Sbrinz cheese from cow's milk, nesoi, subject to add. US note 21 to Ch. 4	0406.90.36	19%	A+
Cheeses	Sbrinz cheese not from cow's milk, nesoi, not subject to gen. note 15 or to add. US note 21 to Ch. 4	0406.90.38	12.20%	A+
Cheeses	Sbrinz cheese, nesoi, subject to gen. note 15 of the HTS	0406.90.34	19%	A+
Cheeses	Swiss or emmenthaler cheese with eye formation, nesoi, subject to add. US note 25 to Ch. 4	0406.90.46	6.40%	A+
Cheeses	Swiss or emmenthaler cheese with eye formation, nesoi, subject to gen. note 15 of the HTS	0406.90.44	6.40%	A+
Chemical Products, Miscellaneous	Additives for lubricating oils containing petroleum oils or oils obtained from bituminous minerals	3811.21.00	8.70%	A+
Chemical Products, Miscellaneous	Additives for lubricating oils, nesoi	3811.29.00	6.50%	A+
Chemical Products, Miscellaneous	Antifreezing preparations and prepared de-icing fluids	3820.00.00	8.70%	A+
Chemical Products, Miscellaneous	Antiknock preparations based on other than lead compounds	3811.19.00	1.5 cents/kg + 9.3%	A+
Chemical Products, Miscellaneous	Antioxidizing preparations and other compound stabilizers for rubber or plastics, nesoi	3812.30.90	5%	A+

Products Eligible for Duty-Free Treatment Under AGOA if Exported to the U.S. from an AGOA Beneficiary Country

Chemical Products, Miscellaneous	Chemical mixtures nesoi, of two or more inorganic compounds, of tungsten	3824.90.35	6.50%	A+
Chemical Products, Miscellaneous	Chemical products, preparations, and residual products of the chemical or allied products industries, nesoi	3824.90.90	5%	A+
Chemical Products, Miscellaneous	Compound plasticizers for rubber or plastics not containing any aromatic or modified aromatic plasticizer nesoi	3812.20.50	5%	A+
Chemical Products, Miscellaneous	Finishing agents, dye carriers and other preparations used in leather and like industries, < 5% by weight aromatic (mod.) substance(s)	3809.93.50	6%	A+
Chemical Products, Miscellaneous	Finishing agents, dye carriers and other preparations used in leather and like industries, > 5% by weight aromatic (mod.) substance(s)	3809.93.10	8.70%	A+
Chemical Products, Miscellaneous	Finishing agents, dye carriers and other preparations used in paper or like industries, 5% or more by wt. aromatic (mod.) substance(s)	3809.92.10	8.70%	A+
Chemical Products, Miscellaneous	Finishing agents, dye carriers and other preparations used in paper or like industries, < 5% by weight of aromatic (mod.) substance(s)	3809.92.50	6%	A+
Chemical Products, Miscellaneous	Fungicides nesoi, put up in forms or packing for retail sale or as preparations or articles	3808.20.50	5%	A+
Chemical Products, Miscellaneous	Herbicides, antisprouting products and plant-growth regulators nesoi, put up for retail sale	3808.30.50	5%	A+
Chemical Products, Miscellaneous	Hydraulic brake fluids and transmission fluids cont. less than 70% by weight of petroleum oils, or bituminous mineral oils	3819.00.00	1.5 cents/kg + 9.3%	A+
Chemical Products, Miscellaneous	Industrial fatty alcohols other than derived from fatty substances of animal or vegetable origin	3823.70.60	2.40%	A+
Chemical Products, Miscellaneous	Industrial fatty alcohols, other than oleyl, derived from fatty substances of animal or vegetable origin	3823.70.40	2%	A+
Chemical Products, Miscellaneous	Industrial monocarboxylic fatty acids or acid oils from refining, nesoi	3823.19.40	3.20%	A+
Chemical Products, Miscellaneous	Insecticides, nesoi, for retail sale or as preparations or articles	3808.10.50	5%	A+
Chemical Products, Miscellaneous	Mixed alkylnaphthalenes, other than those of heading 2707 or 2902	3817.20.00	1.5 cents/kg + 9.3%	A+
Chemical Products, Miscellaneous	Mixed linear alkylbenzenes	3817.10.10	0.4 cents/kg + 10.8%	A+

Products Eligible for Duty-Free Treatment Under AGOA if Exported to the U.S. from an AGOA Beneficiary Country

Chemical Products, Miscellaneous	Mixtures containing acyclic hydrocarbons perhalogenated only with fluorine and chlorine	3824.71.00	3.70%	A+
Chemical Products, Miscellaneous	Mixtures containing perhalogenated derivatives of acyclic hydrocarbons containing two or more different halogens, nesoi	3824.79.00	3.70%	A+
Chemical Products, Miscellaneous	Mixtures nesoi, that are in whole or in part of hydrocarbons derived in whole or in part from petroleum, shale oil or natural gas	3824.90.45	6.50%	A+
Chemical Products, Miscellaneous	Mixtures of halogenated hydrocarbons other than chlorinated only, nesoi	3824.90.47	3.70%	A+
Chemical Products, Miscellaneous	Oleyl alcohol derived from fatty substances of animal or vegetable origin	3823.70.20	5.10%	A+
Chemical Products, Miscellaneous	Organic composite solvents and thinners containing 5 to 25 percent, by weight of one or more aromatic substances	3814.00.10	1.5 cents/kg + 9.3%	A+
Chemical Products, Miscellaneous	Organic composite solvents and thinners, nesoi; prepared paint or varnish removers; nesoi	3814.00.50	6%	A+
Chemical Products, Miscellaneous	Pickling preparations for metal surfaces; soldering, brazing or welding powders and pastes consisting of metal and other materials	3810.10.00	5%	A+
Chemical Products, Miscellaneous	Preparations used for soldering or as cores or coatings for welding electrodes or rods, nesoi	3810.90.50	5%	A+
Chemical Products, Miscellaneous	Preparations used for soldering or cores or coatings for welding electrodes or rods, 5% or more by weight aromatic (or mod.) substance(s)	3810.90.10	1.5 cents/kg + 9.3%	A+
Chemical Products, Miscellaneous	Prepared additives for cements, mortars or concretes containing 5% or more by weight of aromatic or modified aromatic substances	3824.40.10	1.5 cents/kg + 9.3%	A+
Chemical Products, Miscellaneous	Prepared additives for cements, mortars or concretes, nesoi	3824.40.50	5%	A+
Chemical Products, Miscellaneous	Prepared additives for mineral oils (incl. gasoline) or other liquids used for the same purposes as mineral oils, nesoi	3811.90.00	1.5 cents/kg + 9.3%	A+
Chemical Products, Miscellaneous	Prepared binders for foundry molds or cores	3824.10.00	6%	A+
Chemical Products, Miscellaneous	Prepared culture media for development of microorganisms	3821.00.00	5%	A+
Chemical Products, Miscellaneous	Prepared rubber accelerators not containing any aromatic or modified aromatic rubber accelerator nesoi	3812.10.50	5%	A+
Chemical Products, Miscellaneous	Reaction initiators, reaction accelerators and catalytic preparations, nesoi	3815.90.50	5%	A+
Chemical Products, Miscellaneous	Residual lyes from the manufacture of wood pulp, nesoi, excluding tall oil	3804.00.50	3.70%	A+

Products Eligible for Duty-Free Treatment Under AGOA if Exported to the U.S. from an AGOA Beneficiary Country

Chemical Products, Miscellaneous	Resin acids, derivatives of resin acids and rosin, rosin spirit and rosin oils, run gums, nesoi	3806.90.00	4.20%	A+
Chemical Products, Miscellaneous	Rodenticides, nesoi	3808.90.95	5%	A+
Chemical Products, Miscellaneous	Tall oil fatty acids	3823.13.00	3.20%	A+
Chemical Products, Miscellaneous	Terpenic oils, nesoi, produced by treatment of coniferous woods, crude dipentene; sulfite turpentine and other crude para-cymene	3805.90.00	3.70%	A+
Chemicals, Inorganic	Alkali metals, other than sodium	2805.19.00	5.50%	A+
Chemicals, Inorganic	Alloys, dispersions (including cermets), ceramic products and mixtures containing natural uranium or natural uranium compounds	2844.10.50	5%	A+
Chemicals, Inorganic	Bromine	2801.30.20	5.50%	A+
Chemicals, Inorganic	Calcium	2805.21.00	3%	A+
Chemicals, Inorganic	Colloidal precious metals	2843.10.00	5.50%	A+
Chemicals, Inorganic	Double or complex silicates	2842.10.00	3.70%	A+
Chemicals, Inorganic	Hydride, nitride, azide, silicide and boride of tungsten	2850.00.10	5.50%	A+
Chemicals, Inorganic	Rare-earth metals, scandium and yttrium, whether or not intermixed or interalloyed	2805.30.00	5%	A+
Chemicals, Inorganic	Sodium	2805.11.00	5.30%	A+
Chemicals, Inorganic	Tungstates (wolframates)	2841.80.00	5.50%	A+
Chemicals, Inorganic	Tungsten carbide	2849.90.30	7.50%	A+
Chemicals, Inorganic	Tungsten hexachloride	2827.39.40	5.50%	A+
Chemicals, Inorganic	Tungsten oxides	2825.90.30	5.50%	A+
Chemicals, Organic	1,2,4-Benzenetricarboxylic acid 1,2-dianhydride(trimellitic anhydride);naphthalic anhydride;phthalic acid;& 4-sulfo-1,8-naphthalic anhydride	2917.39.04	6.50%	A+
Chemicals, Organic	1,6-Hexamethylene diisocyanate	2929.10.35	7.10%	A+
Chemicals, Organic	1-(1,3-Benzodioxol-5-yl)propan-2-one	2932.92.00	9.30%	A+
Chemicals, Organic	1-Amino-8-hydroxy-3,6-naphthalenedisulfonic acid; and other specified aminohydroxynaphthalenesulfonic acids and their salts	2922.21.10	5.80%	A+
Chemicals, Organic	1-Bromo-2-nitrobenzene; 1-chloro-3,4-dinitrobenzene; 1,2-dichloro-4-nitrobenzene; and o-fluoronitrobenzene	2904.90.30	5.50%	A+
Chemicals, Organic	1-Formylphenylacetic acid, methyl ester	2918.30.10	5.80%	A+
Chemicals, Organic	2'-Aminoacetophenone and other specified aromatic amino-aldehydes, -ketones and -quinones, except those with more than one oxygen function	2922.30.10	5.80%	A+

Products Eligible for Duty-Free Treatment Under AGOA if Exported to the U.S. from an AGOA Beneficiary Country

Chemicals, Organic	2,3-Cresotic acid; m-hydroxybenzoic acid;2-hydroxybenzoic acid, calcium salt; and other specified carboxylic acids w/phenol function	2918.29.04	5.80%	A+
Chemicals, Organic	2-(Trifluoromethyl)phenothiazine	2934.30.12	6.50%	A+
Chemicals, Organic	2-Acetamido-3-chloroanthraquinone; o-acetoacetaldide; o-acetoacetotoluidide; 2,4-acetoacetoxylidide; and 1-amino-5-benzamidoanthraquinone	2924.29.20	6.50%	A+
Chemicals, Organic	2-Acetamidobenzoic acid	2924.22.00	1.5 cents/kg + 11.1%	A+
Chemicals, Organic	2-Amino-4-chlorobenzonitrile (5-chloro-2-cyanoaniline); 2-amino-5-chlorobenzonitrile; 4-amino-2-chlorobenzonitrile; and others specified	2926.90.05	6.50%	A+
Chemicals, Organic	2-Amino-6-chloro-4-nitrophenol and other specified amino-naphthols and amino-phenols, their ethers and esters; salts thereof	2922.29.10	5.80%	A+
Chemicals, Organic	2-Amino-6-methoxybenzothiazole and other specified heterocyclic compounds, cont. a benzothiazole ring-system, not further fused	2934.20.30	5.80%	A+
Chemicals, Organic	2-Amino-N-ethylbenzenesulfonamide; and six other specified sulfonamides	2935.00.10	6.50%	A+
Chemicals, Organic	2-Hydroxy-3-dibenzofurancarboxylic acid	2932.99.35	6.50%	A+
Chemicals, Organic	2-Mercaptobenzothiazole, sodium salt (2-Benzothiazolethiol, sodium salt)	2934.20.20	0.4 cents/kg + 8.9%	A+
Chemicals, Organic	2-Phenylimidazole	2933.29.10	5.80%	A+
Chemicals, Organic	3-(5-Amino-3-methyl-1H-pyrazol-1-yl)benzenesulfonic acid; amino-J-pyrazolone; and another 12 specified chemicals	2933.19.08	5.80%	A+
Chemicals, Organic	4,4'-Bis(dimethylamino)benzhydrol (Michler's hydrol) and other specified aromatic amino-alcohols, their ethers and esters; salts thereof	2922.19.20	5.80%	A+
Chemicals, Organic	4,4'-Diphenyl-bis-phosphonous acid, di(2',2",4',4"-di-tert-butyl)phenyl ester	2931.00.10	1.5 cents/kg + 8.9%	A+
Chemicals, Organic	4,4'-Methylenedianiline	2921.59.30	6.50%	A+
Chemicals, Organic	4-Acetamido-2-aminophenol; p-acetaminobenzaldehyde; acetoacetbenzylamide; p-acetoacetophenetidide; N-acetyl-2,6-xylidine; & other specified	2924.29.31	5.80%	A+
Chemicals, Organic	4-Amino-2-(N,N-diethylamino)toluene hydrochloride; m- and o-phenylenediamine; toluene-2,4- and -2,5-diamine; and toluene-2,5-diamine sulfate	2921.51.10	6.50%	A+
Chemicals, Organic	4-Amino-2-stilbenesulfonic acid and its salts, p-ethylaniline; 2,4,6-trimethylaniline (Mesidine); and specified xylidines	2921.49.10	5.80%	A+
Chemicals, Organic	4-Chloro-o-toluidine hydrochloride; 5-chloro-o-o-toluidine; 6-chloro-2-toluidine-sulfonic acid; 4-chloro-a,a,a-trifluoro-o-toluidine;& other	2921.43.08	5.80%	A+
Chemicals, Organic	4-Ethylguaiacol	2909.50.10	5.50%	A+
Chemicals, Organic	4-Nitro-m-cresol	2908.90.28	5.50%	A+

Products Eligible for Duty-Free Treatment Under AGOA if Exported to the U.S. from an AGOA Beneficiary Country

Chemicals, Organic	5-Amino-2-(p-aminoanilino)benzenesulfonic acid; 4,4-diamino-3-biphenylsulfonic acid; 3,3-dimethylbenzidine (o-tolidine); & other specified	2921.59.08	5.80%	A+
Chemicals, Organic	5-Amino-3-phenyl-1,2,4-thiadiazole(3-Phenyl-5-amino-1,2,4-thiadiazole), other specified aromatic or mod. aromatic heterocyclic compounds	2934.90.05	5.80%	A+
Chemicals, Organic	5-Chloro-2-nitroanisole; 6-chloro-3-nitro-p-dimethoxybenzene; and dimethyl diphenyl ether	2909.30.05	5.50%	A+
Chemicals, Organic	5-Chloro-7-iodo-8-quinolinol (Iodochlorhydroxyquin); decoquinate; diiodohydroxyquin; and oxyquinoline sulfate	2933.40.20	6.50%	A+
Chemicals, Organic	6-Bromo-5-methyl-1H-imidazo-(4,5-b)pyridine; 2-sec-butyl-4-tert-butyl-6-(benzotriazol-2-yl)phenol; 2-methylindoline; and others specified	2933.90.13	5.80%	A+
Chemicals, Organic	6-Chloro-m-cresol [OH=1]; m-chlorophenol; and chlorothymol	2908.10.10	5.50%	A+
Chemicals, Organic	7-Amino-1,3-naphthalenedisulfonic acid, specified naphthalenesulfonic acids and their salts; N-phenyl-2-napthylamine	2921.45.10	6.50%	A+
Chemicals, Organic	7-Nitronaphth[1,2]oxadiazole-5-sulfonic acid and its salts	2934.90.06	6.50%	A+
Chemicals, Organic	8-Methylquinoline and isoquinoline	2933.40.15	5.80%	A+
Chemicals, Organic	Acetone, derived in whole or in part from cumene	2914.11.10	0.1 cents/kg + 10.8%	A+
Chemicals, Organic	Acrylic acid and its salts	2916.11.00	4.20%	A+
Chemicals, Organic	Acyclic amide derivatives, salts thereof	2924.10.80	6.50%	A+
Chemicals, Organic	Acyclic polycarboxylic acids, derived from aromatic hydrocarbons, and their derivatives, nesoi	2917.19.40	1.5 cents/kg + 8.9%	A+
Chemicals, Organic	Adipic acid	2917.12.10	0.1 cents/kg + 11.8%	A+
Chemicals, Organic	Adipic acid salts and esters, nesoi	2917.12.50	9.30%	A+
Chemicals, Organic	Alkylbenzenes and polyalkylbenzenes	2902.90.30	0.4 cents/kg + 6.9%	A+
Chemicals, Organic	Alkylcresols	2907.19.10	5.50%	A+
Chemicals, Organic	Alkylphenols	2907.19.20	7.70%	A+
Chemicals, Organic	alpha,alpha,alpha-Trifluoro-2,6-dinitro-N,N-dipropyl-p-toluidine (Trifluralin)	2921.43.15	9.30%	A+
Chemicals, Organic	Amino-naphthols and other amino-phenols and their derivatives of products described in add'l U.S. note 3 to section VI	2922.29.60	9.30%	A+
Chemicals, Organic	Amino-naphthols and other amino-phenols; their ethers, esters & salts (not containing more than one oxygen function) thereof nesoi	2922.29.80	1.5 cents/kg + 10.1%	A+
Chemicals, Organic	Aminohydroxynaphthalene sulfonic acids and their salts of products described in additional US note 3 to section VI	2922.21.40	9.30%	A+
Chemicals, Organic	Aminohydroxynaphthalene sulfonic acids and their salts, nesoi	2922.21.50	1.5 cents/kg + 10.1%	A+
Chemicals, Organic	Aniline	2921.41.10	1.5 cents/kg + 9.3%	A+
Chemicals, Organic	Aniline derivatives and their salts of products in additional U.S. note 3 to section VI	2921.42.65	9.30%	A+
Chemicals, Organic	Aniline salts	2921.41.20	1 cent/kg + 11.4%	A+

Products Eligible for Duty-Free Treatment Under AGOA if Exported to the U.S. from an AGOA Beneficiary Country

Chemicals, Organic	Anisidines, dianisidines, phenetidines, and their salts, described in additional U.S. note 3 to section VI	2922.22.20	9.30%	A+
Chemicals, Organic	Anthranilic acid and its salts, described in additional US note 3 to section VI	2922.43.10	9.30%	A+
Chemicals, Organic	Anthranilic acid and its salts, nesoi	2922.43.50	1.5 cents/kg + 10.1%	A+
Chemicals, Organic	Anti-infective agents nesoi, of heterocyclic compounds with nitrogen hetero-atom(s) only, cont. pyrimidine, piperazine ring	2933.59.36	6.50%	A+
Chemicals, Organic	Antidepressants, tranquilizers and other pschotherapeutic agents containing a phenothiazine ring-system, not further fused	2934.30.23	10.50%	A+
Chemicals, Organic	Antihistamines, including those principally used as antinauseants	2933.59.21	6.50%	A+
Chemicals, Organic	Aromatic alcohol peroxides, ether peroxides, ketone peroxides and their halogenated, sulfonated, nitrated or nitrosated derivatives, nesoi	2909.60.20	11.30%	A+
Chemicals, Organic	Aromatic alcohol, ether and ketone peroxides and their halogenated, sulfonated, nitrated, nitrosated derivatives, in add. US note 3 sec. VI	2909.60.10	8.70%	A+
Chemicals, Organic	Aromatic aldehyde-alcohols	2912.30.10	7.50%	A+
Chemicals, Organic	Aromatic amino-acids and their esters, excl. those with more than one oxygen function; salts: described in add. U.S. note 3 to sect VI	2922.49.30	9.30%	A+
Chemicals, Organic	Aromatic amino-acids and their esters, not contng more than 1 kind of oxygen function (excluding goods in add U.S. note 3 to sec VI), nesoi	2922.49.37	1.5 cents/kg + 10.1%	A+
Chemicals, Organic	Aromatic amino-acids drugs and their esters, not containing more than one kind of oxygen function	2922.49.27	6.50%	A+
Chemicals, Organic	Aromatic amino-alcohol-phenols, amino-acid-phenols and other amino-compounds with oxygen function described in add. US note 3 to section VI	2922.50.35	9.30%	A+
Chemicals, Organic	Aromatic amino-alcohol-phenols, amino-acid-phenols and other amino-compounds with oxygen function, nesoi	2922.50.40	1.5 cents/kg + 10.1%	A+
Chemicals, Organic	Aromatic amino-alcohols, their ethers and esters, other than those containing more than one oxy func described in add. US note 3 to sect VI	2922.19.60	9.30%	A+
Chemicals, Organic	Aromatic amino-aldehydes, -ketones and -quinones, except those with more than one oxygen function & salts, desc in add US note 3 sec VI	2922.30.25	9.30%	A+
Chemicals, Organic	Aromatic carboxylic acids w/aldehyde or ketone function but w/o other oxygen function & their deriv desc. in add US note 3 to sec VI, nesoi	2918.30.25	9.30%	A+
Chemicals, Organic	Aromatic carboxylic acids with add'l oxygen function and their anhydrides, halide, etc deriv described in add US note 3 to sect VI, nesoi	2918.90.43	9.30%	A+
Chemicals, Organic	Aromatic carboxylic acids with alcohol function, w/o other oxygen functions, and their derivatives, described in add. U.S. note 3 to sec. VI	2918.19.20	9.30%	A+
Chemicals, Organic	Aromatic carboxylic acids with alcohol function, without other oxygen functions, and their derivatives, nesoi	2918.19.30	1.5 cents/kg + 11.1%	A+
Chemicals, Organic	Aromatic carboxylic acids with aldehyde or ketone function, but without other oxygen function, and derivatives, nesoi	2918.30.30	1.5 cents/kg + 11.1%	A+
Chemicals, Organic	Aromatic compounds of thiocarbamates and dithiocarbamates, excluding pesticides	2930.20.20	6.50%	A+
Chemicals, Organic	Aromatic compounds with other nitrogen function, nesoi	2929.90.20	1.2 cents/kg + 10.4%	A+
Chemicals, Organic	Aromatic cyclic amides and their derivatives; salts thereof, nesoi	2924.29.75	1.5 cents/kg + 11.1%	A+

Products Eligible for Duty-Free Treatment Under AGOA if Exported to the U.S. from an AGOA Beneficiary Country

Chemicals, Organic	Aromatic derivatives of hydrocarbons containing only nitro or only nitroso groups, described in additional U.S. note 3 to section VI	2904.20.40	8.70%	A+
Chemicals, Organic	Aromatic derivatives of hydrocarbons containing only nitro or only nitroso groups, nesoi	2904.20.45	1.5 cents/kg + 9.7%	A+
Chemicals, Organic	Aromatic derivatives of hydrocarbons containing only sulfo groups, their salts and ethyl esters, described in add. U.S. note 3 to sec. VI	2904.10.32	8.70%	A+
Chemicals, Organic	Aromatic derivatives of hydrocarbons containing only sulfo groups, their salts and ethyl esters, nesoi	2904.10.37	1.5 cents/kg + 9.7%	A+
Chemicals, Organic	Aromatic dermatological agents and local anesthetics of amino-compounds with oxygen function	2922.50.17	6.50%	A+
Chemicals, Organic	Aromatic drugs of amino-compounds with oxygen function, nesoi	2922.50.25	6.50%	A+
Chemicals, Organic	Aromatic drugs of imines and their derivatives, nesoi	2925.20.20	6.50%	A+
Chemicals, Organic	Aromatic drugs of lactones	2932.29.20	6.50%	A+
Chemicals, Organic	Aromatic epoxides, epoxyalcohols, epoxyphenols and epoxyethers, with a three-membered ring, and their derivatives, nesoi	2910.90.20	5.50%	A+
Chemicals, Organic	Aromatic esters of acetic acid described in additional U.S. note 3 to section VI	2915.39.30	8.70%	A+
Chemicals, Organic	Aromatic esters of acetic acid, nesoi	2915.39.35	1.5 cents/kg + 10.5%	A+
Chemicals, Organic	Aromatic esters of other inorganic acids (excluding hydrogen halides) their salts and their derivatives, nesoi	2920.90.20	6.50%	A+
Chemicals, Organic	Aromatic ether-alcohols and their halogenated, sulfonated, nitrated or nitrosated derivatives, nesoi	2909.49.15	11.30%	A+
Chemicals, Organic	Aromatic ethers and their halogenated, sulfonated, nitrated or nitrosated derivatives, nesoi, described in add. U.S. note 3 to section VI	2909.30.40	8.70%	A+
Chemicals, Organic	Aromatic halogenated, sulfonated, nitrated or nitrosated derivatives of product of heading 2912	2913.00.40	11.30%	A+
Chemicals, Organic	Aromatic heterocyclic compounds nesoi, with nitrogen hetero-atom(s) only, cont. pyrimidine or piperazine ring, in add. U.S. note 3, sec. VI	2933.59.70	9.30%	A+
Chemicals, Organic	Aromatic heterocyclic compounds with oxygen hetero-atom(s) only described in additional U.S. note 3 to section VI, nesoi	2932.99.60	9.30%	A+
Chemicals, Organic	Aromatic heterocyclic compounds with oxygen hetero-atom(s) only, containing an unfused furan ring, nesoi	2932.19.10	6.50%	A+
Chemicals, Organic	Aromatic heterocyclic compounds with oxygen hetero-atom(s) only, nesoi	2932.99.70	1.5 cents/kg + 10.4%	A+
Chemicals, Organic	Aromatic imines and their derivatives; salts thereof (excluding drugs); nesoi	2925.20.60	9.90%	A+
Chemicals, Organic	Aromatic ketone-alcohols and ketone-aldehydes, nesoi	2914.40.40	7.70%	A+
Chemicals, Organic	Aromatic ketone-phenols and ketones with other oxygen function	2914.50.30	7.70%	A+
Chemicals, Organic	Aromatic lactones, nesoi	2932.29.45	1.5 cents/kg + 10.4%	A+
Chemicals, Organic	Aromatic lactones, nesoi, described in additional U.S. note 3 to section VI	2932.29.30	9.30%	A+

Products Eligible for Duty-Free Treatment Under AGOA if Exported to the U.S. from an AGOA Beneficiary Country

Chemicals, Organic	Aromatic monoamine drugs, nesoi	2921.49.43	6.50%	A+
Chemicals, Organic	Aromatic monoamine drugs: antidepressants, tranquilizers and other psychotherapeutic agents	2921.49.37	10.50%	A+
Chemicals, Organic	Aromatic monoamines and their derivatives and salts described in additional US note 3 to section VI, nesoi	2921.45.60	9.30%	A+
Chemicals, Organic	Aromatic monoamines and their derivatives and salts thereof nesoi	2921.45.90	1 cent/kg + 11.4%	A+
Chemicals, Organic	Aromatic monoamines and their derivatives and salts thereof, nesoi	2921.49.50	1 cent/kg + 11.4%	A+
Chemicals, Organic	Aromatic monoamines and their derivatives nesoi; salts thereof, described in additional U.S. note 3 to section VI	2921.49.45	9.30%	A+
Chemicals, Organic	Aromatic monocarboxylic acids, their anhydrides, halides, peroxides, peroxyacids and derivatives described in add'l US note 3 to section VI	2916.39.45	9.30%	A+
Chemicals, Organic	Aromatic nitrile-function compounds excluding products in additional U.S. note 3 to section VI	2926.90.47	11.90%	A+
Chemicals, Organic	Aromatic nitrile-function compounds, nesoi, described in additional U.S. note 3 to section VI	2926.90.44	9.30%	A+
Chemicals, Organic	Aromatic or mod aromatic goods contng unfused imidazole ring (whether or n/hydrogenated) in the structure (exc prod in add US note 3 sec VI)	2933.29.43	1.5 cents/kg + 10.4%	A+
Chemicals, Organic	Aromatic or mod. aromatic compound desc in add US note 3 to section VI contain an unfused pyrazole ring (w/wo hydrogenated) in the structure	2933.19.37	9.30%	A+
Chemicals, Organic	Aromatic or mod. aromatic compounds with nitrogen hetero-atom(s) only excluding products described in add. U.S. note 3 to section VI; nesoi	2933.90.82	1.5 cents/kg + 10.4%	A+
Chemicals, Organic	Aromatic or mod. aromatic goods in add US note 3 to sect VI containing an unfused imidazole ring (whether or n/hydrogenated) in structure	2933.29.35	9.30%	A+
Chemicals, Organic	Aromatic or modified aromatic anti-infective agents of heterocyclic compounds with nitrogen hetero-atom(s) only, nesoi	2933.90.46	6.50%	A+
Chemicals, Organic	Aromatic or modified aromatic anticonvulsants, hypnotics and sedatives, of heterocyclic compounds with nitrogen hetero-atom(s) only, nesoi	2933.90.65	6.50%	A+
Chemicals, Organic	Aromatic or modified aromatic antihistamines of heterocyclic compounds with nitrogen hetero-atom(s) only	2933.90.26	6.50%	A+
Chemicals, Organic	Aromatic or modified aromatic cardiovascular drugs of heterocyclic compounds with nitrogen hetero-atom(s) only, nesoi	2933.90.53	6.50%	A+
Chemicals, Organic	Aromatic or modified aromatic compounds (excluding products in add US note 3 to sec VI) containing an unfused pyrazole ring in the structure	2933.19.43	1.5 cents/kg + 10.4%	A+
Chemicals, Organic	Aromatic or modified aromatic compounds with nitrogen hetero-atom(s) only described in additional U.S. note 3 to section VI	2933.90.79	9.30%	A+
Chemicals, Organic	Aromatic or modified aromatic drugs affecting the CNS, of heterocyclic compounds with nitrogen atom(s) only, nesoi	2933.90.70	6.50%	A+
Chemicals, Organic	Aromatic or modified aromatic drugs of heterocyclic compounds with nitrogen hetero-atom(s) only, nesoi	2933.90.75	6.50%	A+
Chemicals, Organic	Aromatic or modified aromatic drugs of other organic compounds, nesoi	2942.00.05	6.50%	A+
Chemicals, Organic	Aromatic or modified aromatic heterocyclic compounds cont. an unfused thiazole ring, described in add. U.S. note 3 to section VI	2934.10.10	9.30%	A+
Chemicals, Organic	Aromatic or modified aromatic heterocyclic compounds nesoi, with nitrogen hetero-atom(s) only, cont. pyrimidine or piperazine ring	2933.59.80	1.5 cents/kg + 10.4%	A+

Products Eligible for Duty-Free Treatment Under AGOA if Exported to the U.S. from an AGOA Beneficiary Country

Chemicals, Organic	Aromatic or modified aromatic heterocyclic compounds, nesoi	2934.90.44	1.5 cents/kg + 10.4%	A+
Chemicals, Organic	Aromatic or modified aromatic heterocyclic compounds, nesoi, containing an unfused thiazole ring	2934.10.20	1.5 cents/kg + 10.4%	A+
Chemicals, Organic	Aromatic or modified aromatic lactams, nesoi	2933.79.15	1.5 cents/kg + 10.4%	A+
Chemicals, Organic	Aromatic or modified aromatic organic compounds, nesoi, described in additional U.S. note 3 to section VI	2942.00.10	9.30%	A+
Chemicals, Organic	Aromatic organic derivatives of hydrazine or of hydroxylamine	2928.00.25	6.50%	A+
Chemicals, Organic	Aromatic organo-inorganic compounds, nesoi, described in additional U.S. note 3 to section VI	2931.00.30	9.30%	A+
Chemicals, Organic	Aromatic organo-mercury compounds	2931.00.27	6.50%	A+
Chemicals, Organic	Aromatic phosphoric esters and their salts, including lactophosphates, and their derivatives, not used as plasticizers	2919.00.30	6.50%	A+
Chemicals, Organic	Aromatic polyamines and their derivatives and salts thereof, described in additional U.S. note 3 to section VI	2921.59.40	9.30%	A+
Chemicals, Organic	Aromatic polyamines and their derivatives; salts thereof nesoi	2921.59.80	1 cent/kg + 11.4%	A+
Chemicals, Organic	Aromatic polycarboxylic acids, their anhydrides, halides, peroxides, peroxyacids and their derivatives nesoi, in add. U.S. note 3 to sec. VI	2917.39.30	9.30%	A+
Chemicals, Organic	Aromatic salts and esters of chlorocetic acids, described in additional U.S. note 3 to section VI	2915.40.20	8.70%	A+
Chemicals, Organic	Aromatic salts and esters of chlorocetic acids, nesoi	2915.40.30	1.5 cents/kg + 10.5%	A+
Chemicals, Organic	Aromatic sulfonated, nitrated or nitrosated derivatives of hydrocarbons nesoi, described in additional U.S. note 3 to section VI	2904.90.40	8.70%	A+
Chemicals, Organic	Aromatic sulfonated, nitrated or nitrosated derivatives of hydrocarbons, nesoi	2904.90.47	1.5 cents/kg + 9.7%	A+
Chemicals, Organic	Aromatic ureines and their derivatives; salts thereof, nesoi	2924.21.45	1.5 cents/kg + 11.1%	A+
Chemicals, Organic	Aromatic ureines and their derivatives; salts thereof; described in additional U.S. note 3 to section VI	2924.21.20	9.30%	A+
Chemicals, Organic	Aromatic/modified aromatic psychotherapeutic agents, affecting the CNS, of heterocyclic compounds with nitrogen hetero-atom(s) only, nesoi	2933.90.61	10.50%	A+
Chemicals, Organic	Benzaldehyde	2912.21.00	5.50%	A+
Chemicals, Organic	Benzilic acid; and benzilic acid, methyl ester	2918.19.10	5.80%	A+
Chemicals, Organic	Benzoic acid esters, except odoriferous or flavoring compounds, described in additional U.S. note 3 to section VI	2916.31.30	9.30%	A+
Chemicals, Organic	Benzoic acid esters, nesoi	2916.31.50	1.5 cents/kg + 11.1%	A+
Chemicals, Organic	Benzoic anhydride; tert-butyl peroxybenzoate; p-nitrobenzoyl chloride; 2-nitro-m-toluic acid; and 3-nitro-o-toluic acid	2916.39.03	6.50%	A+
Chemicals, Organic	Benzointetrahydropyranyl ester; and Xanthen-9-one	2932.99.39	5.80%	A+
Chemicals, Organic	Benzoyl chloride	2916.32.20	6.50%	A+
Chemicals, Organic	Benzoyl peroxide	2916.32.10	1.5 cents/kg + 11.1%	A+
Chemicals, Organic	Benzyl alcohol	2906.21.00	5.50%	A+

Products Eligible for Duty-Free Treatment Under AGOA if Exported to the U.S. from an AGOA Beneficiary Country

Chemicals, Organic	Benzyl chloride (alpha-Chlorotoluene); benzotrichloride (alpha,alpha,alpha-trichlorotoluene)	2903.69.20	5.50%	A+
Chemicals, Organic	Biligrafin acid; 3,5-diacetamido-2,4,6-triiodobenzoic acid; and metrizoic acid	2924.29.05	5.30%	A+
Chemicals, Organic	Bis-(tribromophenoxy)ethane; pentabromodiphenyl oxide; and tetradecabromodiphenoxy benzene	2909.30.09	8%	A+
Chemicals, Organic	Bitolylene diisocyanate (TODI); o-Isocyanic acid, o-tolyl ester; and Xylene diisocyanate	2929.10.20	5.80%	A+
Chemicals, Organic	Carboxylic acids with phenol function but w/o other oxygen function, described in add'l. U.S. note 3 to section VI	2918.29.65	9.30%	A+
Chemicals, Organic	Cyclanic, cyclenic or cycloterpenic polycarboxylic acids, their anhydrides, halides, peroxides, peroxyacids and their derivatives	2917.20.00	4.20%	A+
Chemicals, Organic	Cyclanic, cyclenic, cycloterpenic mono- or polyamines and their derivative, deriv from any aromatic cmpd (excl goods in add US note 3 sec VI	2921.30.30	1.5 cents/kg + 10.6%	A+
Chemicals, Organic	Cyclanic, cyclenic, cycloterpenic mono- or polyamines, derivatives and salts, from any aromatic compound desc in add US note 3, sec. VI	2921.30.10	9.30%	A+
Chemicals, Organic	Cyclic hydrocarbons, nesoi	2902.90.90	4.20%	A+
Chemicals, Organic	Cyclohexanol, methylcyclohexanols and dimethylcyclohexanols	2906.12.00	1.5 cents/kg + 10%	A+
Chemicals, Organic	Decabromodiphenyl oxide; and octabromodiphenyl oxide	2909.30.07	11.30%	A+
Chemicals, Organic	Derivatives nesoi,of phenols or phenol-alcohols cont. only sulfo groups, their salts and esters, described in add. U.S. note 3 to section VI	2908.20.20	8.70%	A+
Chemicals, Organic	Derivatives of malonylurea (barbituric acid); salts thereof	2933.51.90	3.70%	A+
Chemicals, Organic	Derivatives of phenol or phenol-alcohols containing only sulfo groups, their salts and esters, nesoi	2908.20.60	0.6 cents/kg + 11.1%	A+
Chemicals, Organic	Derivatives of phenols or phenol-alcohols containing only halogen substituents and their salts described in add. U.S. note 3 to sec. VI	2908.10.35	8.70%	A+
Chemicals, Organic	Diazo-, azo- or azoxy-compounds, nesoi, described in additional U.S. note 3 to section VI	2927.00.40	9.30%	A+
Chemicals, Organic	Dibromoethyldibromocyclohexane	2903.59.05	5.40%	A+
Chemicals, Organic	Diphenylamine and its derivatives (except nitrodiphenylamine); salts thereof, described in additional U.S. note 3 to section VI	2921.44.20	9.30%	A+
Chemicals, Organic	Diphenylamine and its derivatives; salts thereof; excluding goods in additional U.S. note 3 to section VI	2921.44.70	1 cent/kg + 11.4%	A+
Chemicals, Organic	Dodecan-1-ol (Lauryl alcohol); hexadecan-1-ol (Cetyl alcohol); octadecan-1-ol (Stearyl alcohol)	2905.17.00	5%	A+
Chemicals, Organic	Drugs containing an unfused pyridine ring (whether or not hydrogenated) in the structure, nesoi	2933.39.41	6.50%	A+
Chemicals, Organic	Drugs of amino-naphthols and -phenols, their ethers and esters, except those cont. more than one oxygen function; salts thereof, nesoi	2922.29.27	6.50%	A+
Chemicals, Organic	Drugs of aromatic organo-inorganic (except organo-sulfur) compounds	2931.00.22	6.50%	A+
Chemicals, Organic	Drugs of quinones	2914.69.20	5.50%	A+
Chemicals, Organic	Esters of salicylic acid and their salts, described in additional U.S. note 3 to section VI	2918.23.30	9.30%	A+

Products Eligible for Duty-Free Treatment Under AGOA if Exported to the U.S. from an AGOA Beneficiary Country

Chemicals, Organic	Esters of salicylic acid and their salts, nesoi	2918.23.50	1.5 cents/kg + 11.1%	A+
Chemicals, Organic	Ether-phenols, ether-alcohol-phenols & their halogenated, sulfonated, nitrated, nitrosated derivatives nesoi, in add. U.S. note 3 to sec. VI	2909.50.45	8.70%	A+
Chemicals, Organic	Ether-phenols, ether-alcohol-phenols and their halogenated, sulfonated, nitrated or nitrosated derivatives, nesoi	2909.50.50	11.30%	A+
Chemicals, Organic	Ethylene dibromide	2903.30.05	5.40%	A+
Chemicals, Organic	Ethylenebistetrabromophthalimide	2925.19.10	9.90%	A+
Chemicals, Organic	Gentisic acid; and hydroxycinnamic acid and its salts	2918.29.20	6.50%	A+
Chemicals, Organic	Halogenated derivatives derived in whole or in part from benzene or other aromatic hydrocarbon, nesoi	2903.59.20	1.5 cents/kg + 10%	A+
Chemicals, Organic	Halogenated products derived in whole or in part from benzene or other aromatic hydrocarbon, described in additional U.S. note 3 to sec. VI	2903.59.15	8.70%	A+
Chemicals, Organic	Halogenated, sulfonated, nitrated or nitrosated derivatives of phenols or phenol-alcohols described in additional U.S. note 3 to section VI	2908.90.40	8.70%	A+
Chemicals, Organic	Halogenated, sulfonated, nitrated or nitrosated derivatives of phenols or phenol-alcohols, nesoi	2908.90.50	0.6 cents/kg + 11.1%	A+
Chemicals, Organic	Heterocyclic compounds containing a benzothiazole ring-system, not further fused, described in add. U.S. note 3 to section VI	2934.20.40	9.30%	A+
Chemicals, Organic	Heterocyclic compounds containing a phenothiazine ring-system (whether or not hydrogenated), not further fused, nesoi	2934.30.50	1.5 cents/kg + 10.4%	A+
Chemicals, Organic	Heterocyclic compounds with nitrogen hetero-atom(s) only containing an unfused pyridine ring, described in add. US note 3 to sec. VI	2933.39.61	9.30%	A+
Chemicals, Organic	Heterocyclic compounds with nitrogen hetero-atom(s) only containing an unfused pyridine ring, nesoi	2933.39.91	1.5 cents/kg + 10.4%	A+
Chemicals, Organic	Heterocyclic compounds with nitrogen hetero-atom(s) only, containing a quinoline ring-system, not further fused, nesoi	2933.40.70	1.5 cents/kg + 10.4%	A+
Chemicals, Organic	Hexachlorobenzene and DDT (1,1,1-Trichloro-2,2-bis(p-chlorophenyl)ethane)	2903.62.00	5.50%	A+
Chemicals, Organic	Hexamethylenediamine and its salts (except Nylon salt), derived in whole or in part from adipic acid	2921.22.10	11.90%	A+
Chemicals, Organic	Hydroquinone (Quinol) and its salts, other than photographic grade	2907.22.50	5.50%	A+
Chemicals, Organic	Isocyanates of products described in additioonal U.S. note 3 to sect VI	2929.10.55	9.30%	A+
Chemicals, Organic	Isophthalic acid	2917.39.15	6.50%	A+
Chemicals, Organic	Isosafrole	2932.91.00	9.30%	A+
Chemicals, Organic	Lactams described in add'l U.S. note 3 to section VI	2933.79.09	9.30%	A+
Chemicals, Organic	m-Aminobenzoic acid, technical; and other specified aromatic amino-acids and their esters, except those with more than one oxygen function	2922.49.10	5.80%	A+
Chemicals, Organic	m-Benzenedisulfonic acid, sodium salt; 1,5-naphthalenedisulfonic acid; and p-toluenesulfonyl chloride	2904.10.10	5.50%	A+
Chemicals, Organic	m-Dichlorobenzene; 1,1-dichloro-2,2-bis(p-ethylphenyl)ethane; and trichlorobenzenes	2903.69.10	5.50%	A+
Chemicals, Organic	m-Diethylaminophenol; m-dimethylaminophenol; 3-ethylamino-p-cresol; and 5-methoxy-m-phenylenediamine	2922.29.15	6.50%	A+

Products Eligible for Duty-Free Treatment Under AGOA if Exported to the U.S. from an AGOA Beneficiary Country

Chemicals, Organic	m-Nitrochlorobenzene	2904.90.08	5.50%	A+
Chemicals, Organic	Methacrylic acid and its salts	2916.13.00	4.20%	A+
Chemicals, Organic	Mixtures of 1,3,6-naphthalenetrisulfonic acid and 1,3,7-naphthalenetrisulfonic acid	2904.10.15	1.5 cents/kg + 8.3%	A+
Chemicals, Organic	Monosodium glutamate	2922.42.10	8.70%	A+
Chemicals, Organic	N'-(4-Chloro-o-tolyl)-N,N-dimethylformamidine; bunamidine hydrochloride; and pentamidine	2925.20.10	6.50%	A+
Chemicals, Organic	N,N-Dimethylaniline	2921.42.10	8.90%	A+
Chemicals, Organic	Naphthols and their salts, other than alpha-Naphthol and 2-Naphthol	2907.15.60	11.30%	A+
Chemicals, Organic	Nicarbazin and trimethoprim	2933.59.22	6.50%	A+
Chemicals, Organic	Nitrated benzene, nitrated toluene (except p-nitrotoluene) or nitrated naphthalene	2904.20.35	1.2 cents/kg + 8.3%	A+
Chemicals, Organic	Nitrophenols, except p-nitrophenol	2908.90.08	5.50%	A+
Chemicals, Organic	Nitrosodiphenylamine	2921.44.10	6.50%	A+
Chemicals, Organic	Nitrotoluenesulfonic acids	2904.90.20	7.60%	A+
Chemicals, Organic	Nonaromatic carboxylic acids with alcohol function, without other oxygen function, and their derivatives, nesoi	2918.19.90	4%	A+
Chemicals, Organic	Nonaromatic derivatives of hydrocarbons containing only sulfo groups, their salts and ethyl esters, nesoi	2904.10.50	4.20%	A+
Chemicals, Organic	Nonaromatic organo-sulfur acids, nesoi	2930.90.49	4.20%	A+
Chemicals, Organic	o-, m-, p-Phenylenediamine, and diaminotoluenes and their derivatives, and salts thereof, nesoi	2921.51.50	1 cent/kg + 11.4%	A+
Chemicals, Organic	o-, m-, p-Phenylenediamine, diaminotoluenes, and their derivatives, and salts thereof, described in additional U.S. note 3 to section VI	2921.51.30	9.30%	A+
Chemicals, Organic	o-Aminobenzenesulfonic acid; 6-chlorometanilic acid; 2-chloro-5-nitroaniline; 4-chloro-3-nitroaniline; dichloroanilines; and other specified	2921.42.18	5.80%	A+
Chemicals, Organic	o-Anisidine; p-anisidine; and p-phenetidine	2922.22.10	6.50%	A+
Chemicals, Organic	o-Dichlorobenzene	2903.61.20	9.40%	A+
Chemicals, Organic	o-Toluenesulfonamide	2935.00.15	6.50%	A+
Chemicals, Organic	Octylphenol, nonylphenol and their isomers; salts thereof	2907.13.00	7.70%	A+
Chemicals, Organic	Oleic, linoleic or linolenic acids	2916.15.10	6.50%	A+
Chemicals, Organic	Other aniline derivatives and their salts	2921.42.90	1 cent/kg + 11.4%	A+

Products Eligible for Duty-Free Treatment Under AGOA if Exported to the U.S. from an AGOA Beneficiary Country

Chemicals, Organic	Other anisidines, dianisidines, phenetidines, and their salts, nesoi	2922.22.50	1.5 cents/kg + 10.1%	A+
Chemicals, Organic	Other aromatic alcohols and their halogenated, sulfonated, nitrated or nitrosated derivatives	2906.29.60	5.50%	A+
Chemicals, Organic	Other aromatic amino-alcohols, their ethers & esters, other than those contain more than one oxy func (exc goods of add. US note 3 sect VI)	2922.19.70	1.5 cents/kg + 10.1%	A+
Chemicals, Organic	Other aromatic amino-alcohols, their ethers and esters, other than those contng > one kind of oxygen func.; salts thereof used as drugs	2922.19.18	6.50%	A+
Chemicals, Organic	Other aromatic amino-aldehydes, amino-ketones and amino-quinones other than those contng > one oxy func (excl good of add US note 3 sec VI)	2922.30.45	1.5 cents/kg + 10.1%	A+
Chemicals, Organic	Other aromatic carboxylic acids with add'l oxygen function and their anhydrides, halide, etc deriv (exclud goods in add US note 3 to sec VI)	2918.90.47	1.5 cents/kg + 11.1%	A+
Chemicals, Organic	Other aromatic cardiovascular drugs of amino-compounds with oxygen function	2922.50.14	6.50%	A+
Chemicals, Organic	Other aromatic compounds with other nitrogen function of products described in additional U.S. note 3 to section VI	2929.90.15	9.30%	A+
Chemicals, Organic	Other aromatic cyclic amides and their derivatives of products in additional U.S. note 3 to section VI	2924.29.70	9.30%	A+
Chemicals, Organic	Other aromatic ether-alcohols, their halogenated, sulfonated, nitrated or nitrosated derivatives described in add. US note 3 to section VI	2909.49.10	8.70%	A+
Chemicals, Organic	Other aromatic ethers and their halogenated, sulfonated, nitrated, or nitrosated derivatives, nesoi	2909.30.60	11.30%	A+
Chemicals, Organic	Other aromatic imides and their derivatives	2925.19.40	9.90%	A+
Chemicals, Organic	Other aromatic monocarboxylic acids, their anhydrides, halides, peroxides, peroxyacids and their derivatives	2916.39.75	1.5 cents/kg + 11.1%	A+
Chemicals, Organic	Other aromatic or modified aromatic drugs containing a pyrimidine ring (whether or not hydrogenated) or piperazine ring in the structure	2933.59.53	6.50%	A+
Chemicals, Organic	Other aromatic or modified aromatic organic compounds (excluding products described in additional U.S. note 3 to section VI)	2942.00.35	10.30%	A+
Chemicals, Organic	Other aromatic organo-inorganic compounds (excluding products described in additional U.S. note 3 to section VI	2931.00.60	11%	A+
Chemicals, Organic	Other aromatic organo-sulfur compounds (excluding pesticides)	2930.90.29	6.50%	A+
Chemicals, Organic	Other aromatic polycarboxylic acids and their derivatives (excluding those described in additional US note 3 to section VI	2917.39.70	11.90%	A+
Chemicals, Organic	Other carboxylic acids w/phenol function but w/o other oxygen function & their derivatives (excluding goods of add. US note 3 to section VI)	2918.29.75	1.5 cents/kg + 11.1%	A+
Chemicals, Organic	Other compounds containing a benzothiazole ring system (whether or not hydrogenated), not further fused	2934.20.80	1.5 cents/kg + 10.4%	A+
Chemicals, Organic	Other diazo-, azo- or azoxy-compounds, nesoi	2927.00.50	11.90%	A+
Chemicals, Organic	Other dichlorobenzonitriles	2926.90.12	6.50%	A+
Chemicals, Organic	Other drugs containing a phenothiazine ring system (whether or not hydrogenated), not further fused, nesoi	2934.30.27	6.50%	A+
Chemicals, Organic	Other drugs containing a quinoline or isoquinoline ring-system (whether or not hydrogenated) not further fused	2933.40.26	6.50%	A+
Chemicals, Organic	Other halogenated derivatives of aromatic hydrocarbons	2903.69.70	5.50%	A+

Products Eligible for Duty-Free Treatment Under AGOA if Exported to the U.S. from an AGOA Beneficiary Country

Chemicals, Organic	Other halogenated, sulfonated, nitrated or nitrosated derivatives of phenol or phenol-alcohols	2908.10.60	0.6 cents/kg + 11.1%	A+
Chemicals, Organic	Other halogenated, sulfonated, nitrated, or nitrosated derivatives of aromatic ketones & quinones whether or not with other oxygen function	2914.70.40	7.70%	A+
Chemicals, Organic	Other heterocyclic compounds of products described in additional U.S. note 3 to section VI	2934.90.39	9.30%	A+
Chemicals, Organic	Other isocyanates, nesoi	2929.10.80	1.2 cents/kg + 10.4%	A+
Chemicals, Organic	Other monophenols	2907.19.80	5.50%	A+
Chemicals, Organic	Other polyphenols, nesoi	2907.29.90	5.50%	A+
Chemicals, Organic	Other sulfonamide drugs (excluding anti-infective agents)	2935.00.60	6.50%	A+
Chemicals, Organic	Other sulfonamides (excluding drugs and certain specified chemicals) described in additional U.S. note 3 to section VI	2935.00.75	9.30%	A+
Chemicals, Organic	Other sulfonamides (excluding drugs and certain specified chemicals) not described in additional U.S. note 3 to section VI	2935.00.95	1.5 cents/kg + 11.1%	A+
Chemicals, Organic	Other sulfonamides used as anti-infective agents	2935.00.48	8.20%	A+
Chemicals, Organic	Other toluidines and their derivatives; and salts thereof	2921.43.80	1 cent/kg + 11.4%	A+
Chemicals, Organic	p-Aminoazobenzenedisulfonic acid; and diazoaminobenzene (1,3-diphenyltriazine)	2927.00.06	5.80%	A+
Chemicals, Organic	p-Anisic acid; clofibrate; 1,6-hexanediol-bis(3,5-dibutyl-4-hydroxyphenyl)propionate; and 3-phenoxybenzoic acid	2918.90.05	5.80%	A+
Chemicals, Organic	p-Chloro-2-benzylpyridine & other specified heterocyclic compounds, w nitrogen hetero-atom(s) only cont. an unfused pyridine ring	2933.39.20	5.80%	A+
Chemicals, Organic	p-Nitro-o-xylene	2904.20.15	5.50%	A+
Chemicals, Organic	p-Nitrotoluene	2904.20.10	5.50%	A+
Chemicals, Organic	Phenylacetic acid (alpha-Toluic acid)	2916.34.10	6.50%	A+
Chemicals, Organic	Phenylacetic acid esters, nesoi	2916.35.55	1.5 cents/kg + 7.2%	A+
Chemicals, Organic	Phenylacetic acid esters, nesoi, described in additional US note 3 to section VI	2916.35.25	9.30%	A+
Chemicals, Organic	Phenylacetic acid salts, nesoi	2916.34.55	1.5 cents/kg + 7.2%	A+
Chemicals, Organic	Phenylacetic acid salts, nesoi, described in additional US note 3 to section VI	2916.34.25	9.30%	A+
Chemicals, Organic	Phenylglycolic (Mandelic) acid salts and esters	2918.17.50	6.50%	A+
Chemicals, Organic	Piperidine	2933.32.10	1.5 cents/kg + 10.4%	A+
Chemicals, Organic	Piperidine salts	2933.32.50	9.30%	A+
Chemicals, Organic	Piperonal (heliotropin)	2932.93.00	4.80%	A+
Chemicals, Organic	Products described in add. US note 3 to sec VI containing quinoline or isoquinoline ring-system (whether or n/hydrogenated), n/further fused	2933.40.60	9.30%	A+

Products Eligible for Duty-Free Treatment Under AGOA if Exported to the U.S. from an AGOA Beneficiary Country

Chemicals, Organic	Products described in add. US note 3 to section VI containing a phenothiazine ring system (whether or not hydrogenated), not further fused	2934.30.43	9.30%	A+
Chemicals, Organic	Psychotherapeutic agents of heterocyclic compounds with nitrogen hetero-atom(s) only, cont. pyrimidine or piperazine ring	2933.59.45	10.50%	A+
Chemicals, Organic	Psychotherapeutic agents of heterocyclic compounds with nitrogen hetero-atom(s) only, containing an unfused pyridine ring	2933.39.30	10.50%	A+
Chemicals, Organic	Quinones, nesoi	2914.69.90	7.70%	A+
Chemicals, Organic	Resorcinol and its salts	2907.21.00	5.50%	A+
Chemicals, Organic	Saturated acyclic monocarboxylic acids, nesoi	2915.90.18	4.20%	A+
Chemicals, Organic	Sodium tetraphenylboron	2931.00.15	5.80%	A+
Chemicals, Organic	Specified acyclic polycarboxylic acids and their derivatives, described in additional U.S. note 3 to section VI	2917.19.20	9.30%	A+
Chemicals, Organic	Specified aromatic amino-alcohol-phenols, amino-acid-phenols and other amino-compounds with oxygen function	2922.50.10	5.80%	A+
Chemicals, Organic	Specified aromatic monoamines and their derivatives; salts thereof	2921.45.20	5.80%	A+
Chemicals, Organic	Specified derivatives of phenols or phenol-alcohols containing only sulfo groups, their salts and esters	2908.20.04	5.50%	A+
Chemicals, Organic	Succinic acid, glutaric acid, and their derivatives, and derivatives of adipic, fumeric and maleic acids, nesoi	2917.19.27	1.5 cents/kg + 10.6%	A+
Chemicals, Organic	Sulfanilic acid	2921.42.22	1 cent/kg + 11.4%	A+
Chemicals, Organic	Terephthalic acid and its salts	2917.36.00	1.5 cents/kg + 11.1%	A+
Chemicals, Organic	Tetrabromobisphenol A	2908.10.25	0.6 cents/kg + 11.1%	A+
Chemicals, Organic	Tetrabromophthalic anhydride	2917.39.17	11.90%	A+
Chemicals, Organic	Toluenediisocyanates (unmixed)	2929.10.10	6.50%	A+
Chemicals, Organic	Toluidines and their derivatives; salts thereof: described in additional U.S. note 3 to section VI	2921.43.40	9.30%	A+
Chemicals, Organic	Tribromocumene	2903.69.27	5.50%	A+
Chemicals, Organic	Unsaturated acyclic monocarboxylic acids, nesoi	2916.19.30	6.10%	A+
Chemicals, Organic	Unsubstituted phenol-alcohols	2907.30.00	5.50%	A+
Clock Parts	Alarm clock movements, complete and assembled, electrically operated, with display nesoi, measuring not over 50 mm in width or diameter	9109.11.20	30 cents each + 5.3% on the battery	A+
Clock Parts	Alarm clock movements, complete and assembled, electrically operated, with display nesoi, measuring over 50 mm, valued not over $5 each	9109.11.40	7.5 cents each 3.2% on the movement + 2.6% on the battery	A+
Clock Parts	Alarm clock movements, complete and assembled, electrically operated, with display nesoi, measuring over 50 mm, valued over $5 each	9109.11.60	22 cents each + 3.2% on the movement + 2.6% on the battery	A+

Products Eligible for Duty-Free Treatment Under AGOA if Exported to the U.S. from an AGOA Beneficiary Country

Clock Parts	Alarm clock movements, complete and assembled, electrically operated, with opto-electronic display only	9109.11.10	3.9% on the movement + 5.3% on the battery	A+
Clock Parts	Assemblies and subassemblies for clock movements consisting of 2 or more pieces or parts fastened or joined inseparably together	9114.90.30	6% + 2.3 cents/jewel + 0.2 cents for each other piece or part, but if consisting in part of a plate or a set of plates the total duty shall not exceed the duty for the complete movement	A+
Clock Parts	Clock cases and cases of a similar type for other goods of chapter 91, of metal	9112.10.00	3.50%	A+
Clock Parts	Clock movements nesoi, complete and assembled, electrically operated, with display nesoi, measuring not over 50 mm in width or diameter	9109.19.20	20 cents each + 3.5% on the battery	A+
Clock Parts	Clock movements nesoi, complete and assembled, electrically operated, with display nesoi, measuring over 50 mm, valued not over $5 each	9109.19.40	12 cents each + 5.1% on the movement + 4.2% on the battery	A+
Clock Parts	Clock movements nesoi, complete and assembled, electrically operated, with display nesoi, measuring over 50 mm, valued over $5 each	9109.19.60	30 cents each + 4.3% on the movement + 3.5% on the battery	A+
Clock Parts	Clock movements nesoi, complete and assembled, electrically operated, with opto-electronic display only	9109.19.10	3.9% on the movement + 5.3% on The battery	A+
Clock Parts	Clock movements, complete and assembled, not electrically operated, measuring not over 50 mm in width or diameter	9109.90.20	20 cents each	A+
Clock Parts	Clock movements, complete and assembled, not electrically operated, measuring over 50 mm in width or diameter, valued not over $5 each	9109.90.40	15 cents each + 6.4%	A+
Clock Parts	Clock movements, complete and assembled, not electrically operated, measuring over 50 mm in width or diameter, valued over $5 each	9109.90.60	30 cents each + 4.3%	A+
Clock Parts	Clock parts, nesi	9114.90.50	4.20%	A+
Clock Parts	Dials for watches and clocks, exceeding 50 mm in width	9114.30.80	4.40%	A+

Products Eligible for Duty-Free Treatment Under AGOA if Exported to the U.S. from an AGOA Beneficiary Country

Clock Parts	Dials for watches and clocks, not exceeding 50 mm in width	9114.30.40	0.4 cents each + 7.2%	A+
Clock Parts	Plates and bridges for clocks, nesi	9114.40.80	4.20%	A+
Clock Parts	Springs, including hair-springs, for clocks	9114.10.80	4.20%	A+
Clocks and Time Devices (excluding watches)	Alarm clocks nesoi, electrically operated, other than with opto-electronic display only	9105.11.80	30 cents each + 6.9% on the case + 5.3% on the battery	A+
Clocks and Time Devices (excluding watches)	Alarm clocks nesoi, electrically operated, with opto-electronic display only	9105.11.40	3.9% on the movement and case + 5.3% on the battery	A+
Clocks and Time Devices (excluding watches)	Alarm clocks nesoi, not electrically operated, movement measuring over 50 mm in width or diameter, valued over $5 each	9105.19.50	23 cents each + 3.2%	A+
Clocks and Time Devices (excluding watches)	Alarm clocks nesoi, not electrically operated, movement measuring n/o 50 mm, designed to operate over 47 hrs w/o rewinding, over 1 jewel	9105.19.30	43 cents each + 2.8 cents/jewel over 7 + 3.7% on the case	A+
Clocks and Time Devices (excluding watches)	Alarm clocks nesoi, not electrically operated, movement measuring n/o 50 mm, designed to operate over 47 hrs w/o rewinding, with 0-1 jewel	9105.19.20	60 cents each + 6.9% on the case	A+
Clocks and Time Devices (excluding watches)	Apparatus for meas., recording or indicating time intervals, w/watch or clock mvmt., AC powered, w/opto-electronic display only	9106.90.75	3.90%	A+
Clocks and Time Devices (excluding watches)	Clocks nesoi, electrically operated, other than with opto-electronic display only	9105.91.80	30 cents each + 6.9% on the case + 5.3% on the battery	A+
Clocks and Time Devices (excluding watches)	Clocks nesoi, electrically operated, with opto-electronic display only	9105.91.40	3.9% on the movement And case + 5.3% on the battery	A+
Clocks and Time Devices (excluding watches)	Clocks nesoi, not electrically operated, movement measuring over 50 mm in width or diameter, valued not over $5 each	9105.99.50	7.5 cents each + 3.2%	A+
Clocks and Time Devices (excluding watches)	Clocks nesoi, not electrically operated, movement measuring over 50 mm in width or diameter, valued over $5 each	9105.99.60	23 cents each + 3.2%	A+
Clocks and Time Devices (excluding watches)	Clocks with watch movements, excluding clocks of heading 9104, electrically operated, with 0-1 jewel in the movement	9103.10.40	24 cents each + 4.5% on the case + 3.5% on the battery	A+
Clocks and Time Devices (excluding watches)	Clocks with watch movements, excluding clocks of heading 9104, electrically operated, with opto-electronic display only	9103.10.20	2.6% on the movement and case + 3.6% on the battery	A+

Products Eligible for Duty-Free Treatment Under AGOA if Exported to the U.S. from an AGOA Beneficiary Country

Clocks and Time Devices (excluding watches)	Clocks with watch movements, excluding clocks of heading 9104, electrically operated, with over 1 jewel in the movement	9103.10.80	48 cents each + 4.6% on the case + 3.5% on the Battery	A+
Clocks and Time Devices (excluding watches)	Clocks with watch movements, excluding clocks of heading 9104, not electrically operated	9103.90.00	24 cents each + 4.6% on the case	A+
Clocks and Time Devices (excluding watches)	Instrument panel clocks for veh., air/spacecraft, vessels, clock mvmt over 50 mm wide, electric, nt optoelectronic display, n/o $10 each	9104.00.10	20 cents each + 4.3% on the movement and case + 3.5% on the battery	A+
Clocks and Time Devices (excluding watches)	Instrument panel clocks for vehicles, air/spacecraft or vessels, w/clock or watch movement < 50 mm wide, nonelectric	9104.00.60	19 cents each + 4.5% on the case	A+
Clocks and Time Devices (excluding watches)	Instrument panel clocks for vehicles, air/spacecraft, vessels, clock movement over 50 mm wide, opto-electronic display only, n/o $10 each	9104.00.05	2.6% on the movement and case + 3.5% on the battery	A+
Clocks and Time Devices (excluding watches)	Instrument panel clocks for vehicles, air/spacecraft, vessels, w/clock movement ov 50 mm wide, opto-electronic display only, ov $10 each	9104.00.25	3.9% on the movement and case + 5.3% on the battery	A+
Clocks and Time Devices (excluding watches)	Instrument panel clocks for vehicles, air/spacecraft, vessels, w/clock movement over 50 mm wide, valued n/o $10 each, nonelectric	9104.00.20	30 cents each + 6.4%	A+
Clocks and Time Devices (excluding watches)	Instrument panel clocks for vehicles, air/spacecraft, vessels, w/watch or clock movement < 50 mm wide, electric, not opto-electronic display	9104.00.50	20 cents each + 4.6% on the case + 3.5% on the battery	A+
Clocks and Time Devices (excluding watches)	Instrument panel clocks for vehicles, air/spacecraft,vessels, w/clock movement ov 50 mm wide, valued ov $10 each, non-electric	9104.00.40	30 cents each + 4.3%	A+
Clocks and Time Devices (excluding watches)	Instrument panel clocks for vehicles, air/spacecraft,vessels, w/clock mvmt ov 50 mm wide, electric, nt optoelectronic display, ov $10 each	9104.00.30	30 cents each + 4.3% on the movement and case + 3.5% on the battery	A+
Clocks and Time Devices (excluding watches)	Instrument panel clocks for vehicles, air/spacecraft,vessels, w/watch or clock movement < 50 mm wide, opto-electronic display only	9104.00.45	2.6% on the movement and case + 3.5% on the battery	A+
Clocks and Time Devices (excluding watches)	Parking meters	9106.20.00	35 cents each + 5.6% + 2 cents/jewel	A+

Products Eligible for Duty-Free Treatment Under AGOA if Exported to the U.S. from an AGOA Beneficiary Country

Clocks and Time Devices (excluding watches)	Time of day recording apparatus & apparatus for measuring, detecting, recording or otherwise indicating intervals of time nesi	9106.90.85	15 cents each + 2.3% + 0.8 cents/jewel	A+
Clocks and Time Devices (excluding watches)	Time registers; time recorders	9106.10.00	36 cents each + 5.6% + 2 cents/jewel	A+
Clocks and Time Devices (excluding watches)	Time switches with clock or watch movements or with synchronous motor, valued over $5 each	9107.00.80	45 cents each + 6.4% + 2.5 cents/jewel	A+
Clocks and Time Devices (excluding watches)	Wall clocks nesoi, electrically operated, other than with opto-electronic display only	9105.21.80	30 cents each + 6.9% on the case + 5.3% on the battery	A+
Clocks and Time Devices (excluding watches)	Wall clocks nesoi, electrically operated, with opto-electronic display only	9105.21.40	3.9% on the movement and case+ 5.3% on the battery	A+
Clocks and Time Devices (excluding watches)	Wall clocks nesoi, not electrically operated, movement measuring over 50 mm in width or diameter, valued not over $5 each	9105.29.40	15 cents each + 6.4%	A+
Clocks and Time Devices (excluding watches)	Wall clocks nesoi, not electrically operated, movement measuring over 50 mm in width or diameter, valued over $5 each	9105.29.50	30 cents each + 4.3%	A+
Clocks and Time Devices (excluding watches)	Wall clocks nesoi, not electrically operated, mvmt measuring n/o 50 mm, 0-1 jewel, constructed/designed to operate over 47 hrs w/o rewinding	9105.29.20	40 cents each + 4.6% on the case	A+
Clocks and Time Devices (excluding watches)	Wall clocks nesoi, not electrically operated, mvmt measuring n/o 50 mm, not designed or constr. to operate over 47 hrs without rewinding	9105.29.10	20 cents each + 4.6% on the case	A+
Clocks and Time Devices (excluding watches)	Wall clocks nesoi, not electrically operated, mvmt measuring n/o 50 mm, ov 1 jewel, constructed/designed to operate ov 47 hrs w/o rewinding	9105.29.30	57 cents each + 3.7 cents/jewel over 7 + 4.9% on the case	A+
Cocoa and Cocoa Products	Chocolate and preps w/cocoa, nesoi, o/2kg but n/o 4.5 kg, n/o 65% sugar, desc in Ch17 US note 3, subj. to Ch17 US note 8, not GN15	1806.20.95	10%	A+
Cocoa and Cocoa Products	Chocolate and preps with cocoa, nesoi, ov 2kg but n/o 4.5 kg, n/o 65% sugar, nesoi	1806.20.99	8.50%	A+
Cocoa and Cocoa Products	Chocolate/oth preps with cocoa, ov 2kg but n/o 4.5 kg, (dairy prod. descr. in Ch.4 US note 1), n/o 65% sugar, subj to Ch.4 nte 10, not GN15	1806.20.81	10%	A+
Cocoa and Cocoa Products	Chocolate/oth preps with cocoa, ov 2kg but n/o 4.5 kg, n/o 65% by wt of sugar, not in blocks 4.5 kg or more, subj to GN 15	1806.20.79	10%	A+
Cocoa and Cocoa Products	Low-fat chocoate crumb, n/o 65% by wt of sugar, ov 2kg but n/o 4.5 kg, subject to add US note 3 to Ch. 18, not GN15	1806.20.85	10%	A+
Coffee	Coffee substitutes containing coffee	0901.90.20	1.5 cents/kg	A+
Copper and Copper Products	Copper, containers a kind normally carried on the person, in the pocket or in the handbag	7419.99.15	3%	

Products Eligible for Duty-Free Treatment Under AGOA if Exported to the U.S. from an AGOA Beneficiary Country

Cutlery	Base metal scissors, tailors' shears and similar shears (o/than pinking shears val o$30/dz), and base metal parts, val. o/$1.75 per dozen	8213.00.90	5.8 cents each + 5.8%	A+
Cutlery	Butchers' or kitchen cleavers with their handles, nesoi, and base metal parts thereof	8214.90.30	1 cent each + 4.9%	A+
Cutlery	Sets of assorted knives w/cutting blades serrated or not (including pruning knives)	8211.10.00	The rate of duty applicable to that article in the set subject to the highest rate of duty	
Cutlery	Table knives w/fixed blades, w/stain. steel handles cont. Ni or ov 10% by wt of Mn, nesoi	8211.91.25	0.4 cents each + 6.8%	
Cutlery	Table knives w/fixed blades, w/stain. steel handles w/Ni or ov 10% by wt. of Mn, w/overall length 25.9cm or less & val. <than 25 cents ea	8211.91.20	0.4 cents each + 6.4%	
Cutlery	Table knives w/fixed blades, w/stain. steel handles, nesoi	8211.91.40	0.3 cents each + 3.7%	
Cutlery	Table knives w/fixed blades, w/stain. steel handles, nesoi, not ov 25.9 cm in overall length & val less than 25 cents each	8211.91.30	0.9 cents each + 10.6%	
Dairy Preparations (excluding Cheeses)	Cajeta not made from cow's milk	1901.90.32	11.20%	A+
Dairy Preparations (excluding Cheeses)	Dairy preps n/o 10% by wt of milk solids (descr. in add US note 1 to Ch. 4), neosi, subject to add US note 10 to Ch.4	1901.90.46	16%	A+
Dairy Preparations (excluding Cheeses)	Dairy preps n/o 10% by wt of milk solids (descr. in add US note 1 to Ch. 4), neosi, subject to gen. note 15 of the HTS	1901.90.44	16%	A+
Dairy Preparations (excluding Cheeses)	Dairy preps o/10% by wt of milk solids (descr. in add US note 1 to Ch. 4), neosi, subject to add US note 10 to Ch.4	1901.90.42	16%	A+
Dairy Preparations (excluding Cheeses)	Dairy preps o/10% by wt of milk solids (descr. in add US note 1 to Ch. 4), neosi, subject to gen. note 15 of the HTS	1901.90.38	16%	A+
Dairy Preparations (excluding Cheeses)	Food preps of flour, etc., nesoi, o/10% by dry wt of sugar, described in add. US note 3 to chap. 17: subj. to add US note 8 to Ch.17	1901.90.56	10%	A+
Dairy Preparations (excluding Cheeses)	Food preps of flour, etc., nesoi, o/5.5% by wt of butterfat, not pkgd for retail sale, nesoi	1901.90.70	10.20%	A+
Dairy Preparations (excluding Cheeses)	Infant formula w/oligossaccharides, for retail sale, n/o 10% milk solids, subject to add US note 2 to Ch. 19, not GN15	1901.10.60	17.50%	A+

Products Eligible for Duty-Free Treatment Under AGOA if Exported to the U.S. from an AGOA Beneficiary Country

Dairy Preparations (excluding Cheeses)	Malt extract and other preps of flour, etc., nesoi, subject to gen. note 15 of the HTS	1901.90.48	10%	A+
Dairy Preparations (excluding Cheeses)	Malt extract, fluid	1901.90.10	3.2 cents/liter	A+
Dairy Preparations (excluding Cheeses)	Malt extract, solid or condensed	1901.90.20	9.60%	A+
Dairy Preparations (excluding Cheeses)	Margarine cheese subject to add. US note 23 to Ch. 4 and entered pursuant to its provisions	1901.90.34	10%	A+
Dairy Preparations (excluding Cheeses)	Margarine cheese subject to gen. note 15 of the HTS and entered pursuant to its provisions	1901.90.33	10%	A+
Dairy Preparations (excluding Cheeses)	Preps for infant use (dairy prod. of add US note 1 to Ch.4), for retail sale, o/10% milk solids, subject to Ch4 US note 10, not GN15	1901.10.35	17.50%	A+
Dairy Preparations (excluding Cheeses)	Preps for infant use (dairy prod. of Ch4 US note 1), retail sale, n/o 10% milk solids, subject to add US note 10 to Ch. 4, not GN15	1901.10.80	17.50%	A+
Dairy Preparations (excluding Cheeses)	Preps for infant use (not dairy prod. of add US note 1 to Ch.4), for retail sale, o/10% milk solids, not GN15, nesoi	1901.10.45	14.90%	A+
Dairy Preparations (excluding Cheeses)	Preps for infant use (not dairy prod. of Ch4 US note 1), retail sale, n/o 10% milk solids, nesoi	1901.10.95	14.90%	A+
Dairy Preparations (excluding Cheeses)	Preps for infant use, for retail sale, n/o 10% milk solids, subject to gen. note 15	1901.10.55	17.50%	A+
Dairy Preparations (excluding Cheeses)	Preps for infant use, for retail sale, o/10% milk solids, subject to gen. note 15	1901.10.05	17.50%	A+
Dairy Preparations (excluding Cheeses)	Preps for infant use, infant formula containing oligossaccharides and > 10% milk solids, described in add'l U.S. note 2: provisional	1901.10.15	17.50%	A+
Dairy Products	Butter subject to general note 15 (outside quota)	0405.10.05	12.3 cents/kg	A+
Dairy Products	Butter subject to quota pursuant to chapter 4 additional US note 6	0405.10.10	12.3 cents/kg	A+

Products Eligible for Duty-Free Treatment Under AGOA if Exported to the U.S. from an AGOA Beneficiary Country

Dairy Products	Butter substitute dairy spreads, containing 45% or less butterfat by weight	0405.20.40	13.1 cents/kg	A+
Dairy Products	Butter substitute dairy spreads, over 45% butterfat weight, subject to general note 15 (outside quota)	0405.20.10	15.4 cents/kg	A+
Dairy Products	Butter substitute dairy spreads, over 45% butterfat weight, subject to quota pursuant to chapter 4 additional US note 14	0405.20.20	15.4 cents/kg	A+
Dairy Products	Condensed milk, sweetened, in airtight containers, subject to add. US note 11 to Ch.4	0402.99.10	3.9 cents/kg	A+
Dairy Products	Condensed milk, sweetened, in airtight containers, subject to gen. note 15 of the HTS	0402.99.03	3.9 cents/kg	A+
Dairy Products	Condensed milk, sweetened, not in airtight containers, subject to add. US note 11 to Ch. 4	0402.99.30	3.3 cents/kg	A+
Dairy Products	Condensed milk, sweetened, not in airtight containers, subject to gen. note 15 of the HTS	0402.99.06	3.3 cents/kg	A+
Dairy Products	Curdled milk/cream/kephir & other fermentd or acid. milk/cream descr.in gen. note 15	0403.90.87	20%	A+
Dairy Products	Curdled milk/cream/kephir & other fermentd or acid. milk/cream subject to add US note 10 to Ch.4	0403.90.90	20%	A+
Dairy Products	Dairy products of nat. milk constituents (except protein conc.), descr. in add. US nte 1 to Ch. 4 and sub to Ch4 US note 10	0404.90.30	14.50%	A+
Dairy Products	Dairy products of nat. milk constituents (except protein conc.), descr. in add. US nte 1 to Ch. 4 and subj to GN 15	0404.90.28	14.50%	A+
Dairy Products	Fats and oils derived from milk, other than butter or dairy spreads, subject to general note 15 (outside quota)	0405.90.05	10%	A+
Dairy Products	Fats and oils derived from milk, other than butter or dairy spreads, subject to quota pursuant to chapter 4 additional US note 14	0405.90.10	10%	A+
Dairy Products	Fermented milk o/than dried fermented milk or o/than dried milk with added lactic ferments	0403.90.85	17%	A+
Dairy Products	Fluid buttermilk	0403.90.20	0.34 cents/liter	A+
Dairy Products	Fluid whey, whether or not concentrated or containing added sweeteners	0404.10.20	0.34 cents/liter	A+
Dairy Products	Milk & cream (except condensed milk), concentrated in non-solid forms, sweetened, subject to add. US note 10 to Ch. 4	0402.99.70	17.50%	A+
Dairy Products	Milk & cream (except condensed milk), concentrated in non-solid forms, sweetened, subject to gen. note 15 of the HTS	0402.99.68	17.50%	A+
Dairy Products	Milk & cream in powder granules/other solid forms fat content by weight not exceeding 1.5% whether/not sweetened, described in addl note 7	0402.10.10	3.3 cents/kg	A+
Dairy Products	Milk & cream, concen in non-solid forms, not sweetened, in airtight containers, subject to add. US note 11 to Ch.4	0402.91.10	2.2 cents/kg	A+
Dairy Products	Milk & cream, concen in non-solid forms, not sweetened, not in airtight containers, subject to add. US note 11 to Ch. 4	0402.91.30	3.3 cents/kg	A+
Dairy Products	Milk & cream, concen in non-solid forms, not sweetened, not in airtight containers, subject to gen. note 15 of the HTS	0402.91.06	3.3 cents/kg	A+
Dairy Products	Milk & cream, concen or sweetened, in powder, granules or other solid forms, w/fat content by weight not o/1.5%, subj to GN15	0402.10.05	3.3 cents/kg	A+
Dairy Products	Milk & cream, concen, in non-solid forms, not sweetened, in airtight containers, subject to gen. note 15 of the HTS	0402.91.03	2.2 cents/kg	A+
Dairy Products	Milk & cream, concen, not sweetened, in powder, granules or other solid forms, w/fat content o/1.5% but not o/3%, subj Ch4 US note 7	0402.21.05	3.3 cents/kg	A+
Dairy Products	Milk & cream, concen, not sweetened, in powder, granules or other solid forms, w/fat content o/1.5% but not o/3%, subj to GN15	0402.21.02	3.3 cents/kg	A+

Products Eligible for Duty-Free Treatment Under AGOA if Exported to the U.S. from an AGOA Beneficiary Country

Dairy Products	Milk & cream, concen, not sweetened, in powder, granules or other solid forms, w/fat content o/3% but not o/35%, subject to gen. note 15	0402.21.27	6.8 cents/kg	A+
Dairy Products	Milk & cream, concen, not sweetened, in powder, granules or other solid forms, w/fat content o/35%, subject to add. US note 9 to Ch.4	0402.21.75	13.7 cents/kg	A+
Dairy Products	Milk & cream, concen, not sweetened, in powder, granules or other solid forms, w/fat content o/35%, subject to gen. note 15	0402.21.73	13.7 cents/kg	A+
Dairy Products	Milk & cream, concen, not sweetened, in powder/granules/oth solid forms, fat cont o/3% but not o/35%, subj to Ch 4 US note 7	0402.21.30	6.8 cents/kg	A+
Dairy Products	Milk & cream, concen, sweetened, in powder, granules or other solid forms, w/fat content o/1.5%, subject to add. US note 10 to Ch.4	0402.29.10	17.50%	A+
Dairy Products	Milk & cream, concen, sweetened, in powder, granules or other solid forms, w/fat content o/1.5%, subject to gen. note 15	0402.29.05	17.50%	A+
Dairy Products	Milk and cream, not concentrated, not sweetened, fat content o/45%, subject to add. US note 6 to Ch. 4	0401.30.50	12.3 cents/kg	A+
Dairy Products	Milk and cream, not concentrated, not sweetened, fat content o/45%, subject to gen. note 15 of the HTS	0401.30.42	12.3 cents/kg	A+
Dairy Products	Milk and cream, not concentrated, not sweetened, fat content o/6% but not o/45%, subject to add. US note 5 to Ch. 4	0401.30.05	3.2 cents/liter	A+
Dairy Products	Milk and cream, not concentrated, not sweetened, fat content o/6% but not o/45%, subject to gen. note 15 of the HTS	0401.30.02	3.2 cents/liter	A+
Dairy Products	Milk and cream, unconcentrated, unsweetened, fat content over 1% but n/o 6%, for not over 11,356,236 liters entered in any calender year	0401.20.20	0.43 cents/liter	A+
Dairy Products	Milk and cream, unconcentrated, with no added sweeteners, fat content, by weight, not more than 1 percent	0401.10.00	0.34 cents/liter	A+
Dairy Products	Modified whey (except protein conc.), subject to gen. note 15 of the HTS	0404.10.08	13%	A+
Dairy Products	Modified whey (except protein conc.), wheth/not conc. or sweetened, subject to add US note 10 to Ch.4	0404.10.11	13%	A+
Dairy Products	Other dairy spreads of a type provided in ch. 4 add. US note 1, subject to quota pursuant to chapter 4 additional US note 10	0405.20.60	10%	A+
Dairy Products	Other dairy spreads of a type provided in chapter 4 additional US note 1, subject to general note 15 (outside quota)	0405.20.50	10%	A+
Dairy Products	Products consisting of natural milk constituents (except protein conc.), whether or not sweetened, not descr. in add US note 1 to Ch. 4	0404.90.70	8.50%	A+
Dairy Products	Sour cream, dried, n/o 6% by wt. butterfat, subject to add. US note 12 to Ch. 4	0403.90.41	3.3 cents/kg	A+
Dairy Products	Sour cream, dried, n/o 6% by wt. butterfat, subject to gen. note 15 of the HTS	0403.90.37	3.3 cents/kg	A+
Dairy Products	Sour cream, dried, o/35% but n/o 45% by wt. butterfat, subject to add. US note 9 to Ch. 4	0403.90.61	13.7 cents/kg	A+
Dairy Products	Sour cream, dried, o/35% but n/o 45% by wt. butterfat, subject to gen. note 15 of the HTS	0403.90.57	13.7 cents/kg	A+
Dairy Products	Sour cream, dried, o/6% but n/o 35% by wt. butterfat, subject to add. US note 8 to Ch. 4	0403.90.51	6.8 cents/kg	A+
Dairy Products	Sour cream, dried, o/6% but n/o 35% by wt. butterfat, subject to gen. note 15 of the HTS	0403.90.47	6.8 cents/kg	A+
Dairy Products	Sour cream, fluid, n/o 45% by wt. butterfat, subject to add. US note 5 to Ch.4	0403.90.04	3.2 cents/liter	A+
Dairy Products	Sour cream, fluid, n/o 45% by wt. butterfat, subject to gen. note 15 of the HTS	0403.90.02	3.2 cents/liter	A+
Dairy Products	Sour cream, o/45% by wt. butterfat, subject to add. US note 6 to Ch 4	0403.90.74	12.3 cents/kg	A+

Products Eligible for Duty-Free Treatment Under AGOA if Exported to the U.S. from an AGOA Beneficiary Country

Dairy Products	Sour cream, o/45% by wt. butterfat, subject to gen. note 15 of the HTS	0403.90.72	12.3 cents/kg	A+
Dairy Products	Whey (except modified whey), dried, whether or not conc. or sweetened, subject to add. US note 12 to Ch. 4	0404.10.50	3.3 cents/kg	A+
Dairy Products	Whey (except modified whey), dried, whether or not conc. or sweetened, subject to gen. note 15 of the HTS	0404.10.48	3.3 cents/kg	A+
Dairy Products	Yogurt, in dry form, whether or not flavored or containing add fruit or cocoa, subject to add. US note 10 to Ch. 4	0403.10.10	20%	A+
Dairy Products	Yogurt, in dry form, whether or not flavored or containing add fruit or cocoa, subject to gen. note 15 of the HTS	0403.10.05	20%	A+
Dairy Products	Yogurt, not in dry form, whether or not flavored or containing add fruit or cocoa	0403.10.90	17%	A+
Dyes, Pigments, and Coloring Matter	Acid dyes, whether or not premetallized, and preparations based thereon, acid black 31, and other specified acid or mordant dyes	3204.12.17	9.60%	A+
Dyes, Pigments, and Coloring Matter	Basic black 7 and other specified basic dyes and preparations based thereon	3204.13.10	6.50%	A+
Dyes, Pigments, and Coloring Matter	Basic blue 3; basic red 14; and basic yellow 1, 11, 13; and preparations based thereon	3204.13.25	11.90%	A+
Dyes, Pigments, and Coloring Matter	Basic dyes and preparations based thereon, described in add'l U.S note 3 to section VIvi	3204.13.60	9.90%	A+
Dyes, Pigments, and Coloring Matter	Basic dyes and preparations based thereon, nesoi	3204.13.80	11.90%	A+
Dyes, Pigments, and Coloring Matter	Basic orange 22, basic red 13 dyes, and preparations based thereon	3204.13.20	9.60%	A+
Dyes, Pigments, and Coloring Matter	Color lakes and preparations based thereon, described in additional U.S. note 3 to section VI	3205.00.40	9.90%	A+
Dyes, Pigments, and Coloring Matter	Color lakes and preparations based thereon, nesoi	3205.00.50	11.90%	A+
Dyes, Pigments, and Coloring Matter	Coloring preparations based on iron oxides, as specified in note 3 to this chapter 32	3206.49.20	6.50%	A+
Dyes, Pigments, and Coloring Matter	Copper phthalocyanine ([Phthalocyanato(2-)]copper) not ready for use as a pigment	3204.17.20	10.90%	A+
Dyes, Pigments, and Coloring Matter	Direct black 51 and other specified basic dyes and preparations based thereon	3204.14.20	6.50%	A+
Dyes, Pigments, and Coloring Matter	Direct black 62 and other specified basic dyes and preparations based thereon	3204.14.10	9.60%	A+
Dyes, Pigments, and Coloring Matter	Direct blue 86; direct red 83; direct yellow 28 dyes; and preparations based thereon	3204.14.25	11.90%	A+
Dyes, Pigments, and Coloring Matter	Direct dyes and preparations based thereon, nesoi	3204.14.50	11.90%	A+

Products Eligible for Duty-Free Treatment Under AGOA if Exported to the U.S. from an AGOA Beneficiary Country

Dyes, Pigments, and Coloring Matter	Direct dyes nesoi, and preparations based thereon, described in additional U.S. note 3 to section VI	3204.14.30	9.90%	A+
Dyes, Pigments, and Coloring Matter	Disperse blue 19 and other specified dispersed dyes and preparations based thereon	3204.11.10	6.50%	A+
Dyes, Pigments, and Coloring Matter	Disperse blue 30 and preparations based thereon	3204.11.15	9.60%	A+
Dyes, Pigments, and Coloring Matter	Disperse dyes and preparations based thereon, nesoi	3204.11.50	11.90%	A+
Dyes, Pigments, and Coloring Matter	Disperse dyes described in add'l U.S. note 3 to section VI	3204.11.35	9.90%	A+
Dyes, Pigments, and Coloring Matter	Glass frit and other glass, in the form of granules or flakes	3207.40.50	9.30%	A+
Dyes, Pigments, and Coloring Matter	Inorganic products of a kind used as luminophores	3206.50.00	6.50%	A+
Dyes, Pigments, and Coloring Matter	Nonrefractory surfacing preparations for facades, indoor walls, floors, ceilings or the like, not based on rubber	3214.90.50	8.30%	A+
Dyes, Pigments, and Coloring Matter	Other pigments and preparations based thereon, nesoi	3204.17.90	11.90%	A+
Dyes, Pigments, and Coloring Matter	Pigments and preparations based thereon, pigment black 1, and other specified pigments, nesoi	3204.17.04	6.50%	A+
Dyes, Pigments, and Coloring Matter	Pigments and preparations based thereon, products described in add'l U.S. note 3 to section VI, nesoi	3204.17.60	9.90%	A+
Dyes, Pigments, and Coloring Matter	Prepared driers for paints and varnishes	3211.00.00	3.70%	A+
Dyes, Pigments, and Coloring Matter	Reactive black 1; blue 1, 2, 4; orange 1; red 1, 2, 3, 5, 6, and yellow 1; and preparations based thereon	3204.16.10	9.60%	A+
Dyes, Pigments, and Coloring Matter	Reactive dyes and preparations based thereon nesoi, described in additional U.S. note 3 to section VI	3204.16.30	9.90%	A+
Dyes, Pigments, and Coloring Matter	Solubilized vat blue 5 and specified solubilized vat dyes and preparations based thereon	3204.15.30	6.50%	A+
Dyes, Pigments, and Coloring Matter	Solubilized vat orange 3, vat blue 2, vat red 44; and vat yellow 4, 20 and preparations based thereon	3204.15.35	9.60%	A+

Products Eligible for Duty-Free Treatment Under AGOA if Exported to the U.S. from an AGOA Beneficiary Country

Dyes, Pigments, and Coloring Matter	Solvent black 2 and other specified solvent dyes and preparations based thereon	3204.19.11	6.50%	A+
Dyes, Pigments, and Coloring Matter	Solvent dyes and preparations based thereon nesoi	3204.19.25	11.90%	A+
Dyes, Pigments, and Coloring Matter	Solvent dyes and preparations based thereon, products described in add'l U.S. note 3 to section VI	3204.19.20	9.90%	A+
Dyes, Pigments, and Coloring Matter	Specified reactive dye mixtures and preparations based thereon	3204.16.20	6.50%	A+
Dyes, Pigments, and Coloring Matter	Sulfur black, "Colour Index Nos. 53185, 53190 and 53195" and preparations based thereon	3204.19.30	1.3 cents/kg + 9.5%	A+
Dyes, Pigments, and Coloring Matter	Synthetic organic coloring matter and preparations based thereon nesoi, including mixtures of items from subheading 320411 to 320419	3204.19.50	11.90%	A+
Dyes, Pigments, and Coloring Matter	Synthetic organic coloring matter and preparations based thereon, nesoi, described in additional U.S. note 3 to section VI	3204.19.40	9.90%	A+
Dyes, Pigments, and Coloring Matter	Synthetic reactive dyes and preparations based thereon, nesoi	3204.16.50	11.90%	A+
Dyes, Pigments, and Coloring Matter	Vat blue 1 (synthetic indigo) dye, "Colour Index No. 73000" and preparations based thereon	3204.15.10	1.3 cents/kg + 9.7%	A+
Dyes, Pigments, and Coloring Matter	Vat brown 3; vat orange 2, 7; and vat violet 9, 13 dyes and preparations based thereon	3204.15.20	11.90%	A+
Dyes, Pigments, and Coloring Matter	Vat dyes (incl. those usable as pigments) and preparations based thereon, described in add. U.S. note 3 to sec. VI	3204.15.40	9.90%	A+
Dyes, Pigments, and Coloring Matter	Vat dyes (including those usable in that state as pigments) and preparations based thereon, nesoi	3204.15.80	11.90%	A+
Eggs	Birds' eggs, not in shell, dried, whether or not containing added sweeteners	0408.91.00	47.6 cents/kg	A+
Eggs	Birds' eggs, not in shell, other than dried, whether or not containing added sweeteners	0408.99.00	9.7 cents/kg	A+
Eggs	Egg yolks, dried, whether or not containing added sweeteners	0408.11.00	47.6 cents/kg	A+
Eggs	Egg yolks, other than dried, whether or not containing added sweeteners	0408.19.00	9.7 cents/kg	A+
Essential Oils	Essential oils of lemon	3301.13.00	3.80%	A+
Explosives and Pyrotechnic Products	Ferrocerium and other pyrophoric alloys in all forms	3606.90.30	5.90%	A+
Fats and Oils (Animal and Vegetable)	Corn (maize) oil, crude, and its fractions, not chemically modified	1515.21.00	3.40%	A+
Fats and Oils (Animal and Vegetable)	Corn (maize) oil, other than crude, and its fractions, whether or not refined, not chemically modified	1515.29.00	3.40%	A+
Fats and Oils (Animal and Vegetable)	Cottonseed oil, crude, and its fractions, whether or not gossypol has been removed	1512.21.00	5.6 cents/kg	A+

Products Eligible for Duty-Free Treatment Under AGOA
if Exported to the U.S. from an AGOA Beneficiary Country

Fats and Oils (Animal and Vegetable)	Cottonseed oil, other than crude, and its fractions, whether or not refined, but not chemically modified	1512.29.00	5.6 cents/kg	A+
Fats and Oils (Animal and Vegetable)	Crude peanut (ground-nut) oil	1508.10.00	7.5 cents/kg	A+
Fats and Oils (Animal and Vegetable)	Crude soybean oil, whether or not degummed	1507.10.00	19.10%	A+
Fats and Oils (Animal and Vegetable)	Degras; residues resulting from the treatment of fatty substances or animal or vegetable waxes	1522.00.00	3.80%	A+
Fats and Oils (Animal and Vegetable)	Denatured rapeseed, colza or mustard oil, other than crude, and their fractions, whether or not refined, nesi	1514.90.50	1.3 cents/kg	A+
Fats and Oils (Animal and Vegetable)	Edible mixt. & preps (ex. dairy products descr. in add. US note 1 to Ch. 4), nesoi	1517.90.90	8.8 cents/kg	A+
Fats and Oils (Animal and Vegetable)	Edible mixt. & preps, dairy products described in add. US note 1 to Ch 4: subject to add. US note 10 to Ch. 4	1517.90.50	11 cents/kg	A+
Fats and Oils (Animal and Vegetable)	Edible mixt. & preps. dairy products described in add. US note 1 to Ch 4: subject to gen. note 15 of the HTS	1517.90.45	11 cents/kg	A+
Fats and Oils (Animal and Vegetable)	Fats of bovine animals, sheep or goats, other than those of heading 1503	1502.00.00	0.43 cents/kg	A+
Fats and Oils (Animal and Vegetable)	Fish-liver oils and their fractions, other than cod-liver oil and its fractions	1504.10.40	2.50%	A+
Fats and Oils (Animal and Vegetable)	Lard stearin, lard oil, oleostearin, oleo-oil, and tallow oil, not emulsified or mixed or otherwise prepared	1503.00.00	2 cents/kg	A+
Fats and Oils (Animal and Vegetable)	Linseed oil, crude, and its fractions, not chemically modified	1515.11.00	6.3 cents/kg	A+
Fats and Oils (Animal and Vegetable)	Linseed oil, other than crude, and its fractions, whether or not refined, not chemically modified	1515.19.00	6.3 cents/kg	A+
Fats and Oils (Animal and Vegetable)	Linseed or flaxseed oil, and their fractions, boiled, oxidized, dehydrated, sulfurized, blown or otherwise chemically modified	1518.00.20	6.3 cents/kg	A+
Fats and Oils (Animal and Vegetable)	Margarine, excluding liquid margarine	1517.10.00	12.3 cents/kg	A+
Fats and Oils (Animal and Vegetable)	Peanut (ground-nut) oil, other than crude, and its fractions, whether or not refined, but not chemically modified	1508.90.00	7.5 cents/kg	A+
Fats and Oils (Animal and Vegetable)	Pig fat (including lard) and poultry fat, other than that of head 0209 or 1503	1501.00.00	3 cents/kg	A+
Fats and Oils (Animal and Vegetable)	Rapeseed oil, hydrogenated or hardened	1516.20.10	7.70%	A+

Products Eligible for Duty-Free Treatment Under AGOA if Exported to the U.S. from an AGOA Beneficiary Country

Fats and Oils (Animal and Vegetable)	Rapeseed, colza or mustard oil, crude, and their fractions, not chemically modified, nesi	1514.10.90	6.40%	A+
Fats and Oils (Animal and Vegetable)	Rapeseed, colza or mustard oil, other than crude, and their fractions, whether or not refined, not chemically modified, nesi	1514.90.90	6.40%	A+
Fats and Oils (Animal and Vegetable)	Soybean oil, other than crude, and its fractions, whether or not refined, but not chemically modified, nesi	1507.90.40	19.10%	A+
Fats and Oils (Animal and Vegetable)	Sunflower seed or safflower oil, other than crude, and their fractions, whether or not refined, but not chemically modified	1512.19.00	1.7 cents/kg + 3.4%	A+
Fats and Oils (Animal and Vegetable)	Sunflower-seed or safflower oil, crude, and their fractions, whether or not refined, not chemically modified	1512.11.00	1.7 cents/kg + 3.4%	A+
Fats and Oils (Animal and Vegetable)	Vegetable fats and oils nesi, partly or wholly hydrogenated, interesterified, reesterified or elaidinized, not further prepared	1516.20.90	8.8 cents/kg	A+
Feed for Animals	Acorns and horse-chestnuts, of a kind used in animal feeding	2308.10.00	1.40%	A+
Feed for Animals	Animal feeds containing egg, other than mixed feeds or mixed feed ingredients, not containing milk or milk derivatives	2309.90.60	1.90%	A+
Feed for Animals	Animal feeds w/milk or milk derivatives, n/o 10% by wt of milk solids, subject to add note 2 to Ch. 23, not GN15	2309.90.44	7.50%	A+
Feed for Animals	Animal feeds w/milk or milk derivatives, n/o 10% by wt of milk solids, subject to gen. note 15 of the HTS	2309.90.42	7.50%	A+
Feed for Animals	Animal feeds w/milk or milk derivatives, o/10% by wt of milk solids, subject to add note 2 to Ch. 23, not GN15	2309.90.24	7.50%	A+
Feed for Animals	Animal feeds w/milk or milk derivatives, o/10% by wt of milk solids, subject to gen. note 15 of the HTS	2309.90.22	7.50%	A+
Feed for Animals	Other preps nes of a kind used in animal feeding, not cont milk or egg prods	2309.90.95	1.40%	A+
Feed for Animals	Vegetable materials and vegetable waste, vegetable residues and by products, nesi, of a kind used in animal feeding	2308.90.80	1.40%	A+
Food Residues/Wastes	Bran, sharps (middlings) and other residues, derived from the sifting, milling or other working of leguminous plants	2302.50.00	1.40%	A+
Food Residues/Wastes	Oilcake and other solid residues, resulting from the extraction of soybean oil	2304.00.00	0.45 cents/kg	A+
Food Residues/Wastes	Oilcake and other solid residues, resulting from the extraction of vegetable fats or oils, of cotton seeds	2306.10.00	0.56 cents/kg	A+
Food Residues/Wastes	Residues of starch manufacture and similar residues	2303.10.00	1.40%	A+
Foodstuffs (Miscellaneous Preparations)	Butter substitutes n/o 10% by wt of milk solids, n/o 45% butterfat, neosi	2106.90.38	13.1 cents/kg	A+
Foodstuffs (Miscellaneous Preparations)	Butter substitutes n/o 10% by wt of milk solids, o/45% butterfat, subject to add US note 14 to Ch 4, not GN15	2106.90.34	15.4 cents/kg	A+
Foodstuffs (Miscellaneous Preparations)	Butter substitutes n/o 10% by wt of milk solids, o/45% butterfat, subject to gen. note 15 to the HTS	2106.90.32	15.4 cents/kg	A+

Products Eligible for Duty-Free Treatment Under AGOA if Exported to the U.S. from an AGOA Beneficiary Country

Foodstuffs (Miscellaneous Preparations)	Butter substitutes o/10% by wt of milk solids, n/o 45% butterfat, neosi	2106.90.28	13.1 cents/kg	A+
Foodstuffs (Miscellaneous Preparations)	Butter substitutes o/10% by wt of milk solids, o/45% butterfat, subject to add US note 14 to Ch.4, not GN15	2106.90.24	15.4 cents/kg	A+
Foodstuffs (Miscellaneous Preparations)	Butter substitutes o/10% by wt of milk solids, o/45% butterfat, subject to gen. note 15 to the HTS	2106.90.22	15.4 cents/kg	A+
Foodstuffs (Miscellaneous Preparations)	Edible ice (dairy prod. described in add US note 1 to Ch. 4), subject to add US note 10 to Ch. 4, not GN15	2105.00.30	20%	A+
Foodstuffs (Miscellaneous Preparations)	Edible ice (dairy prod. described in add US note 1 to Ch. 4), subject to gen note 15 of the HTS	2105.00.25	20%	A+
Foodstuffs (Miscellaneous Preparations)	Edible ice, except ice cream, not described in add US note 1 to Ch. 4, nesoi	2105.00.50	17%	A+
Foodstuffs (Miscellaneous Preparations)	Food preps, nesoi, n/o 10% by wt of milk solids, dairy prods, descr. in add US note 1 to Ch.4: subject to add US note 10 to Ch.4, not GN15	2106.90.85	10%	A+
Foodstuffs (Miscellaneous Preparations)	Food preps, nesoi, n/o 10% by wt of milk solids, subject to gen. note 15 of the HTS	2106.90.83	10%	A+
Foodstuffs (Miscellaneous Preparations)	Food preps, nesoi, n/o 10% milk solids, o/10% sugar, descr. in add US note 3 to Ch.17, subject to add US note 8 to Ch. 17, not GN15	2106.90.95	10%	A+
Foodstuffs (Miscellaneous Preparations)	Food preps, nesoi, o/10% by wt of milk solids, dairy prods, descr. in add US note 1 to Ch.4: subject to add US note 10 to Ch.4, not GN15	2106.90.64	10%	A+
Foodstuffs (Miscellaneous Preparations)	Food preps, nesoi, o/10% by wt of milk solids, subject to gen. note 15 of the HTS	2106.90.62	10%	A+
Foodstuffs (Miscellaneous Preparations)	Food preps, nesoi, o/10% milk solids, o/10% sugar, descr. in add US note 3 to Ch.17, subject to add US note 8 to Ch. 17, not GN15	2106.90.78	10%	A+
Foodstuffs (Miscellaneous Preparations)	Ice cream, whether or not w/cocoa, subject to add. US note 5 to Ch. 21, not GN15	2105.00.10	20%	A+
Foodstuffs (Miscellaneous Preparations)	Ice cream, whether or not w/cocoa, subject to gen. note 15 of the HTS	2105.00.05	20%	A+
Foodstuffs (Miscellaneous Preparations)	Orange juice, fortified with vitamins or minerals	2106.90.48	7.85 cents/liter	A+
Foodstuffs (Miscellaneous Preparations)	Roasted chicory and other roasted coffee substitutes and extracts, essences and concentrates thereof	2101.30.00	2.1 cents/kg	A+
Foodstuffs (Miscellaneous Preparations)	Tomato sauces, nesi	2103.20.40	11.60%	A+
Footwear	Footwear w/outer soles & uppers of rubber or plastics, nesoi, covering ankle, designed as protection against liquids, chemicals, weather	6402.91.50	37.50%	
Footwear	Footwear w/outer soles & uppers of rubber or plastics, nesoi, covering ankle, nesoi, valued n/o $3/pair	6402.91.60	48%	

Products Eligible for Duty-Free Treatment Under AGOA if Exported to the U.S. from an AGOA Beneficiary Country

Footwear	Footwear w/outer soles & uppers of rubber or plastics, nesoi, covering ankle, nesoi, valued o/$6.50 but n/o $12/pair	6402.91.80	90 cents/pr. + 20%	
Footwear	Footwear w/outer soles & uppers of rubber or plastics, nesoi, covering ankle, nesoi, valued over $12/pair	6402.91.90	20%	
Footwear	Footwear w/outer soles & uppers of rubber or plastics, nesoi, covering ankle, nesoi, valued over $3 but n/o $6.50/pair	6402.91.70	90 cents/pr. + 37.5%	
Footwear	Footwear w/outer soles & uppers of rubber or plastics, nesoi, covering ankle, w/ext. surf. of uppers o/90% rubber or plastics	6402.91.40	6%	
Footwear	Footwear w/outer soles & uppers of rubber or plastics, nesoi, n/cov. ankle, nesoi, design. as protection against liquids/chemicals/weather	6402.99.20	37.50%	
Footwear	Footwear w/outer soles & uppers of rubber or plastics, nesoi, n/cov. ankle, nesoi, valued n/o $3/pair	6402.99.60	48%	
Footwear	Footwear w/outer soles & uppers of rubber or plastics, nesoi, n/cov. ankle, nesoi, valued o/$3 but n/o $6.50/pair	6402.99.70	90 cents/pr. + 37.5%	
Footwear	Footwear w/outer soles & uppers of rubber or plastics, nesoi, n/cov. ankle, nesoi, valued o/$6.50 but n/o $12/pair	6402.99.80	90 cents/pr. + 20%	
Footwear	Footwear w/outer soles & uppers of rubber or plastics, nesoi, n/cov. ankle, nesoi, valued over $12/pair	6402.99.90	20%	
Footwear	Footwear w/outer soles & uppers of rubber or plastics, nesoi, n/cov. ankle, w/ext. surf. of uppers o/90% rubber or plastics, nesoi	6402.99.18	6%	
Footwear	Footwear w/outer soles & uppers of rubber or plastics, nesoi, n/cov. ankle, w/ext. surf. uppers o/90% rubber/plastics, w/base of cork	6402.99.10	12.50%	
Footwear	Footwear w/outer soles & uppers of rubber or plastics, nesoi, n/cov. ankle, w/ext. surf. uppers o/90% rubber/plastics, w/base of wood	6402.99.05	8%	
Footwear	Footwear w/outer soles & uppers of rubber or plastics, nesoi, n/cov. ankle, w/open toes or heels or of the slip-on type	6402.99.30	37.50%	
Footwear	Footwear w/outer soles & uppers of rubber or plastics, nesoi, w/metal toe-cap, designed as a protection against liquids, chemicals, weather	6402.30.50	37.50%	
Footwear	Footwear w/outer soles & uppers of rubber or plastics, nesoi, w/metal toe-cap, not protective, valued n/o $3/pair	6402.30.60	24%	
Footwear	Footwear w/outer soles & uppers of rubber or plastics, nesoi, w/metal toe-cap, not protective, valued o/$6.50 but n/o $12/pair	6402.30.80	90 cents/pr. + 20%	
Footwear	Footwear w/outer soles & uppers of rubber or plastics, nesoi, w/metal toe-cap, not protective, valued over $12/pair	6402.30.90	20%	
Footwear	Footwear w/outer soles & uppers of rubber or plastics, nesoi, w/metal toe-cap, not protective, valued over $3 but n/o $6.50/pair	6402.30.70	90 cents/pr. + 37.5%	
Footwear	Footwear w/outer soles and uppers of leather, nesoi, covering the ankle, n/welt, for men, youths and boys	6403.51.60	8.50%	
Footwear	Footwear w/outer soles and uppers of leather, nesoi, covering the ankle, n/welt, for persons other than men, youths and boys	6403.51.90	10%	
Footwear	Footwear w/outer soles and uppers of leather, nesoi, covering the ankle, welt	6403.51.30	5%	
Footwear	Footwear w/outer soles and uppers of leather, not cov. ankle, n/welt, for men, youths and boys	6403.59.60	8.50%	
Footwear	Footwear w/outer soles and uppers of leather, not cov. ankle, n/welt, for persons other than men, youths and boys	6403.59.90	10%	
Footwear	Footwear w/outer soles and uppers of leather, not covering the ankle, welt, nesoi	6403.59.30	5%	
Footwear	Footwear w/outer soles of leather/comp. leath., n/o 50% by wt. rub./plast. or rub./plast./text. & 10%+ by wt. rub./plast., val. n/o $2.50/pr	6404.20.20	15%	
Footwear	Footwear w/outer soles of leather/comp. leath., n/o 50% by wt. rub./plast. or rub./plast./text. & 10%+ by wt. rub./plast., val. o/$2.50/pr	6404.20.40	10%	

Products Eligible for Duty-Free Treatment Under AGOA if Exported to the U.S. from an AGOA Beneficiary Country

Footwear	Footwear w/outer soles of leather/comp. leather & uppers of textile, nesoi	6404.20.60	37.50%	
Footwear	Footwear w/outer soles of rub./plast. & upp. of textile, nesoi, val. n/o $3/pr, nesoi	6404.19.50	48%	
Footwear	Footwear w/outer soles of rub./plast. & upp. of textile, nesoi, val. n/o $3/pr, w/soles affixed to upp. w/adhesives & w/o foxing	6404.19.40	37.50%	
Footwear	Footwear w/outer soles of rub./plast. & upp. of textile, nesoi, val. o/$12/pr	6404.19.90	9%	
Footwear	Footwear w/outer soles of rub./plast. & upp. of textile, nesoi, val. o/$3 but n/o $6.50/pr, nesoi	6404.19.70	90 cents/pr. + 37.5%	
Footwear	Footwear w/outer soles of rub./plast. & upp. of textile, nesoi, val. o/$3 but n/o $6.50/pr, w/soles affixed to upp. w/adhesives & w/o foxing	6404.19.60	37.50%	
Footwear	Footwear w/outer soles of rub./plast. & upp. of textile, nesoi, val. o/$6.50 but n/o $12/pr	6404.19.80	90 cents/pr. + 20%	
Footwear	Footwear w/outer soles of rub./plast. & upp. of textile, nesoi, w/open toes/heels or slip-on type, 10% or more by wt. of rubb./plastic	6404.19.35	37.50%	
Footwear	Footwear w/outer soles of rub./plast. & upp. of textile, nesoi, w/open toes/heels or slip-on type, less than 10% rubber/plastics by wt	6404.19.30	12.50%	
Footwear	Footwear w/outer soles of rub./plast. & upp. of veg. fibers, nesoi, w/open toes/heels or slip-on type, less than 10% rubber/plastics by wt.	6404.19.25	7.50%	
Footwear	Footwear w/outer soles of rubber or plastics, nesoi, w/metal toe-cap, w/ext. surf. uppers o/90% rubber or plastics	6402.30.30	6%	
Footwear	Footwear w/outer soles of rubber/plastics & uppers of textile, nesoi, designed as a protection against liquids, chemicals & weather	6404.19.20	37.50%	
Footwear	Footwear w/outer soles of rubber/plastics & uppers of textile, nesoi, w/ext. surf. of uppers over 50% leather	6404.19.15	10.50%	
Footwear	Footwear w/outer soles of rubber/plastics/comp. leather & uppers of leather, cov. ankle, n/welt, for persons other than men/youths/boys	6403.91.90	10%	
Footwear	Footwear w/outer soles of rubber/plastics/comp. leather & uppers of leather, n/cov. ankle, for women/child./infants, val. over $2.50/pair	6403.99.90	10%	
Footwear	Footwear w/outer soles of rubber/plastics/comp. leather & uppers of leather, n/cov. ankle, for women/child./infants, val.n/o $2.50/pr	6403.99.75	7%	
Footwear	Footwear w/outer soles of rubber/plastics/comp. leather & uppers of leather, n/cov. ankle, made on a base wood	6403.99.20	8%	
Footwear	Footwear w/outer soles of rubber/plastics/comp. leather & uppers of leather, n/cov. ankle, n/welt, for men, youths and boys, nesoi	6403.99.60	8.50%	
Footwear	Footwear w/outer soles of rubber/plastics/comp. leather & uppers of leather, n/cov. ankle, welt, nesoi	6403.99.40	5%	
Footwear	Footwear w/outer soles of rubber/plastics/composition leather & uppers of leather, covering the ankle, n/welt, for men,youths and boys	6403.91.60	8.50%	
Footwear	Footwear w/outer soles of rubber/plastics/composition leather & uppers of leather, covering the ankle, welt	6403.91.30	5%	
Footwear	Footwear w/outer soles of rubber/plastics/leather/comp. leather & uppers of leather, w/protective metal toe-cap, n/welt	6403.40.60	8.50%	
Footwear	Footwear w/outer soles of rubber/plastics/leather/comp. leather & uppers of leather, w/protective metal toe-cap, welt	6403.40.30	5%	
Footwear	Footwear, nesoi, w/outer soles and uppers other than of rubber/plastics/leather/comp. leather/textile materials	6405.90.90	12.50%	
Footwear	Footwear, nesoi, w/outer soles of other than rubber/plastics/leather/comp.leather & uppers of leather/composition leather, nesoi	6405.10.00	10%	
Footwear	Footwear, nesoi, w/outer soles of other than rubber/plastics/leather/comp.leather & uppers of vegetable fibers, nesoi	6405.20.30	7.50%	

Products Eligible for Duty-Free Treatment Under AGOA if Exported to the U.S. from an AGOA Beneficiary Country

Footwear	Footwear,nesoi,w/outer sole other than rubber/plastics/leather/comp. leather & upper of text. material other than veg. fibers or wool felt	6405.20.90	12.50%	
Footwear	Formed upper for footwear, of materials other than leather/comp.leather or textile, w/over 90% of ext. surf. rub./plast. not for fw w/foxing	6406.10.45	6%	
Footwear	Formed uppers for footwear, of leather/composition leather, for men, youths and boys	6406.10.05	8.50%	
Footwear	Formed uppers for footwear, of leather/composition leather, for women, misses, children and infants	6406.10.10	10%	
Footwear	Formed uppers for footwear, of materials other than leather/comp.leather or textile materials, nesoi	6406.10.50	26.20%	
Footwear	Formed uppers for footwear, of textile materials, nesoi, valued n/o $3/pr	6406.10.25	33.60%	
Footwear	Formed uppers for footwear, of textile materials, nesoi, valued o/$12/pr	6406.10.40	7.50%	
Footwear	Formed uppers for footwear, of textile materials, nesoi, valued o/$3 but n/o $6.50/pr	6406.10.30	63 cents/pr. + 26.2%	
Footwear	Formed uppers for footwear, of textile materials, nesoi, valued o/$6.50 but n/o $12/pr	6406.10.35	62 cents/pr. + 13.7%	
Footwear	Formed uppers for footwear, of textile materials, w/o 50% of external surface leather	6406.10.20	10.50%	
Footwear	Golf shoes w/outer soles of rubber or plastics and uppers > 90% of ext. surface area rubber or plastics	6402.19.05	6%	
Footwear	Golf shoes, w/outer soles rubber/plastics/leather/comp. leather & upper of leather, for persons other than men/youths/boys	6403.19.50	10%	
Footwear	Golf shoes, w/outer soles rubber/plastics/leather/comp. leather & uppers of leather, n/welt, for men/youths/boys	6403.19.30	8.50%	
Footwear	Golf shoes, w/outer soles rubber/plastics/leather/comp. leather & uppers of leather, welt, for men/youths/boys	6403.19.10	5%	
Footwear	Sandals w/outer soles & uppers of rubber or plastics, not cov. ankle, produced in one piece by molding	6402.99.14	3%	
Footwear	Sports & athletic footwear w/outer soles of rubber/plastics & uppers of textile, val. n/o $3/pair, w/soles fixed w/adhesives w/o foxing	6404.11.40	37.50%	
Footwear	Sports & athletic footwear w/outer soles of rubber/plastics & uppers of textile, val. o/$3 but n/o $6.50/pr, w/soles fixed w/adhesives	6404.11.60	37.50%	
Footwear	Sports & athletic footwear w/outer soles of rubber/plastics & uppers of textile, valued n/o $3/pair, nesoi	6404.11.50	48%	
Footwear	Sports & athletic footwear w/outer soles of rubber/plastics & uppers of textile, valued o/$12/pair	6404.11.90	20%	
Footwear	Sports & athletic footwear w/outer soles of rubber/plastics & uppers of textile, valued o/$3 but n/o $6.50/pr, nesoi	6404.11.70	90 cents/pr. + 37.5%	
Footwear	Sports & athletic footwear w/outer soles of rubber/plastics & uppers of textile, valued o/$6.50 but n/o $12/pair	6404.11.80	90 cents/pr. + 20%	
Footwear	Sports & athletic footwear w/outer soles of rubber/plastics & uppers of textile, w/ext. surf. of uppers over 50% leather	6404.11.20	10.50%	
Footwear	Sports footwear (o/than ski fwear & golf shoes), w/outer soles of rubber or plastics & uppers >90% ext. surf. area rubber or plast.	6402.19.15	5.10%	
Footwear	Sports footwear w/outer soles and uppers of rubber or plastics, nesi, valued over $12/pair	6402.19.90	9%	

Products Eligible for Duty-Free Treatment Under AGOA if Exported to the U.S. from an AGOA Beneficiary Country

Footwear	Sports footwear w/outer soles and uppers of rubber or plastics, nesi, valued over $3 but not over $6.50/pair	6402.19.50	76 cents/pr. + 32%	
Footwear	Sports footwear w/outer soles and uppers of rubber or plastics, nesi, valued over $6.50 but not over $12/pair	6402.19.70	76 cents/pr. + 17%	
Footwear	Sports footwear, nesoi, w/outer soles rubber/plastics/leather/comp. leather & uppers of leather, n/welt, for men/youths/boys	6403.19.40	4.30%	
Footwear	Turn or turned footwear w/outer soles and uppers of leather, not covering the ankle	6403.59.15	2.50%	
Footwear	Waterproof footwear, not mechanically asmbld, w/outer soles and uppers of rubber or plastics, nesoi, not cover ankle	6401.99.90	37.50%	
Footwear	Waterproof footwear, not mechanically asmbld., w/outer soles and upper of rubber or plastics, nesoi, covering ankle but not knee	6401.92.90	37.50%	
Footwear	Waterproof footwear, not mechanically asmbld., w/over 90% of ext. surf. area of soles & uppers PVC, covering/ankle but not knee	6401.92.60	4.60%	
Footwear	Waterproof footwear not mechanically assembled, w/outer soles & uppers of rubber or plastics, covering the knee	6401.91.00	37.50%	
Footwear	Waterproof footwear, not mechanically assembled, w/outer soles & uppers of rubber or plastics, w/metal toecap	6401.10.00	37.50%	
Footwear	Waterproof protect. footwear, not mechanically asmbld., w/outer soles and uppers of rubber or plastics, not cover ankle, w/closures	6401.99.60	37.50%	
Footwear	Waterproof protect. footwear, not mechanically asmbld., w/outer soles and uppers of rubber or plastics, not cover ankle, w/o closures	6401.99.30	25%	
Fruit Juices	Citrus juice of any single citrus fruit, nesi, (including lemon), concentrated	2009.30.60	7.9 cents/liter	
Fruit Juices	Citrus juice of any single citrus fruit, nesi, (including lemon), not concentrated	2009.30.40	3.4 cents/liter	
Fruit Juices	Grape juice (including grape must), concentrated or not concentrated	2009.60.00	4.4 cents/liter	A+
Fruit Juices	Grapefruit juice, nesi, frozen or not frozen, concentrated or not concentrated, nesi	2009.20.40	7.9 cents/liter	
Fruit Juices	Grapefruit juice, not frozen, not concentrated, and not made from a juice of 1.5 or more degree of concentration	2009.20.20	4.5 cents/liter	
Fruit Juices	Mixtures of fruit juices, or mixtures of vegetable and fruit juices, concentrated or not concentrated	2009.90.40	7.4 cents/liter	A+
Fruit Juices	Orange juice, frozen, unfermented and not containing added spirit	2009.11.00	7.85 cents/liter	
Fruit Juices	Orange juice, not frozen, concentrated, or not concentrated	2009.19.45	7.85 cents/liter	
Fruit Juices	Orange juice,nt concentrated & nt made from a juice of 1.5 or more degree concentration,not frozen,unfermented & not containing added spirit	2009.19.25	4.5 cents/liter	
Fruit Juices	Pineapple juice, concentrated (in concentrations greater than 3.5 degrees)	2009.40.40	1 cent/liter	A+
Fruit Juices	Pineapple juice, not concentrated, or not having a degree of concentration of more than 3.5 degrees	2009.40.20	4.2 cents/liter	A+
Fruit Juices	Prune juice, concentrated or not concentrated	2009.80.40	0.64 cents/liter	A+
Fruit Preparations	Apples, otherwise prepared or preserved, nesi	2008.99.05	0.9 cents/kg	A+
Fruit Preparations	Avocados, otherwise prepared or preserved, nesi	2008.99.10	10.6 cents/kg	A+
Fruit Preparations	Blueberries, otherwise prepared or preserved, nesi.	2008.99.18	2.20%	A+
Fruit Preparations	Cherries, otherwise prepared or preserved, nesi	2008.60.00	6.9 cents/kg + 4.5%	A+

Products Eligible for Duty-Free Treatment Under AGOA if Exported to the U.S. from an AGOA Beneficiary Country

Fruit Preparations	Cherries, preserved by sugar (drained, glace or crystallized)	2006.00.20	9.9 cents/kg + 6.4%	A+
Fruit Preparations	Citron (other than peel or pulp), otherwise prepared or preserved, nesi	2008.30.85	14%	A+
Fruit Preparations	Citrus fruit or peel of citrus or other fruit, except mixtures, preserved by sugar (drained, glace or crystallized)	2006.00.60	6 cents/kg	A+
Fruit Preparations	Citrus fruit pastes and purees, being cooked preparations	2007.91.10	11.20%	A+
Fruit Preparations	Clementines, wilkings and similar citrus hybrids (other than peel or pulp), otherwise prepared or preserved, nesi	2008.30.55	1.4 cents/kg	
Fruit Preparations	Currant and berry fruit jellies	2007.99.70	1.40%	A+
Fruit Preparations	Currant and other berry jams, nesi	2007.99.15	1.40%	A+
Fruit Preparations	Dates, otherwise prepared or preserved, nesi	2008.99.25	22.40%	A+
Fruit Preparations	Fruit pastes and purees, nesi, and nut pastes and purees, being cooked preparations	2007.99.65	10%	A+
Fruit Preparations	Fruits, nuts, and other edible parts of plants, nesi, prepared or preserved by vinegar or acetic acid	2001.90.60	14%	A+
Fruit Preparations	Grapefruit (other than peel or pulp), otherwise prepared or preserved, nesi	2008.30.70	1.1 cents/kg	A+
Fruit Preparations	Grapes, otherwise prepared or preserved, nesi	2008.99.29	7%	A+
Fruit Preparations	Homogenized cooked preparations of fruit put up for retail sale as infant food or for dietetic purposes, in cont. not over 250 grams, net	2007.10.00	12%	A+
Fruit Preparations	Kumquats (other than peel or pulp), otherwise prepared or preserved, nesi	2008.30.80	0.55 cents/kg	A+
Fruit Preparations	Limes (other than peel or pulp), otherwise prepared or preserved, nesi	2008.30.65	14%	A+
Fruit Preparations	Mixtures of fruit or edible parts of plants, in airtight cont. excl. apricots, citrus, peaches or pears (incl. canned tropical fruit salad)	2008.92.10	5.60%	A+
Fruit Preparations	Mixtures of nuts or other seeds otherwise prepared or preserved, nesi	2008.19.85	22.40%	A+
Fruit Preparations	Mixtures of vegetables, fruit, nuts, fruit-peel or other parts of plants, preserved by sugar (drained, glace or crystallized)	2006.00.50	16%	A+
Fruit Preparations	Nectarines, otherwise prepared or preserved, nesi	2008.99.42	16%	A+
Fruit Preparations	Orange pulp, otherwise prepared or preserved, nesi	2008.30.35	11.20%	A+
Fruit Preparations	Oranges (other than peel or pulp), otherwise prepared or preserved, nesi	2008.30.40	1.4 cents/kg	A+
Fruit Preparations	Papaya pastes and purees, being cooked preparations	2007.99.55	14%	A+
Fruit Preparations	Peach jam	2007.99.35	7%	A+
Fruit Preparations	Pears, otherwise prepared or preserved, nesi	2008.40.00	15.30%	A+
Fruit Preparations	Peel of citrus fruit, nesi, otherwise prepared or preserved, nesi	2008.30.30	11.3 cents/kg	A+
Fruit Preparations	Peel of lemons, otherwise prepared or preserved, nesi	2008.30.20	4.2 cents/kg	A+
Fruit Preparations	Pineapples, otherwise prepared or preserved, nesi	2008.20.00	0.35 cents/kg	A+

Products Eligible for Duty-Free Treatment Under AGOA if Exported to the U.S. from an AGOA Beneficiary Country

Fruit Preparations	Pineapples, preserved by sugar (drained, glace or crystallized)	2006.00.40	2.10%	A+
Fruit Preparations	Plums (including prune plums and sloes), otherwise prepared or preserved, nesi	2008.99.60	11.20%	A+
Fruit Preparations	Satsumas, prepared or preserved, in airtight containers, aggregate quantity o/40,000 metric tons/calandar yr	2008.30.46	0.28 cents/kg	A+
Fruit Preparations	Strawberries, otherwise prepared or preserved, nesi	2008.80.00	11.90%	A+
Fruit Preparations	Strawberry pastes and purees, being cooked preparations	2007.99.60	12%	A+
Fruit Preparations	Watermelon seeds, otherwise prepared or preserved, nesi	2008.19.50	6.40%	A+
Fruits	Apricots, fresh	0809.10.00	0.2 cents/kg	A+
Fruits	Avocados, fresh or dried	0804.40.00	11.2 cents/kg	A+
Fruits	Barberries, dried	0813.40.15	3.5 cents/kg	A+
Fruits	Boysenberries, frozen, in water or containing added sweetening	0811.90.22	11.20%	A+
Fruits	Cantaloupes, fresh, if entered during the period from August 1 through September 15, inclusive	0807.19.10	12.80%	A+
Fruits	Cherries, dried	0813.40.30	10.6 cents/kg	A+
Fruits	Cherries, provisionally preserved, but unsuitable in that state for immediate consumption	0812.10.00	13.4 cents/kg	A+
Fruits	Citrus fruit, provisionally preserved, but unsuitable in that state for immediate consumption	0812.90.20	1.8 cents/kg	A+
Fruits	Dates, fresh or dried, other than whole	0804.10.80	29.80%	A+
Fruits	Dates, fresh or dried, whole, with or without pits, packed in units weighing (with immediate container, if any) not over 4.6 kg	0804.10.20	13.2 cents/kg	A+
Fruits	Dates, fresh or dried, whole, with pits, packed in units weighing over 4.6 kg	0804.10.40	1 cent/kg	A+
Fruits	Dates, fresh or dried, whole, without pits, packed in units weighing over 4.6 kg	0804.10.60	2.8 cents/kg	A+
Fruits	Figs, fresh or dried, other than whole (including fig paste)	0804.20.80	8.8 cents/kg	A+
Fruits	Figs, fresh or dried, whole, in units weighing more than 0.5 kg each	0804.20.40	7.9 cents/kg	A+
Fruits	Figs, provisionally preserved, but unsuitable in that state for immediate consumption	0812.90.30	2.6 cents/kg	A+
Fruits	Fruit and nuts nesi, including mixtures containing nuts, provisionally preserved, but not for immediate consumption	0812.90.90	0.1 cents/kg	A+
Fruits	Fruit nesi, dried, other than that of headings 0801 to 0806, and excluding mixtures	0813.40.90	2.50%	A+
Fruits	Grapefruit, fresh or dried, entered during the period August 1 through September 30, inclusive	0805.40.40	1.9 cents/kg	
Fruits	Grapefruit, fresh or dried, if entered during the month of October	0805.40.60	1.5 cents/kg	
Fruits	Grapefruit, fresh or dried, if entered during the period November 1 through the following July 31, inclusive	0805.40.80	2.5 cents/kg	
Fruits	Grapes, dried, other than raisins	0806.20.90	3.5 cents/kg	A+
Fruits	Grapes, fresh, if entered during the period February 15 through March 31, inclusive	0806.10.20	$1.13/m3	A+
Fruits	Grapes, fresh, if entered during the period July 1 through the following February 14, inclusive	0806.10.60	$1.80/m3	A+
Fruits	Lemons, fresh or dried	0805.30.20	2.2 cents/kg	A+
Fruits	Mandarins (including tangerines and satsumas); clementines, wilkings and similar citrus hybrids, fresh or dried	0805.20.00	1.9 cents/kg	
Fruits	Mixtures of nuts or dried fruits of Chapter 8	0813.50.00	14%	A+
Fruits	Mixtures of two or more fruits, provisionally preserved, but unsuitable in that state for consumption	0812.90.10	11.20%	A+
Fruits	Oranges, fresh or dried	0805.10.00	1.9 cents/kg	

Products Eligible for Duty-Free Treatment Under AGOA if Exported to the U.S. from an AGOA Beneficiary Country

Fruits	Other melons nesoi, fresh, if entered during the period from June 1 through November 30, inclusive	0807.19.80	28%	A+
Fruits	Papayas, frozen, in water or containing added sweetening	0811.90.40	11.20%	A+
Fruits	Peaches, dried	0813.40.40	1.4 cents/kg	A+
Fruits	Peaches, including nectarines, fresh, if entered during the period from June 1 through November 30, inclusive	0809.30.20	0.2 cents/kg	A+
Fruits	Pears and quinces, fresh, if entered during the period from July 1 through the following March 31, inclusive	0808.20.40	0.3 cents/kg	A+
Fruits	Peel of citrus fruit, excl. orange or citron and peel, nesi, of melon, fresh, frozen, dried or provisionally preserved	0814.00.80	1.6 cents/kg	A+
Fruits	Pineapples, fresh or dried, not reduced in size, in bulk	0804.30.20	0.51 cents/kg	A+
Fruits	Pineapples, fresh or dried, not reduced in size, in crates or other packages	0804.30.40	1.1 cents/kg	A+
Fruits	Pineapples, fresh or dried, reduced in size	0804.30.60	0.44 cents/kg	A+
Fruits	Pineapples, provisionally preserved, but unsuitable in that state for immediate consumption	0812.90.40	0.25 cents/kg	A+
Fruits	Plums, prunes and sloes, fresh, if entered during the period from June 1 through December 31, inclusive	0809.40.40	0.5 cents/kg	A+
Fruits	Prunes and plums, dried, (except if presoaked in brine)	0813.20.20	14%	A+
Fruits	Prunes and plums, soaked in brine and dried	0813.20.10	2 cents/kg	A+
Fruits	Raisins, made from dried seedless grapes	0806.20.10	1.8 cents/kg	A+
Fruits	Raisins, made from other than seedless grapes	0806.20.20	2.8 cents/kg	A+
Fruits	Raspberries and loganberries, fresh, if entered during the period from September 1 through the following June 30, inclusive	0810.20.10	0.18 cents/kg	A+
Fruits	Strawberries, provisionally preserved, but unsuitable in that state for immediate consumption	0812.20.00	0.8 cents/kg	A+
Fruits	Watermelons, fresh, if entered during the period April 1 through November 30, inclusive	0807.11.40	17%	A+
Furskin Articles	Artificial fur and articles thereof	4304.00.00	6.50%	A+
Glass and Glassware	Drinking glasses of glass (o/than Pb crystal), nesoi, cut or engraved, valued over $3 but n/over $5 each	7013.29.30	11.30%	A+
Glass and Glassware	Drinking glasses of glass (o/than Pb crystal), nesoi, cut or engraved, valued over $5 each	7013.29.40	5%	A+
Glass and Glassware	Drinking glasses of glass (o/than Pb crystal), nesoi, n/cut or engraved, valued over $3 but n/over $5 each	7013.29.50	10.50%	A+
Glass and Glassware	Drinking glasses of glass (o/than Pb crystal), nesoi, n/cut or engraved, valued over $5 each	7013.29.60	5%	A+
Glass and Glassware	Drinking glasses of glass (o/than Pb crystal), nesoi, valued n/over $0.30 each	7013.29.10	32.30%	A+
Glass and Glassware	Drinking glasses of glass (o/than Pb crystal), nesoi, valued over $0.30 but n/over $3 each	7013.29.20	25.50%	A+
Glass and Glassware	Drinking glasses of lead crystal, valued n/over $1 each	7013.21.10	17%	A+
Glass and Glassware	Drinking glasses of lead crystal, valued o/$1 but n/over $3 each	7013.21.20	14%	A+
Glass and Glassware	Drinking glasses of lead crystal, valued o/$3 but n/over $5 each	7013.21.30	7.30%	A+
Glass and Glassware	Drinking glasses of pressed and toughened (specially tempered) glass	7013.29.05	12.50%	A+
Glass and Glassware	Float glass & surface ground or polished glass, nonwired, in sheets, colored thru mass, opacified, flashed, 10 mm or more thick, not worked	7005.21.20	5.60%	A+
Glass and Glassware	Float glass & surface ground or polished glass, nonwired, in sheets, colored thru mass, opacified, flashed, under 10 mm thick, not worked	7005.21.10	14.5 cents/m2 + 0.4%	A+

Products Eligible for Duty-Free Treatment Under AGOA if Exported to the U.S. from an AGOA Beneficiary Country

Glass and Glassware	Float glass & surface ground or polished glass, nonwired, in sheets, less than 10 mm thick, w/area n/o 0.65 M2 & not for LCD's	7005.29.08	18.7 cents/m2	A+
Glass and Glassware	Float glass & surface ground or polished glass, nonwired, in sheets, less than 10 mm thick, w/area over 0.65 M2 & not for LCD's	7005.29.18	14.5 cents/m2	A+
Glass and Glassware	Glass fiber slivers	7019.19.90	4.20%	A+
Glass and Glassware	Glass in balls (o/than microspheres of heading 7018), unworked, n/o 6mm in diameter	7002.10.10	3.90%	A+
Glass and Glassware	Glass microspheres not exceeding 1 mm in diameter	7018.20.00	5%	A+
Glass and Glassware	Glass-ceramic ware of a kind used for household, office, indoor decoration or similar purposes, nesoi	7013.10.50	26%	A+
Glass and Glassware	Glassware for table or kitchen purposes (o/than drinking glasses), nesoi, cut or engraved, valued over $3 but n/over $5 each	7013.39.30	12.80%	A+
Glass and Glassware	Glassware for table or kitchen purposes (o/than drinking glasses), nesoi, cut or engraved, valued over $5 each	7013.39.40	7.20%	A+
Glass and Glassware	Glassware for table or kitchen purposes (o/than drinking glasses), nesoi, n/cut or engraved, valued over $3 but n/o $5 each	7013.39.50	15%	A+
Glass and Glassware	Glassware for table or kitchen purposes (o/than drinking glasses), nesoi, n/cut or engraved, valued over $5 each	7013.39.60	7.20%	A+
Glass and Glassware	Glassware for table or kitchen purposes (o/than drinking glasses), nesoi, valued n/over $3 each	7013.39.20	25.50%	A+
Glass and Glassware	Glassware for table or kitchen purposes (o/than drinking glasses), of lead crystal, valued n/over $1 each	7013.31.10	17%	A+
Glass and Glassware	Glassware for table or kitchen purposes (o/than drinking glasses), of lead crystal, valued over $1 but n/over $3 each	7013.31.20	14%	A+
Glass and Glassware	Glassware for table or kitchen purposes (o/than drinking glasses), of low coefficient of heat expansion glass, n/o $3 each	7013.32.20	25.50%	A+
Glass and Glassware	Glassware for table or kitchen purposes (o/than drinking glasses), of low coefficient of heat expansion glass, over $3 but n/o $5 each	7013.32.30	12.80%	A+
Glass and Glassware	Glassware for table or kitchen purposes (o/than drinking glasses), of low coefficient of heat expansion, over $5 each	7013.32.40	7.20%	A+
Glass and Glassware	Glassware for table or kitchen purposes (o/than drinking glasses), of pressed and toughened glass, nesoi	7013.39.10	12.50%	A+
Glass and Glassware	Glassware for table or kitchen purposes (o/than drinking glasses), of pressed and toughened low coefficient of heat expansion glass	7013.32.10	12.50%	A+
Glass and Glassware	Glassware for toilet/office/indoor decor. & similar purposes, of lead crystal, valued n/over $1 each	7013.91.10	20%	A+
Glass and Glassware	Glassware for toilet/office/indoor decor. & similar purposes, of lead crystal, valued over $1 but n/over $3 each	7013.91.20	14%	A+
Glass and Glassware	Glassware for toilet/office/indoor decor. & similar purposes, of lead crystal, valued over $3 but n/over $5 each	7013.91.30	10.50%	A+
Glass and Glassware	Glassware for toilet/office/indoor decor. & similar purposes, of pressed and toughened (specially tempered) glass	7013.99.20	12.50%	A+
Glass and Glassware	Glassware for toilet/office/indoor decor. or similar purposes, nesoi, cut or engraved, valued over $3 but n/over $5 each	7013.99.60	15%	A+
Glass and Glassware	Glassware for toilet/office/indoor decor. or similar purposes, nesoi, cut or engraved, valued over $5 each	7013.99.70	7.20%	A+
Glass and Glassware	Glassware for toilet/office/indoor decor. or similar purposes, nesoi, n/cut or engraved, valued over $3 but n/over $5 each	7013.99.80	12.80%	A+
Glass and Glassware	Glassware for toilet/office/indoor decor. or similar purposes, nesoi, n/cut or engraved, valued over $5 each	7013.99.90	7.20%	A+
Glass and Glassware	Glassware for toilet/office/indoor decor. or similar purposes, nesoi, valued n/over $0.30 each	7013.99.40	38%	A+

Products Eligible for Duty-Free Treatment Under AGOA if Exported to the U.S. from an AGOA Beneficiary Country

Glass and Glassware	Glassware for toilet/office/indoor decor. or similar purposes, nesoi, valued over $0.30 but n/over $3 each	7013.99.50	30%	A+
Glass and Glassware	Glassware, nesoi, decorated/colored within the body prior to solidification; millefiori glassware; glassware colored & w/bubbles etc	7013.99.10	17%	A+
Glass and Glassware	Woven glass fiber articles (other than fabrics), nesoi	7019.90.10	4.80%	A+
Grain Milling Products	Flakes, granules and pellets, of potatoes	1105.20.00	1.3 cents/kg	A+
Grain Milling Products	Grains of barley, hulled, pearled, clipped, sliced, kibbled or otherwise worked, but not rolled or flaked	1104.21.00	1.20%	A+
Grain Milling Products	Groats and meal of cereals other than wheat, oats, corn (maize) or rice	1103.19.00	9%	A+
Grain Milling Products	Groats and meal of wheat	1103.11.00	0.5 cents/kg	A+
Grain Milling Products	Malt, not roasted	1107.10.00	0.3 cents/kg	A+
Grain Milling Products	Malt, roasted	1107.20.00	0.42 cents/kg	A+
Grain Milling Products	Potato starch	1108.13.00	0.56 cents/kg	A+
Grain Milling Products	Rolled or flaked grains of barley	1104.11.00	2 cents/kg	A+
Grain Milling Products	Rolled or flaked grains of cereals, other than of barley or oats	1104.19.00	0.45 cents/kg	A+
Grain Milling Products	Rye flour	1102.10.00	0.23 cents/kg	A+
Grain Milling Products	Wheat or meslin flour	1101.00.00	0.7 cents/kg	A+
Grains, Seeds, and Nuts (Miscellaneous)	Alfalfa (lucerne) meal and pellets	1214.10.00	1.40%	A+
Grains, Seeds, and Nuts (Miscellaneous)	Apricot, peach or plum stones and kernels	1212.30.00	1.5 cents/kg	A+
Grains, Seeds, and Nuts (Miscellaneous)	Cauliflower seeds of a kind used for sowing	1209.91.10	5.9 cents/kg	A+
Grains, Seeds, and Nuts (Miscellaneous)	Cotton seeds, whether or not broken	1207.20.00	0.47 cents/kg	A+
Grains, Seeds, and Nuts (Miscellaneous)	Flaxseed (linseed), whether or not broken	1204.00.00	0.39 cents/kg	A+
Grains, Seeds, and Nuts (Miscellaneous)	Flours and meals of oil seeds or oleaginous fruits other than those of mustard or soybeans	1208.90.00	1.40%	A+
Grains, Seeds, and Nuts (Miscellaneous)	Flours and meals of soybeans	1208.10.00	1.90%	A+
Grains, Seeds, and Nuts (Miscellaneous)	Kentucky blue grass seed of a kind used for sowing	1209.24.00	1.2 cents/kg	A+
Grains, Seeds, and Nuts (Miscellaneous)	Parsley seeds of a kind used for sowing	1209.91.50	0.68 cents/kg	A+

Products Eligible for Duty-Free Treatment Under AGOA if Exported to the U.S. from an AGOA Beneficiary Country

Grains, Seeds, and Nuts (Miscellaneous)	Peanuts (ground-nuts), not roasted or cooked, in shell, subject to add. US note 2 to Ch.12	1202.10.40	9.35 cents/kg	A+
Grains, Seeds, and Nuts (Miscellaneous)	Peanuts (ground-nuts), not roasted or cooked, in shell, subject to gen note 15 of the HTS	1202.10.05	9.35 cents/kg	A+
Grains, Seeds, and Nuts (Miscellaneous)	Peanuts (ground-nuts), not roasted or cooked, shelled, subject to add. US note 2 to Ch.12	1202.20.40	6.6 cents/kg	A+
Grains, Seeds, and Nuts (Miscellaneous)	Peanuts (ground-nuts), not roasted or cooked, shelled, subject to gen note 15 of the HTS	1202.20.05	6.6 cents/kg	A+
Grains, Seeds, and Nuts (Miscellaneous)	Rape or colza seeds, whether or not broken	1205.00.00	0.58 cents/kg	A+
Grains, Seeds, and Nuts (Miscellaneous)	Rye grass seed of a kind used for sowing	1209.25.00	1.4 cents/kg	A+
Grains, Seeds, and Nuts (Miscellaneous)	Sugar beet, fresh, chilled, frozen or dried, whether or not ground	1212.91.00	39.7 cents/t	A+
Grains, Seeds, and Nuts (Miscellaneous)	White and ladino clover seed of a kind used for sowing	1209.22.20	1.6 cents/kg	A+
Gums, Saps and Resins	Mucilages and thickeners derived from vegetable products other than locust beans, locust bean seeds or guar seeds, and excluding agar-agar	1302.39.00	3.20%	A+
Gums, Saps and Resins	Saps and extracts of hops	1302.13.00	89 cents/kg	A+
Honey	Natural honey	0409.00.00	1.9 cents/kg	A+
Iron and Steel	Alloy (o/th stainless, silicon elect., hi-speed, or tool) steel, width 600mm+, hot-rolled flat-rolled prod., in coils, w/thick less 4.75mm	7225.30.70	3.80%	A+
Iron and Steel	Alloy (o/th stainless, silicon elect., hi-speed, or tool) steel, width 600mm+, hot-rolled flat-rolled prod., n/coils, w/thick less 4.75mm	7225.40.70	3.80%	A+
Iron and Steel	Alloy (o/th stainless, silicon elect., hi-speed, or tool) steel, width 600mm+, hot-rolled flat-rolled products, in coils, w/thick 4.75mm+	7225.30.30	1.50%	A+
Iron and Steel	Alloy (o/th stainless, silicon elect., hi-speed, or tool) steel, width 600mm+, hot-rolled flat-rolled products, n/coils, w/thick 4.75mm+	7225.40.30	1.50%	A+
Iron and Steel	Alloy (o/than stainless) steel, ingots and other primary forms	7224.10.00	2%	A+
Iron and Steel	Alloy (o/than stainless) steel, semifinished products	7224.90.00	2%	A+
Iron and Steel	Alloy ball-bearing tool steel, bars and rods, not further worked than hot-rolled, hot-drawn or extruded	7228.30.20	2.40%	A+
Iron and Steel	Alloy heat-resisting steel, width 600mm+, cold-rolled flat-rolled products, w/thickness less than 4.75 mm	7225.50.70	1.60%	A+
Iron and Steel	Alloy high-speed steel, bars and rods in irregularly wound coils, hmot-rolled	7227.10.00	2.10%	A+
Iron and Steel	Alloy high-speed steel, bars and rods, o/than hot-rolled and in irregularly wound coils	7228.10.00	4.60%	A+
Iron and Steel	Alloy high-speed steel, width 600mm+, flat-rolled products	7225.20.00	4.20%	A+

Products Eligible for Duty-Free Treatment Under AGOA if Exported to the U.S. from an AGOA Beneficiary Country

Iron and Steel	Alloy high-speed steel, width less th/600mm, flat-rolled products of high-speed steel	7226.20.00	5%	A+
Iron and Steel	Alloy high-speed steel, wire	7229.10.00	4%	A+
Iron and Steel	Alloy silico-manganese steel, bars and rods, cold formed, o/than hot-rolled and in irregularly wound coils	7228.20.50	3%	A+
Iron and Steel	Alloy silico-manganese steel, bars and rods, not cold-formed, o/than hot-rolled and in irregularly wound coils	7228.20.10	2.40%	A+
Iron and Steel	Alloy silico-manganese steel, wire	7229.20.00	3.60%	A+
Iron and Steel	Alloy silicon electrical steel (grain-oriented), width 300mm+ but less th/600mm, flat-rolled products	7226.11.10	2.30%	A+
Iron and Steel	Alloy silicon electrical steel (grain-oriented), width 600mm+, flat-rolled products	7225.11.00	2.30%	A+
Iron and Steel	Alloy silicon electrical steel (grain-oriented), width less th/300mm, flat-rolled products	7226.11.90	2.80%	A+
Iron and Steel	Alloy silicon electrical steel (o/than grain-oriented), width 300mm+ but less th/600mm, flat-rolled products	7226.19.10	2.30%	A+
Iron and Steel	Alloy silicon electrical steel (o/than grain-oriented), width less th/300mm, flat-rolled products	7226.19.90	2.80%	A+
Iron and Steel	Alloy silicon electrical steel (other than grain-oriented), width 600mm+, flat-rolled products	7225.19.00	2.30%	A+
Iron and Steel	Alloy steel (n/plated or coated w/zinc), width less than 600mm, flat-rolled products further worked than cold-rolled, nesoi	7226.99.00	2.50%	A+
Iron and Steel	Alloy steel (o/ than tool), width 600mm+, cold-rolled flat-rolled products, w/thickness 4.75 mm or more	7225.50.60	2.30%	A+
Iron and Steel	Alloy steel (o/th heat-resisting), width 600mm+, cold-rolled flat-rolled products, w/thickness less than 4.75 mm	7225.50.80	1.60%	A+
Iron and Steel	Alloy steel (o/than hi-speed, silico-mang./tool), bars and rods, not further worked than hot-rolled, hot-drawn or extruded	7228.30.80	2.40%	A+
Iron and Steel	Alloy steel (o/than hi-speed/silico-mang.), flat wire	7229.90.10	2.30%	A+
Iron and Steel	Alloy steel (o/than hi-speed/silico-mang.), round wire	7229.90.50	3.60%	A+
Iron and Steel	Alloy steel (o/than hi-speed/silico-mang.), wire (o/than flat or round wire)	7229.90.90	2.50%	A+
Iron and Steel	Alloy steel (o/than silicon elect./tool), width 300mm+ but less th/600mm, hot-rolled flat-rolled products, w/thickness less than 4.75 mm	7226.91.70	3.80%	A+
Iron and Steel	Alloy steel (o/than silicon elect./tool), width less th/300mm, hot-rolled flat-rolled products, w/thickness less than 4.75 mm	7226.91.80	2.50%	A+
Iron and Steel	Alloy steel (o/than silicon elect./tool), width less th/600mm, hot-rolled flat-rolled products, w/thickness of 4.75 mm or more	7226.91.50	1.50%	A+
Iron and Steel	Alloy steel (o/than tool), bars and rods, cold-formed	7228.60.80	3%	A+
Iron and Steel	Alloy steel (o/than tool), bars and rods, further worked than hot-rolled, forged but not cold-formed	7228.60.60	2.40%	A+
Iron and Steel	Alloy steel (o/than tool), bars and rods, not further worked than cold-formed or cold-finished	7228.50.50	3%	A+
Iron and Steel	Alloy steel (o/than tool), width 300mm+ but less th/600mm, cold-rolled flat-rolled products	7226.92.50	1.60%	A+
Iron and Steel	Alloy steel (o/than tool), width less th/300mm, cold-rolled flat-rolled products, w/thickness n/o 0.25 mm	7226.92.70	2%	A+
Iron and Steel	Alloy steel (o/than tool), width less th/300mm, cold-rolled flat-rolled products, w/thickness o/0.25 mm	7226.92.80	2.40%	A+
Iron and Steel	Alloy steel hollow drill bars and rods	7228.80.00	2.30%	A+
Iron and Steel	Alloy steel, angles, shapes and sections, hot-rolled & not drilled/not punched and not otherwise advanced	7228.70.30	0.80%	A+
Iron and Steel	Alloy steel, angles, shapes and sections, o/than hot-rolled & not drilled/punced and not otherwise advanced	7228.70.60	2.10%	A+

Products Eligible for Duty-Free Treatment Under AGOA if Exported to the U.S. from an AGOA Beneficiary Country

Iron and Steel	Alloy steel, bars and rods, not further worked than forged	7228.40.00	2.40%	A+
Iron and Steel	Alloy steel, width less th/600mm, flat-rolled products further worked than cold-rolled, electrolytically plated or coated with zinc	7226.93.00	2.50%	A+
Iron and Steel	Alloy steel, width less th/600mm, flat-rolled products further wrkd than cold-rolled, plated or coated with zinc o/than electrolytically	7226.94.00	2.50%	A+
Iron and Steel	Alloy tool steel (o/th hi-speed), width 600mm+, cold-rolled flat-rolled products	7225.50.10	4%	A+
Iron and Steel	Alloy tool steel (o/than ball-bearing/chipper knife), bars and rods, not further worked than hot-rolled, hot-drawn or extruded	7228.30.60	4.20%	A+
Iron and Steel	Alloy tool steel (o/than hi-speed), bars & rods in irregular wound coils, hot-rolled, n/tempered, treated or partly manufactured	7227.90.10	0.80%	A+
Iron and Steel	Alloy tool steel (o/than hi-speed), bars and rods in irregularly wound coils, hot-rolled, nesoi	7227.90.20	1.70%	A+
Iron and Steel	Alloy tool steel (o/than hi-speed), bars and rods, further worked than hot-rolled, forged, cold-formed or cold-finished	7228.60.10	4.20%	A+
Iron and Steel	Alloy tool steel (o/than hi-speed), bars and rods, not further worked than cold-formed or cold-finished	7228.50.10	4.20%	A+
Iron and Steel	Alloy tool steel (o/than hi-speed), width 300mm+ but less th/600mm, cold-rolled flat-rolled products	7226.92.10	4%	A+
Iron and Steel	Alloy tool steel (o/than hi-speed), width 600m+, hot-rolled flat-rolled products, in coils, w/thick. of 4.75 mm or more	7225.30.10	3.80%	A+
Iron and Steel	Alloy tool steel (o/than hi-speed), width 600m+, hot-rolled flat-rolled products, in coils, w/thick. of less than 4.75 mm	7225.30.50	3.80%	A+
Iron and Steel	Alloy tool steel (o/than hi-speed), width 600m+, hot-rolled flat-rolled products, n/coils, w/thick. of 4.75 mm or more	7225.40.10	3.80%	A+
Iron and Steel	Alloy tool steel (o/than hi-speed), width 600m+, hot-rolled flat-rolled products, n/coils, w/thick. of less than 4.75 mm	7225.40.50	3.80%	A+
Iron and Steel	Alloy tool steel (o/than hi-speed), width less th/300mm, cold-rolled flat-rolled products	7226.92.30	4.20%	A+
Iron and Steel	Alloy tool steel (o/than hi-speed/chipper knife), width 300mm+ but less th/600mm, hot-rolled flat-rolled products	7226.91.15	3.80%	A+
Iron and Steel	Alloy tool steel (o/than hi-speed/chipper knife), width less th/300mm, hot-rolled flat-rolled products	7226.91.25	4.60%	A+
Iron and Steel	Ferroalloys nesoi	7202.99.50	5%	A+
Iron and Steel	Ferrochromium containing by weight more than 3 percent but not more than 4 percent of carbon	7202.49.10	1.90%	A+
Iron and Steel	Ferromanganese containing by weight more than 4 percent of carbon	7202.11.50	1.50%	A+
Iron and Steel	Ferromolybdenum	7202.70.00	4.50%	A+
Iron and Steel	Ferroniobium	7202.93.00	5%	A+
Iron and Steel	Ferrosilicon containing by weight more than 80% but not more than 90% of silicon	7202.21.75	1.90%	A+
Iron and Steel	Ferrosilicon containing by weight more than 90% of silicon	7202.21.90	5.80%	A+
Iron and Steel	Ferrotitanium and ferrosilicon titanium	7202.91.00	3.70%	A+
Iron and Steel	Ferrozirconium	7202.99.10	4.20%	A+
Iron and Steel	Free-cutting steel, bars and rods in irregularly wound coils, hot-rolled	7213.20.00	0.80%	A+
Iron and Steel	Free-cutting steel, bars and rods, not further worked than cold-formed or cold-finished, not in coils	7215.10.00	3%	A+
Iron and Steel	Free-cutting steel, bars and rods, not further worked than hot-rolled, hot-drawn or hot-extruded, n/coils, nesoi	7214.30.00	1.90%	A+
Iron and Steel	Iron and nonalloy steel ingots	7206.10.00	1.70%	A+
Iron and Steel	Iron or nonalloy steel semifinished products, w/0.25% or more of carbon	7207.20.00	1.70%	A+
Iron and Steel	Iron or nonalloy steel semifinished products, w/less than 0.25% carbon, o/than w/rect. cross section	7207.19.00	1.70%	A+

Products Eligible for Duty-Free Treatment Under AGOA if Exported to the U.S. from an AGOA Beneficiary Country

Iron and Steel	Iron or nonalloy steel semifinished products, w/less than 0.25% carbon, w/rect. cross sect. (exclud. sq.), nesoi	7207.12.00	1.70%	A+
Iron and Steel	Iron or nonalloy steel semifinished products, w/less than 0.25% carbon, w/rect. cross sect.(incl. sq.), w/width less than twice thickness	7207.11.00	1.70%	A+
Iron and Steel	Iron/nonalloy steel nesoi, bars and rods, not further wkd. than cold-formed or cold-finished, not in coils	7215.50.00	3%	A+
Iron and Steel	Iron/nonalloy steel, angle, shapes & sections nesoi,cold-formed/cold-finished from flat-rolled prod. & furth wkd th/cold-formed/cold-finish	7216.91.00	1.80%	A+
Iron and Steel	Iron/nonalloy steel, angles, shapes & sections nesoi, not further worked than hot-rolled, hot-drawn or extruded	7216.50.00	0.40%	A+
Iron and Steel	Iron/nonalloy steel, angles, shapes & sections nesoi,further wkd. than cold-formed or cold-finished and not from flat-rolled products	7216.99.00	1.80%	A+
Iron and Steel	Iron/nonalloy steel, bars and rods, cold-formed, plated or coated with metal	7215.90.30	3%	A+
Iron and Steel	Iron/nonalloy steel, bars and rods, not cold-formed, plated or coated with metal	7215.90.10	1.30%	A+
Iron and Steel	Iron/nonalloy steel, bars and rods, not further worked than hot-rolled, hot-drawn or hot-extruded, w/non-rectangular X-sect, not in coils	7214.99.00	1.90%	A+
Iron and Steel	Iron/nonalloy steel, bars and rods, not further worked than hot-rolled, hot-drawn or hot-extruded, w/rectangular (o/than square) X-section	7214.91.00	1.90%	A+
Iron and Steel	Iron/nonalloy steel, concrete reinforcing bars and rods, not further worked than hot-rolled, hot-drawn or hot-extruded, n/coils	7214.20.00	2%	A+
Iron and Steel	Iron/nonalloy steel, flat wire, <0.25% carbon, not plated or coated, w/thick n/o 0.25 mm	7217.10.10	1.70%	A+
Iron and Steel	Iron/nonalloy steel, flat wire, <0.25% carbon, not plated or coated, w/thick o/0.25mm but n/o 1.25 mm	7217.10.20	1.30%	A+
Iron and Steel	Iron/nonalloy steel, flat wire, <0.25% carbon, not plated or coated, w/thick o/1.25 mm	7217.10.30	2%	A+
Iron and Steel	Iron/nonalloy steel, flat wire, plated or coated with base metal other than zinc	7217.30.15	2.10%	A+
Iron and Steel	Iron/nonalloy steel, flat wire, plated or coated with zinc	7217.20.15	2.10%	A+
Iron and Steel	Iron/nonalloy steel, flat wire, w/0.25% or more carbon, not plated or coated	7217.10.70	1.30%	A+
Iron and Steel	Iron/nonalloy steel, forged bars and rods, not in coils	7214.10.00	1.90%	A+
Iron and Steel	Iron/nonalloy steel, H-sections, not further worked than hot-rolled, hot-drawn or extruded, w/height 80 mm or more	7216.33.00	0.40%	A+
Iron and Steel	Iron/nonalloy steel, I-sections (standard beams), not further worked than hot-rolled, hot-drawn or extruded, w/height 80 mm or more	7216.32.00	0.40%	A+
Iron and Steel	Iron/nonalloy steel, L or T-sections, not further worked than hot-rolled, hot-drawn or extruded, w/height 80 mm or more	7216.40.00	0.40%	A+
Iron and Steel	Iron/nonalloy steel, L-sections, not further worked than hot-rolled, hot-drawn or extruded, w/height under 80 mm	7216.21.00	0.40%	A+
Iron and Steel	Iron/nonalloy steel, neosi, width 300mm+ but less th/600mm, hot-rolled flat-rolled products, not pickled, not clad/plated/coated	7211.19.75	2%	A+
Iron and Steel	Iron/nonalloy steel, neosi, width 300mm+ but less th/600mm, hot-rolled flat-rolled products, pickled, not clad/plated/coated	7211.19.60	2%	A+
Iron and Steel	Iron/nonalloy steel, neosi, width less th/300mm, hot-rolled flat-rolled products, w/thick 1.25mm or less, not clad/plated/coated	7211.19.30	1.40%	A+
Iron and Steel	Iron/nonalloy steel, neosi, width less th/300mm, hot-rolled flat-rolled products, w/thick o/1.25 mm but n/o 4.75 mm, n/clad/plated/coated	7211.19.20	2.30%	A+
Iron and Steel	Iron/nonalloy steel, nesoi, width 300mm+ but less th/600mm, cold-rolled flat-rolled, <0.25% carbon, not clad/plated/coated	7211.23.60	2%	A+

Products Eligible for Duty-Free Treatment Under AGOA if Exported to the U.S. from an AGOA Beneficiary Country

Iron and Steel	Iron/nonalloy steel, nesoi, width less th/300mm, cold-rolled flat-rolled, <0.25% carbon, w/thick n/o 0.25mm, not clad/plated/coated	7211.23.45	1%	A+
Iron and Steel	Iron/nonalloy steel, nesoi, width less th/300mm, cold-rolled flat-rolled, <0.25% carbon, w/thick o/0.25mm n/o 1.25mm, not clad/plated	7211.23.30	1.40%	A+
Iron and Steel	Iron/nonalloy steel, nesoi, width less th/300mm, cold-rolled flat-rolled, <0.25% carbon, w/thick o/1.25mm, not clad/plated/coated	7211.23.20	2.30%	A+
Iron and Steel	Iron/nonalloy steel, round wire, <0.25% carbon, not plated or coated, w/diameter less than 1.5 mm	7217.10.40	2.10%	A+
Iron and Steel	Iron/nonalloy steel, round wire, <0.25% carbon, not plated or coated, w/diameter of 1.5 mm or more	7217.10.50	0.60%	A+
Iron and Steel	Iron/nonalloy steel, round wire, <0.25% carbon, plated or coated with base metal other than zinc, w/diam. of 1.5 mm or more	7217.30.30	0.60%	A+
Iron and Steel	Iron/nonalloy steel, round wire, <0.25% carbon, plated or coated with zinc, w/diameter of 1.5 mm or more	7217.20.30	0.60%	A+
Iron and Steel	Iron/nonalloy steel, round wire, w/0.25% or more carbon and/or <1.5mm diam, plated or coated with base metal other than zinc	7217.30.45	2.10%	A+
Iron and Steel	Iron/nonalloy steel, round wire, w/0.25% or more carbon and/or <1.5mm diam, plated or coated with zinc	7217.20.45	2.10%	A+
Iron and Steel	Iron/nonalloy steel, round wire, w/0.25% or more carbon, not plated or coated	7217.10.80	2.10%	A+
Iron and Steel	Iron/nonalloy steel, T-sections, not further worked than hot-rolled, hot-drawn or extruded, w/height under 80 mm	7216.22.00	0.40%	A+
Iron and Steel	Iron/nonalloy steel, U,I or H-sections, not further worked than hot-rolled, hot-drawn or extruded, w/height under 80 mm	7216.10.00	0.40%	A+
Iron and Steel	Iron/nonalloy steel, U-sections, not further worked than hot-rolled, hot-drawn or extruded, w/height of 80 mm or more	7216.31.00	0.40%	A+
Iron and Steel	Iron/nonalloy steel, width 300+ but less th/600mm, flat-rolled products, plated or coated with zinc (other than electrolytically)	7212.30.50	2.60%	A+
Iron and Steel	Iron/nonalloy steel, width 300mm+ but less th/600mm, cold-rolled flat-rolled, w/0.25% or more carbon, not clad/plated/coated	7211.29.60	2%	A+
Iron and Steel	Iron/nonalloy steel, width 600mm+, cold-rolled flat-rolled products, in coils, w/thick 0.361mm+ but less 5mm, not clad/plated/coated	7209.18.60	2%	A+
Iron and Steel	Iron/nonalloy steel, width 600mm+, cold-rolled flat-rolled products, in coils, w/thick 0.5mm or more but n/o 1mm, not clad/plated/coated	7209.17.00	2%	A+
Iron and Steel	Iron/nonalloy steel, width 600mm+, cold-rolled flat-rolled products, in coils, w/thick 3mm+, not clad/plated/coated	7209.15.00	2%	A+
Iron and Steel	Iron/nonalloy steel, width 600mm+, cold-rolled flat-rolled products, in coils, w/thick o/1mm but less than 3mm, not clad/plated/coated	7209.16.00	2%	A+
Iron and Steel	Iron/nonalloy steel, width 600mm+, cold-rolled flat-rolled products, not in coils, w/thick 0.5mm+ but n/o 1mm, not clad/plated/coated	7209.27.00	2%	A+
Iron and Steel	Iron/nonalloy steel, width 600mm+, cold-rolled flat-rolled products, not in coils, w/thick 3mm or more, not clad/plated/coated	7209.25.00	2%	A+
Iron and Steel	Iron/nonalloy steel, width 600mm+, cold-rolled flat-rolled products, not in coils, w/thick less than 0.5mm, not clad/plated/coated	7209.28.00	2%	A+
Iron and Steel	Iron/nonalloy steel, width 600mm+, cold-rolled flat-rolled products, not in coils, w/thick o/1mm but less than 3mm, not clad/plated/coated	7209.26.00	2%	A+
Iron and Steel	Iron/nonalloy steel, width 600mm+, flat-rolled products further worked than cold-rolled, not clad/plated/coated, nesoi	7209.90.00	2%	A+
Iron and Steel	Iron/nonalloy steel, width 600mm+, flat-rolled products, clad	7210.90.10	2.60%	A+
Iron and Steel	Iron/nonalloy steel, width 600mm+, flat-rolled products, electrolytically coated or plated with base metal, nesoi	7210.90.60	2.30%	A+
Iron and Steel	Iron/nonalloy steel, width 600mm+, flat-rolled products, electrolytically plated or coated with zinc	7210.30.00	2.60%	A+
Iron and Steel	Iron/nonalloy steel, width 600mm+, flat-rolled products, painted/varnished or coated w/plastic, nesoi	7210.70.60	2.60%	A+

Products Eligible for Duty-Free Treatment Under AGOA if Exported to the U.S. from an AGOA Beneficiary Country

Iron and Steel	Iron/nonalloy steel, width 600mm+, flat-rolled products, plated or coated with aluminum o/than aluminum-zinc alloy	7210.69.00	2.60%	A+
Iron and Steel	Iron/nonalloy steel, width 600mm+, flat-rolled products, plated or coated with aluminum-zinc alloys	7210.61.00	2.60%	A+
Iron and Steel	Iron/nonalloy steel, width 600mm+, flat-rolled products, plated or coated with chromium oxides or with chromium and chromium oxides	7210.50.00	2.30%	A+
Iron and Steel	Iron/nonalloy steel, width 600mm+, flat-rolled products, plated or coated with lead, including terneplate	7210.20.00	1.60%	A+
Iron and Steel	Iron/nonalloy steel, width 600mm+, flat-rolled products, plated or coated with tin, less than 0.5 mm thick	7210.12.00	1.40%	A+
Iron and Steel	Iron/nonalloy steel, width 600mm+, flat-rolled products, plated or coated with tin, w/thick. 0.5 mm or more	7210.11.00	1.40%	A+
Iron and Steel	Iron/nonalloy steel, width 600mm+, flat-rolled products, plated or coated with zinc (other than electrolytically), corrugated	7210.41.00	2.60%	A+
Iron and Steel	Iron/nonalloy steel, width 600mm+, flat-rolled products, plated or coated with zinc (other than electrolytically), not corrugated	7210.49.00	2.60%	A+
Iron and Steel	Iron/nonalloy steel, width 600mm+, hot-rolled flat-rolled products, in coils, w/thick 3mm or mor but less 4.75mm, pickled, not clad/plated	7208.26.00	2%	A+
Iron and Steel	Iron/nonalloy steel, width 600mm+, hot-rolled flat-rolled products, in coils, w/thick 3mm or more & less 4.75mm, not pickld/clad/plated	7208.38.00	2%	A+
Iron and Steel	Iron/nonalloy steel, width 600mm+, hot-rolled flat-rolled products, in coils, w/thick 4.75mm or more & n/o 10mm, not pickled/clad/plated	7208.37.00	2.40%	A+
Iron and Steel	Iron/nonalloy steel, width 600mm+, hot-rolled flat-rolled products, in coils, w/thick 4.7mm or more, pickled, not clad/plated/coated	7208.25.60	2%	A+
Iron and Steel	Iron/nonalloy steel, width 600mm+, hot-rolled flat-rolled products, in coils, w/thick less than 3mm, not pickled/clad/plated/coated	7208.39.00	2%	A+
Iron and Steel	Iron/nonalloy steel, width 600mm+, hot-rolled flat-rolled products, in coils, w/thick less than 3mm, pickled, not clad/plated/coated	7208.27.00	2%	A+
Iron and Steel	Iron/nonalloy steel, width 600mm+, hot-rolled flat-rolled products, in coils, w/thick o/10mm, not pickled/clad/plated/coated	7208.36.00	2.40%	A+
Iron and Steel	Iron/nonalloy steel, width 600mm+, hot-rolled flat-rolled products, neosi, not in coils, w/thick less than 3mm, not clad/plated/coated	7208.54.00	2%	A+
Iron and Steel	Iron/nonalloy steel, width 600mm+, hot-rolled flat-rolled products, w/pattern in relief,not coils,w/thick < 4.75mm, not clad/plated/coated	7208.40.60	2%	A+
Iron and Steel	Iron/nonalloy steel, width 600mm+, hot-rolled flat-rolled products, w/patterns in relief, in coils, pickled, not clad/plated/coated	7208.10.15	2%	A+
Iron and Steel	Iron/nonalloy steel, width less th/300mm, cold-rolled flat-rolled, w/0.25% or more carbon,w/thick 0.25mm or less, not clad/plated/coated	7211.29.45	1%	A+
Iron and Steel	Iron/nonalloy steel, width less th/300mm, cold-rolled flat-rolled, w/0.25% or more carbon,w/thick o/0.25mm, not clad/plated/coated	7211.29.20	1.40%	A+
Iron and Steel	Iron/nonalloy steel, width less th/300mm, flat-rolled products, plated/coated w/zinc (other than electrolytically), w/thick 0.25mm or less	7212.30.30	1%	A+
Iron and Steel	Iron/nonalloy steel, width less th/300mm, flat-rolled products, plated/coated with zinc (other than electrolytically), w/thick o/0.25mm	7212.30.10	1.40%	A+
Iron and Steel	Iron/nonalloy steel, width less th/600mm, flat-rolled products, clad	7212.60.00	2.60%	A+
Iron and Steel	Iron/nonalloy steel, width less th/600mm, flat-rolled products, electrolytically plated or coated with zinc	7212.20.00	2.60%	A+
Iron and Steel	Iron/nonalloy steel, width less th/600mm, flat-rolled products, plated or coated with tin	7212.10.00	1.40%	A+
Iron and Steel	Iron/nonalloy steel, wire (other than flat or round), <0.25% carbon, not plated or coated	7217.10.60	2.20%	A+
Iron and Steel	Iron/nonalloy steel, wire (other than flat or round), <0.25% carbon, plated or coated with base metal other than zinc	7217.30.60	2.20%	A+

Products Eligible for Duty-Free Treatment Under AGOA if Exported to the U.S. from an AGOA Beneficiary Country

Iron and Steel	Iron/nonalloy steel, wire (other than flat or round), <0.25% carbon, plated or coated with zinc	7217.20.60	2.20%	A+
Iron and Steel	Iron/nonalloy steel, wire (other than flat or round), w/0.25% or more of carbon, not plated or coated	7217.10.90	2.20%	A+
Iron and Steel	Iron/nonalloy steel, wire (other than flat or round), w/0.25% or more of carbon, plated or coated with base metal other than zinc	7217.30.75	2.10%	A+
Iron and Steel	Iron/nonalloy steel, wire (other than flat or round), w/0.25% or more of carbon, plated or coated with zinc	7217.20.75	2.10%	A+
Iron and Steel	Iron/nonalloy steel, wire, coated with plastics	7217.90.10	0.40%	A+
Iron and Steel	Iron/nonalloy steel, wire, plated or coated with materials other than base metals or plastics	7217.90.50	2.10%	A+
Iron and Steel	Iron/nonalloy steel,width 600mm+,hot-rolled flat-rolled product,in coil,w/pattern in relief,w/thick 4.75mm+,not pickld,not clad/plated/coatd	7208.10.30	2.40%	A+
Iron and Steel	Iron/nonalloy steel,width 600mm+,hot-rolled flat-rolled product,in coil,w/pattern in relief,w/thick <4.75mm,not pickld,not clad/plated/coatd	7208.10.60	2%	A+
Iron and Steel	Iron/nonalloy, concrete reinforcing bars and rods in irregularly wound coils, hot-rolled	7213.10.00	2%	A+
Iron and Steel	Nonalloy hi-strength steel, width 300mm+ but less th/600mm, hot-rolled flat-rolled products, not clad/plated/coated	7211.19.45	2%	A+
Iron and Steel	Nonalloy hi-strength steel, width 600mm+, cold-rolled flat-rolled products, in coils, w/thick less than 0.5mm, not clad/plated/coated	7209.18.15	2%	A+
Iron and Steel	Nonalloy hi-strength steel, width 600mm+, hot-rolled flat-rolled products, in coils, w/thick 4.75mm+, pickled, not clad/plated/coated	7208.25.30	2.40%	A+
Iron and Steel	Nonalloy hi-strength steel, width less th/300mm, cold-rolled flat-rolled, <0.25% carbon, w/thick o/1.25mm, not clad/plated/coated	7211.23.15	1.40%	A+
Iron and Steel	Nonalloy hi-strength steel, width less th/300mm, hot-rolled flat-rolled products, not clad/plated/coated	7211.19.15	2.30%	A+
Iron and Steel	Nonalloy steel(blackplate), width 600mm+, cold-rolled flat-rolled products, in coils, w/thick less than 0.361mm, not clad/plated/coated	7209.18.25	1.30%	A+
Iron and Steel	Stainless steel, angles, shapes & sections, hot-rolled, not drilled/punched or otherwise advanced	7222.40.30	0.80%	A+
Iron and Steel	Stainless steel, angles, shapes & sections, other than hot-rolled and not drilled/punched or otherwise advanced	7222.40.60	2.10%	A+
Iron and Steel	Stainless steel, bars and rods in irregularly wound coils, hot-rolled	7221.00.00	1.90%	A+
Iron and Steel	Stainless steel, bars and rods, further worked than cold-formed or cold-finished, nesoi	7222.30.00	4.20%	A+
Iron and Steel	Stainless steel, bars and rods, hot-rolled, hot-drawn or extruded, of circular cross-section	7222.11.00	4.20%	A+
Iron and Steel	Stainless steel, bars and rods, hot-rolled, hot-drawn or extruded, other than of circular cross-section	7222.19.00	4.20%	A+
Iron and Steel	Stainless steel, bars and rods, not further worked than cold-formed or cold-finished, nesoi	7222.20.00	4.20%	A+
Iron and Steel	Stainless steel, flat wire	7223.00.50	1.30%	A+
Iron and Steel	Stainless steel, ingots and other primary forms	7218.10.00	2.10%	A+
Iron and Steel	Stainless steel, round wire	7223.00.10	3.60%	A+
Iron and Steel	Stainless steel, semifinished products of rectangular (other than square) cross-section	7218.91.00	2.10%	A+
Iron and Steel	Stainless steel, semifinished products, other than of rectangular (other than square) cross-section	7218.99.00	2.10%	A+
Iron and Steel	Stainless steel, wire (other than round or flat wire)	7223.00.90	2.50%	A+
Iron and Steel Products	Alloy steel (o/stainless), welded, w/circ. x-sect & ext. diam. 406.4mm or less, tubes, pipes, hollow prof., w/wall thick. less th/1.65 mm	7306.50.10	3%	A+

Products Eligible for Duty-Free Treatment Under AGOA if Exported to the U.S. from an AGOA Beneficiary Country

Iron and Steel Products	Alloy steel (o/stainless), welded, w/circ. x-sect & ext. diam. 406.4mm or less, tubes, pipes, hollow prof., w/wall thick. of 1.65 mm+	7306.50.50	2%	A+
Iron and Steel Products	Alloy steel (o/than stainless), seamless, cold-drawn/cold-rolled, tubes, pipes, etc., w/circ. cross sect., for mfr of ball/roller bearings	7304.51.10	2.70%	A+
Iron and Steel Products	Alloy steel (o/than stainless), seamless, n/cold-drawn/cold-rolled, tubes, pipes, etc. w/circ. cross sect., for boilers, heaters, etc	7304.59.20	3%	A+
Iron and Steel Products	Alloy steel (o/than stainless), seamless, n/cold-drawn/cold-rolled, tubes, pipes, etc. w/circ. cross sect., for mfr ball/roller bearings	7304.59.10	2.70%	A+
Iron and Steel Products	Alloy steel (o/than stainless), seamless, tubes, pipes and hollow profiles, o/than circ. cross sect., w/wall thickness less than 4 mm	7304.90.70	3%	A+
Iron and Steel Products	Alloy steel (o/than stainless), seamless, tubes, pipes and hollow profiles, o/than circ. cross sect., w/wall thickness of 4 mm or more	7304.90.30	1.30%	A+
Iron and Steel Products	Alloy steel, angles, shapes and sections of alloy steel, welded	7301.20.50	1.60%	A+
Iron and Steel Products	Alloy steel, long. welded, w/circ. cross sect. & ext. diam. o/406.4mm, tubes and pipes, o/than used in oil/gas drill. or pipelines	7305.31.60	2%	A+
Iron and Steel Products	Alloy steel, rails for railway or tramway tracks	7302.10.50	1.40%	A+
Iron and Steel Products	Alloy steel, seamed o/than welded, w/non-circ. x-sect or circ. x-sect w/ext. diam. 406.4mm or less, tubes, pipes and hollow profiles	7306.90.50	2%	A+
Iron and Steel Products	Alloy steel, seamed, circ. w/cross sect. & ext. diam o/406.4mm, line pipe, long. submerg. arc weld., used for oil/gas pipelines	7305.11.50	2%	A+
Iron and Steel Products	Alloy steel, seamed, w/circ. cross sect. & ext. diam o/406.4mm, line pipe, long. welded nesoi, used for oil/gas pipelines	7305.12.50	2%	A+
Iron and Steel Products	Alloy steel, seamed, w/circ. cross sect. & ext. diam o/406.4mm, line pipe, not long. welded, used for oil/gas pipelines	7305.19.50	2%	A+
Iron and Steel Products	Alloy steel, seamed, w/circ. cross sect. & ext. diam. o/406.4mm, casing pipe, n/threaded/coupled, of kind for drilling for oil/gas	7305.20.80	1.30%	A+
Iron and Steel Products	Alloy steel, seamed, w/circ. cross sect. & ext. diam. o/406.4mm, casing pipe, threaded/coupled, of kind for drilling for oil/gas	7305.20.60	2.50%	A+
Iron and Steel Products	Alloy steel, seamed, w/circ. cross sect. & ext. diam. o/406.4mm, not welded, tubes and pipes, o/than used in oil/gas drill. or pipelines	7305.90.50	2%	A+
Iron and Steel Products	Alloy steel, seamed, w/ext. diam 406.4mm or less or o/than circ. x-sect, n/threaded/coupled, casing of kind used in drilling for oil/gas	7306.20.40	1.30%	A+
Iron and Steel Products	Alloy steel, seamed, w/ext. diam 406.4mm or less or o/than circ. x-sect, threaded/coupled, casing of kind used in drilling for oil/gas	7306.20.30	2.50%	A+
Iron and Steel Products	Alloy steel, seamed, w/ext. diam 406.4mm or less or o/than circ. x-sect, tubing of a kind used for drilling for oil/gas	7306.20.80	2%	A+
Iron and Steel Products	Alloy steel, seamless casing pipe, not threaded or coupled, of a kind used in drilling for oil or gas	7304.29.40	1.30%	A+
Iron and Steel Products	Alloy steel, seamless casing pipe, threaded or coupled, of a kind used in drilling for oil or gas	7304.29.30	2.50%	A+
Iron and Steel Products	Alloy steel, seamless drill pipe, of a kind used in drilling for oil or gas	7304.21.60	3%	A+
Iron and Steel Products	Alloy steel, seamless tubing, of a kind used in drilling for oil or gas	7304.29.60	3%	A+
Iron and Steel Products	Alloy steel, weld. o/than long. weld., w/circ. x-sect. & ext. diam. o/406.4mm, tubes and pipes, o/than used in oil/gas drill. or pipelines	7305.39.50	2%	A+
Iron and Steel Products	Alloy steel, welded, w/non-circ. x-sect, tubes, pipes and hollow profiles, w/wall thickness less than 4 mm	7306.60.70	3%	A+
Iron and Steel Products	Alloy steel, welded, w/non-circ. x-sect, tubes, pipes and hollow profiles, w/wall thickness of 4 mm or more	7306.60.30	1.80%	A+
Iron and Steel Products	Cast iron or steel, fittings for tubes or pipes, nesoi	7307.19.90	6.20%	A+

Products Eligible for Duty-Free Treatment Under AGOA if Exported to the U.S. from an AGOA Beneficiary Country

Iron and Steel Products	Iron (o/than cast) or nonalloy steel, seamless casing pipe, not threaded or coupled, of a kind used in drilling for oil or gas	7304.29.20	0.20%	A+
Iron and Steel Products	Iron (o/than cast) or nonalloy steel, seamless casing pipe, threaded or coupled, of a kind used in drilling for oil or gas	7304.29.10	2.40%	A+
Iron and Steel Products	Iron (o/than cast) or nonalloy steel, seamless drill pipe, of a kind used in drilling for oil or gas	7304.21.30	3.20%	A+
Iron and Steel Products	Iron (o/than cast) or nonalloy steel, seamless, tubes, pipes and hollow profiles, o/than circ. cross sect., w/wall thickness less than 4 mm	7304.90.50	3.20%	A+
Iron and Steel Products	Iron (o/than cast) or nonalloy steel, seamless, tubes, pipes and hollow profiles, o/than circ. cross sect., w/wall thickness of 4 mm or more	7304.90.10	0.20%	A+
Iron and Steel Products	Iron (o/than cast) or nonalloy, seamless tubing, of a kind used in drilling for oil or gas	7304.29.50	3.20%	A+
Iron and Steel Products	Iron or nonalloy steel, angles, shapes and sections, welded	7301.20.10	1.10%	A+
Iron and Steel Products	Iron or nonalloy steel, long. welded, w/circ. cross sect. & ext. diam. o/406.4mm, tubes and pipes, o/th used in oil/gas drill.etc	7305.31.40	0.80%	A+
Iron and Steel Products	Iron or nonalloy steel, not cast, butt welding fittings for tubes/pipes, w/inside diam. less than 360mm	7307.93.30	6.20%	A+
Iron and Steel Products	Iron or nonalloy steel, rails for railway or tramway tracks	7302.10.10	0.10%	A+
Iron and Steel Products	Iron or nonalloy steel, seamed o/welded, w/non-circ. x-sect. or circ. x-sect. w/ext. diam. 406.4mm or less, tubes, pipes & hollow profiles	7306.90.10	0.80%	A+
Iron and Steel Products	Iron or nonalloy steel, seamed, w/circ. cross sect. & ext. diam o/406.4mm, line pipe, long. submerg. arc weld., used for oil/gas	7305.11.10	0.80%	A+
Iron and Steel Products	Iron or nonalloy steel, seamed, w/circ. cross sect. & ext. diam o/406.4mm, line pipe, long. welded nesoi, used for oil/gas	7305.12.10	0.80%	A+
Iron and Steel Products	Iron or nonalloy steel, seamed, w/circ. cross sect. & ext. diam. o/406.4mm, casing pipe, n/threaded/coupled, of kind for drill. for oil/gas	7305.20.40	0.20%	A+
Iron and Steel Products	Iron or nonalloy steel, seamed, w/circ. cross sect. & ext. diam. o/406.4mm, casing pipe, threaded/coupled, of kind for drilling for oil/gas	7305.20.20	2.40%	A+
Iron and Steel Products	Iron or nonalloy steel, seamed, w/circ. cross sect. & ext. diam. o/406.4mm, not welded, tubes and pipes, o/th used in oil/gas drill.etc	7305.90.10	0.80%	A+
Iron and Steel Products	Iron or nonalloy steel, seamed, w/circ. cross sect.& ext. diam o/406.4mm, line pipe, not long. welded, used for oil/gas	7305.19.10	0.80%	A+
Iron and Steel Products	Iron or nonalloy steel, seamed, w/ext. diam 406.4mm or less or o/than circ. x-sect, n/threaded/coupled, casing kind used drill for oil/gas	7306.20.20	0.20%	A+
Iron and Steel Products	Iron or nonalloy steel, seamed, w/ext. diam 406.4mm or less or o/than circ. x-sect, threaded/coupled, casing of kind used in drill. oil/gas	7306.20.10	2.40%	A+
Iron and Steel Products	Iron or nonalloy steel, seamed, w/ext. diam. 406.4mm or less or o/than circ. x-sect. tubing of a kind used for drilling for oil/gas	7306.20.60	0.80%	A+
Iron and Steel Products	Iron or nonalloy steel, weld. o/than long. weld., w/circ. x-sect. & ext. diam. o/406.4mm, tubes and pipes, o/th used in oil/gas drill.etc	7305.39.10	0.80%	A+
Iron and Steel Products	Iron or nonalloy steel, welded, w/circ. x-sect & ext. diam. 406.4mm or less, pipes, tubes & holl. prof., w/wall thick. of 1.65 mm or more	7306.30.50	0.80%	A+
Iron and Steel Products	Iron or nonalloy steel, welded, w/circ. x-sect & ext. diam. 406.4mm or less, tubes, pipes, hollow profiles, w/wall thick. less than 1.65 mm	7306.30.10	3.20%	A+
Iron and Steel Products	Iron or nonalloy steel, welded, w/non-circ. x-sect. tubes, pipes and hollow profiles, w/wall thickness less than 4 mm	7306.60.50	3.20%	A+

Products Eligible for Duty-Free Treatment Under AGOA if Exported to the U.S. from an AGOA Beneficiary Country

Iron and Steel Products	Iron or nonalloy steel, welded, w/non-circ. x-sect. tubes, pipes and hollow profiles, w/wall thickness of 4 mm or more	7306.60.10	0.20%	A+
Iron and Steel Products	Iron or steel (o/than stainless), stranded wire, not elect. insul., not fitted with fittings or made up into articles	7312.10.30	2%	A+
Iron and Steel Products	Iron or steel sheet piling, whether or not drilled, punched or made from assembled elements	7301.10.00	0.30%	A+
Iron and Steel Products	Iron or steel, coach screws	7318.11.00	12.50%	A+
Iron and Steel Products	Iron or steel, columns, pillars, posts, beams and girders, nesoi	7308.90.60	1.60%	A+
Iron and Steel Products	Iron or steel, containers of a kind normally carried on the person, in the pocket or in the handbag, nesoi	7326.90.35	7.80%	
Iron and Steel Products	Iron or steel, fish plates and sole plates for jointing or fixing rails	7302.40.00	0.40%	A+
Iron and Steel Products	Iron or steel, leaf springs & leaves therefore, suitable for motor vehicle suspension (o/than for motor vehicles w/a G.V.W. o/4 metric tons)	7320.10.60	3.20%	A+
Iron and Steel Products	Iron or steel, nails, tacks, corrugated nails, staples & similar arts., of one piece construction, made of round wire, nesoi	7317.00.55	0.20%	A+
Iron and Steel Products	Iron or steel, not in part alloy steel, columns, pillars, posts, beams and girders	7308.90.30	1.10%	A+
Iron and Steel Products	Iron or steel, self-tapping screws, w/shanks or threads 6 mm or more in diameter	7318.14.50	8.60%	A+
Iron and Steel Products	Iron or steel, self-tapping screws, w/shanks or threads less than 6 mm in diameter	7318.14.10	6.20%	A+
Iron and Steel Products	Iron or steel, sleepers (cross-ties) for railway or tramway track construction	7302.20.00	0.40%	A+
Iron and Steel Products	Iron/steel (o/stainless), ropes, cables & cordage (o/than stranded wire), n/elect. insul., fitted with fittings or made up into articles	7312.10.70	2.30%	A+
Iron and Steel Products	Iron/steel (o/stainless), ropes, cables & cordage, o/th of brass plate wire (o/than stranded wire), n/elect. insul., w/o fittings etc.	7312.10.90	1.60%	A+
Iron and Steel Products	Iron/steel, fencing, of wire, welded at the intersection, plated or coated with zinc, whether or not covered w/plastic material	7314.31.10	0.1 cents/kg	A+
Iron and Steel Products	Iron/steel, grill, netting and fencing, of wire, not welded at the intersection, coated with plastics	7314.42.00	0.1 cents/kg	A+
Iron and Steel Products	Iron/steel, grill, netting and fencing, of wire, not welded at the intersection, plated or coated with zinc	7314.41.00	0.1 cents/kg	A+
Iron and Steel Products	Stainless steel, ropes, cables and cordage (o/than stranded wire), not elect. insul., fitted with fittings or made up into articles	7312.10.50	2.30%	A+
Iron and Steel Products	Stainless steel, ropes, cables and cordage (o/than stranded wire), not elect. insul., not fitted with fittings or made up into articles	7312.10.60	1.80%	A+
Iron and Steel Products	Stainless steel, seamless, cold-drawn/cold-rolled, tubes, pipes and hollow profiles, w/circular cross section & extern. diam less than 19mm	7304.41.30	3%	A+
Iron and Steel Products	Stainless steel, seamless, cold-drawn/cold-rolled, tubes, pipes and hollow profiles, w/circular cross section & extern. diam of 19mm or more	7304.41.60	3%	A+
Iron and Steel Products	Stainless steel, seamless, not cold-drawn/cold-rolled, tubes, pipes and hollow profiles, w/circular cross section	7304.49.00	3%	A+
Iron and Steel Products	Stainless steel, welded, w/circ. x-sect & ext. diam. 406.4mm or less, tubes, pipes, hollow profiles, w/wall thick. less than 1.65 mm	7306.40.10	3%	A+
Iron and Steel Products	Stainless steel, welded, w/circ. x-sect & ext. diam. 406.4mm or less, tubes, pipes, hollow profiles, w/wall thick. of 1.65 mm or more	7306.40.50	2%	A+
Jewelry	Synthetic or reconstructed precious or semiprecious stones, unworked or simply sawn or roughly shaped	7104.20.00	3%	A+

Products Eligible for Duty-Free Treatment Under AGOA if Exported to the U.S. from an AGOA Beneficiary Country

Leather and Skins	Leather of animals, nesi, without hair on, not including chamois, patent, patent laminated or metallized, not fancy	4107.90.30	3.30%	A+
Leather and Skins	Leather of swine, w/o hair on, not incl. chamois, patent, patent laminated or metallized leather, nesi	4107.10.30	4.20%	A+
Leather and Skins	Patent laminated leather or metallized leather, of calf or kip	4109.00.40	3.60%	A+
Leather and Skins	Patent leather	4109.00.30	2.30%	A+
Leather and Skins	Sheep or lamb skin leather, w/o wool on, excl. leather of heading 4108 or 4109, parchment-dressed or prepared after tanning, not fancy	4105.20.30	2%	A+
Leather and Skins	Sheep or lamb skin leather, w/o wool on, not incl. chamois, patent, patent laminated or metallized leather, pretanned other than vegetable	4105.12.00	2%	A+
Leather and Skins	Sheep or lamb skin leather, without wool on, not including chamois, patent, patent laminated or metallized leather, retanned, nesi	4105.19.20	2%	A+
Leather and Skins	Wet blues of sheep or lamb skin leather, without wool on, not including chamois, patent, patent laminated or metallized leather, retanned	4105.19.10	2%	A+
Leather and Skins	Wet blues of swine leather, w/o hair on, not incl. chamois, patent, patent laminated or metallized leather	4107.10.20	4.20%	A+
Leather and Skins	Whole bovine skin leather, w/o hair on, fancy, n/o 2.6 sq m not incl. chamois, patent, patent laminated or metallized leather	4104.10.80	3.60%	A+
Leather and Skins	Whole bovine skin leather, w/o hair on, not fancy, n/o 2.6 sq m not incl. chamois, patent, patent laminated or metallized leather	4104.10.60	2.40%	A+
Leather Articles	Articles of a kind normally carried in the pocket or handbag, with outer surface 85% or more silk or silk waste	4202.32.85	8%	
Leather Articles	Articles of a kind normally carried in the pocket or handbag, with outer surface of leather, composition or patent leather, nesi	4202.31.60	8%	
Leather Articles	Articles of apparel, of leather or of composition leather, nesi	4203.10.40	6%	
Leather Articles	Articles of kind usu. carried in pocket or handbag (o/t lea., shtng. of plas., tex. mat., vul. fib. or paperbd.), pap. cov., of mat. nesi	4202.39.50	7.80%	
Leather Articles	Cases, bags & sim. cont., nesi, of mat. (o/t lea., plas. shtng., tex. mat., vul. fib. or paperbd.), pap. cov., except of wood or plastic	4202.99.50	7.80%	
Leather Articles	Cases, bags and containers nesi, with outer surface of leather, of composition leather or patent leather	4202.91.00	4.50%	
Leather Articles	Cases, bags and similar containers, nesi, with outer surface of vulcanized fiber or of paperboard	4202.99.90	20%	
Leather Articles	Gloves not wholly of horsehide or cowhide leather not specially designed for use in sports, nesi	4203.29.18	14%	
Leather Articles	Gloves not wholly of horsehide or cowhide leather not specially designed for use in sports, with fourchettes or sidewalls	4203.29.15	14%	
Leather Articles	Gloves, mittens and mitts of leather or composition leather, nesi, lined, for persons other than men	4203.29.50	12.60%	
Leather Articles	Gloves, mittens and mitts of leather or composition leather, nesi, not lined, for persons other than men	4203.29.40	12.60%	
Leather Articles	Gloves, mittens and mitts of leather or composition leather, nesi, not seamed	4203.29.20	12.60%	
Leather Articles	Gloves, wholly of horsehide or cowhide (except calfskin) leather, not specially designed for use in sports, nesi	4203.29.08	14%	
Leather Articles	Gloves, wholly of horsehide or cowhide leather not specially designed for use in sports, with fourchettes or sidewalls	4203.29.05	12.60%	
Leather Articles	Handbags w. or w/o shld. strap or w/o handle of mat. (o/t leather, shtng. of plas., tex. mat., vul. fib. or paperbd.), pap.cov. of mat. nesi	4202.29.50	7.80%	
Leather Articles	Handbags with or w/o shoulder strap or w/o handle, with outer surface containing 85% or more of silk, not braided	4202.22.70	7%	

Products Eligible for Duty-Free Treatment Under AGOA if Exported to the U.S. from an AGOA Beneficiary Country

Leather Articles	Handbags with or without shoulder straps or without handle, with outer surface of vulcanized fiber or of paperboard, not covered with paper	4202.29.90	20%	
Leather Articles	Handbags, with or without shoulder strap or without handle, with outer surface of leather, composition or patent leather, nesi, n/o $20 ea.	4202.21.60	10%	
Leather Articles	Handbags, with or without shoulder strap or without handle, with outer surface of leather, composition or patent leather, nesi, over $20 ea.	4202.21.90	9%	
Leather Articles	Handbags, with or without shoulder strap or without handle, with outer surface of reptile leather	4202.21.30	5.30%	
Leather Articles	Handbags, with or without shoulder straps or without handle, with outer surface of sheeting of plastics	4202.22.15	17.60%	
Leather Articles	Men's gloves, mittens and mitts of leather or composition leather, nesi, seamed	4203.29.30	14%	
Leather Articles	Travel, sports and similar bags with outer surface of plastic sheeting	4202.92.45	20%	
Leather Articles	Trunks, suitcases, vanity & all other cases, occupational luggage & like containers, surface of leather, composition or patent leather	4202.11.00	8%	
Leather Articles	Trunks, suitcases, vanity and attache cases, occupational luggage and similar containers, with outer surface of plastics	4202.12.20	20%	
Leather Articles	Trunks, suitcases, vanity cases, attache cases, occupational luggage & like containers surface of vulcanized fiber or paperboard nesi	4202.19.00	20%	
Leather Preparations	Preparations nesoi, for the treatment of leather, furskins or other materials nesoi	3403.91.50	6.50%	A+
Lubricating Preparations	Lubricating preparations (incl. lubricant-based preparations), nesoi	3403.99.00	6.50%	A+
Lubricating Preparations	Lubricating preparations containing 50% but less than 70% by weight of petroleum oils or of oils obtained from bituminous minerals	3403.19.10	0.20%	A+
Machinery and Parts	Ball bearings other than ball bearings with integral shafts	8482.10.50	9%	A+
Machinery and Parts	Ball bearings with integral shafts	8482.10.10	2.40%	A+
Machinery and Parts	Balls, needles and rollers for ball or roller bearings	8482.91.00	4.40%	A+
Machinery and Parts	Bearing housings nesi; plain shaft bearings	8483.30.80	4.50%	A+
Machinery and Parts	Housed bearings (incorporating ball or roller bearings), nesi	8483.20.80	4.50%	A+
Machinery and Parts	Inner or outer rings or races for ball bearings	8482.99.05	9.90%	A+
Machinery and Parts	Inner or outer rings or races for other bearings, nesi	8482.99.25	5.80%	A+
Machinery and Parts	Inner or outer rings or races for taper roller bearings	8482.99.15	5.80%	A+
Machinery and Parts	Parts of articles of subheading 8483.20	8483.90.70	5.50%	A+
Machinery and Parts	Parts of ball bearings (including parts of ball bearings with integral shafts), nesi	8482.99.35	9.90%	A+
Machinery and Parts	Parts of bearing housings and plain shaft bearings, nesi	8483.90.30	4.50%	A+
Machinery and Parts	Parts of other ball or roller bearings, nesi	8482.99.65	5.80%	A+
Machinery and Parts	Parts of tapered roller bearings, nesi	8482.99.45	5.80%	A+
Machinery and Parts	Parts of transmission equipment, nesi	8483.90.80	2.80%	A+

Products Eligible for Duty-Free Treatment Under AGOA if Exported to the U.S. from an AGOA Beneficiary Country

Machinery and Parts	Shaft couplings (other than universal joints)	8483.60.80	2.80%	A+
Machinery and Parts	Tapered roller bearings, including cone and tapered roller assemblies	8482.20.00	5.80%	A+
Manufactured Articles (Miscellaneous)	Brooms (o/than whiskbrooms), wholly or in part broom corn, val. n/o 96 cents ea, first 121478 dz in calendar yr, class. in 9603.10	9603.10.40	8%	A+
Manufactured Articles (Miscellaneous)	Brooms (o/than whiskbrooms), wholly or in part broom corn, val. n/o 96 cents ea, in excess of 121478 dz in calendar yr., class in 9603.10	9603.10.50	32 cents each	A+
Manufactured Articles (Miscellaneous)	Brooms (o/than whiskbrooms), wholly or in part broom corn, val. ov 96 cents each	9603.10.60	32%	A+
Manufactured Articles (Miscellaneous)	Ink pads (whether or not inked and with or without boxes)	9612.20.00	3.50%	A+
Manufactured Articles (Miscellaneous)	Pens, for drawing w/India ink	9608.31.00	0.4 cents each + 2.7%	A+
Manufactured Articles (Miscellaneous)	Pens, fountain, stylograph and other pens, nesoi	9608.39.00	0.4 cents each + 2.7%	A+
Manufactured Articles (Miscellaneous)	Powder puffs and pads for the application of cosmetics or toilet preparations	9616.20.00	4.30%	A+
Manufactured Articles (Miscellaneous)	Sets of pens, mechanical pencils, etc. from two or more subheadings 9608.10 - 9608.40	9608.50.00	The rate applicable to each article in the absence of this subheading	A+
Manufactured Articles (Miscellaneous)	Wiskbrooms, wholly or pt. of broom corn, n/o $0.96 each, first 61,655 doz in calendar year classif. in 9603.10.05-9603.10.35	9603.10.05	8%	A+
Manufactured Articles (Miscellaneous)	Wiskbrooms, wholly or pt. of broom corn, n/o $0.96 each, in excess of first 61,655 dz in calendar year classif. in 9603.10.05-9603.10.35	9603.10.15	5 cents each	A+
Manufactured Articles (Miscellaneous)	Wiskbrooms, wholly or pt. of broom corn, over $0.96 each	9603.10.35	14%	A+
Mattresses	Mattresses, of cotton	9404.29.10	3%	A+
Meat	Boneless meat of lamb, fresh or chilled	0204.23.20	0.7 cents/kg	A+
Meat	Boneless meat of lamb, frozen	0204.43.20	0.7 cents/kg	A+
Meat	Boneless meat of sheep, nesi, fresh or chilled	0204.23.40	2.8 cents/kg	A+
Meat	Boneless meat of sheep, nesi, frozen	0204.43.40	2.8 cents/kg	A+
Meat	Bovine carcasses and halves, fresh or chld., descr. in add. US note 3 to Ch. 2	0201.10.10	4.4 cents/kg	A+
Meat	Bovine carcasses and halves, fresh or chld., descr. in gen. note 15 of the HTS	0201.10.05	4.4 cents/kg	A+

Products Eligible for Duty-Free Treatment Under AGOA if Exported to the U.S. from an AGOA Beneficiary Country

Meat	Bovine carcasses and halves, frozen, descr. in add. US note 3 to Ch. 2	0202.10.10	4.4 cents/kg	A+
Meat	Bovine carcasses and halves, frozen, descr. in gen. note 15 of the HTS	0202.10.05	4.4 cents/kg	A+
Meat	Bovine meat cuts (except high-qual. beef cuts), boneless, processed, fresh or chld., descr in add. US note 3 to Ch. 2	0201.30.30	10%	A+
Meat	Bovine meat cuts (except high-qual. beef cuts), boneless, processed, fresh or chld., descr in gen. note 15 of the HTS	0201.30.04	10%	A+
Meat	Bovine meat cuts (except high-qual. beef cuts), boneless, processed, frozen, descr in add. US note 3 to Ch. 2	0202.30.30	10%	A+
Meat	Bovine meat cuts (except high-qual. beef cuts), boneless, processed, frozen, descr in gen. note 15 of the HTS	0202.30.04	10%	A+
Meat	Bovine meat cuts (except high-qual. beef cuts), w/bone in, processed, fresh or chld., descr in add. US note 3 to Ch. 2	0201.20.30	10%	A+
Meat	Bovine meat cuts (except high-qual. beef cuts), w/bone in, processed, fresh or chld., descr in gen. note 15 of the HTS	0201.20.04	10%	A+
Meat	Bovine meat cuts (except high-qual. beef cuts), w/bone in, processed, frozen, descr in add. US note 3 to Ch. 2	0202.20.30	10%	A+
Meat	Bovine meat cuts (except high-qual. beef cuts), w/bone in, processed, frozen, descr in gen. note 15 of the HTS	0202.20.04	10%	A+
Meat	Bovine meat cuts, boneless, not processed, fresh or chld., descr in add. US note 3 to Ch. 2	0201.30.50	4.4 cents/kg	A+
Meat	Bovine meat cuts, boneless, not processed, fresh or chld., descr in gen. note 15 of the HTS	0201.30.06	4.4 cents/kg	A+
Meat	Bovine meat cuts, boneless, not processed, frozen, descr in add. US note 3 to Ch. 2	0202.30.50	4.4 cents/kg	A+
Meat	Bovine meat cuts, boneless, not processed, frozen, descr in gen. note 15 of the HTS	0202.30.06	4.4 cents/kg	A+
Meat	Bovine meat cuts, w/bone in, not processed, fresh or chld., descr in add. US note 3 to Ch. 2	0201.20.50	4.4 cents/kg	A+
Meat	Bovine meat cuts, w/bone in, not processed, fresh or chld., descr in gen. note 15 of the HTS	0201.20.06	4.4 cents/kg	A+
Meat	Bovine meat cuts, w/bone in, not processed, frozen, descr in add. US note 3 to Ch. 2	0202.20.50	4.4 cents/kg	A+
Meat	Bovine meat cuts, w/bone in, not processed, frozen, descr in gen. note 15 of the HTS	0202.20.06	4.4 cents/kg	A+
Meat	Carcasses and half-carcasses of lamb, fresh or chilled	0204.10.00	0.7 cents/kg	A+
Meat	Carcasses and half-carcasses of lamb, frozen	0204.30.00	0.7 cents/kg	A+
Meat	Carcasses and half-carcasses of sheep, other than lamb, fresh or chilled	0204.21.00	2.8 cents/kg	A+
Meat	Carcasses and half-carcasses of sheep, other than lamb, frozen	0204.41.00	2.8 cents/kg	A+
Meat	Chickens, not cut in pieces, fresh or chilled	0207.11.00	8.8 cents/kg	A+
Meat	Chickens, not cut in pieces, frozen	0207.12.00	8.8 cents/kg	A+
Meat	Cuts and offal of chickens, fresh or chilled	0207.13.00	17.6 cents/kg	A+
Meat	Cuts and offal of chickens, frozen	0207.14.00	17.6 cents/kg	A+
Meat	Cuts and offal of ducks, geese or guineas, frozen	0207.36.00	17.6 cents/kg	A+
Meat	Cuts and offal of turkeys, fresh or chilled	0207.26.00	17.6 cents/kg	A+
Meat	Cuts and offal of turkeys, frozen	0207.27.00	17.6 cents/kg	A+
Meat	Cuts and offal, other than fatty livers, of ducks, geese or guineas, fresh or chilled	0207.35.00	17.6 cents/kg	A+
Meat	Cuts of lamb meat with bone in, fresh or chilled	0204.22.20	0.7 cents/kg	A+
Meat	Cuts of lamb meat with bone in, frozen	0204.42.20	0.7 cents/kg	A+
Meat	Cuts of sheep meat with bone in, nesi, fresh or chilled	0204.22.40	2.8 cents/kg	A+
Meat	Cuts of sheep meat with bone in, nesi, frozen	0204.42.40	2.8 cents/kg	A+
Meat	Ducks, geese or guineas, not cut in pieces, fresh or chilled	0207.32.00	8.8 cents/kg	A+

Products Eligible for Duty-Free Treatment Under AGOA if Exported to the U.S. from an AGOA Beneficiary Country

Meat	Fatty livers of ducks, geese or guineas, fresh or chilled	0207.34.00	17.6 cents/kg	A+
Meat	Fresh or chilled retail cuts of ham, shoulders and cuts thereof, with bone in	0203.12.10	1.4 cents/kg	A+
Meat	Hams, shoulders and cuts thereof with bone in, salted, in brine, dried or smoked	0210.11.00	1.4 cents/kg	A+
Meat	High-qual. beef cuts w/bone in, processed, fresh or chld., descr in gen. note 15 of the HTS	0201.20.02	4%	A+
Meat	High-qual. beef cuts w/bone in, processed, frozen, descr in gen. note 15 of the HTS	0202.20.02	4%	A+
Meat	High-qual. beef cuts, boneless, processed, fresh or chld., descr in add. US note 3 to Ch. 2	0201.30.10	4%	A+
Meat	High-qual. beef cuts, boneless, processed, fresh or chld., descr in gen. note 15 of the HTS	0201.30.02	4%	A+
Meat	High-qual. beef cuts, w/bone in, processed, fresh or chld., descr in add. US note 3 to Ch. 2	0201.20.10	4%	A+
Meat	High-qual. beef cuts, w/bone in, processed, frozen, descr in add. US note 3 to Ch. 2	0202.20.10	4%	A+
Meat	Meat and edible meat offal of rabbits or hares, fresh, chilled or frozen	0208.10.00	6.40%	A+
Meat	Meat of swine nesi, retail cuts, fresh or chilled	0203.19.20	1.4 cents/kg	A+
Meat	Meat of swine other than hams, shoulders, bellies (streaky) and cuts thereof, salted, in brine, dried or smoked	0210.19.00	1.4 cents/kg	A+
Meat	Other meat and edible meat offal nesi, fresh, chilled or frozen	0208.90.40	6.40%	A+
Meat	Turkeys, not cut in pieces, fresh or chilled	0207.24.00	15 cents/kg	A+
Meat	Turkeys, not cut in pieces, valued 88 cents or more per kg, frozen	0207.25.40	10%	A+
Meat	Turkeys, not cut in pieces, valued less than 88 cents/kg, frozen	0207.25.20	8.8 cents/kg	A+
Meat (Prepared)	Homogenized preparations of meat, meat offal or blood, nesi	1602.10.00	1.90%	A+
Meat (Prepared)	Prepared or preserved liver of goose	1602.20.20	4.9 cents/kg	A+
Meat (Prepared)	Prepared or preserved meat of bovine animals, not containing cereals or vegetables, nesi	1602.50.60	1.80%	A+
Meat (Prepared)	Prepared or preserved pork hams and cuts thereof, not containing cereals or vegetables, nesi	1602.41.90	1.4 cents/kg	A+
Meat (Prepared)	Prepared or preserved pork shoulders and cuts thereof, other than boned and cooked and packed in airtight containers	1602.42.40	1.4 cents/kg	A+
Metal Articles (Miscellaneous)	Base metal (o/than iron/steel/aluminum/zinc) mountings, fittings & similar articles, suitable for motor vehicles, & base metal pts thereof	8302.30.60	3.50%	A+
Metal Articles (Miscellaneous)	Padlocks, base metal, not of cylinder or pin tumbler construction, not ov 3.8cm wide	8301.10.20	2.30%	A+
Metal Articles (Miscellaneous)	Padlocks, base metal, not of cylinder or pin tumbler construction, ov 3.8cm but n/o 6.4cm wide	8301.10.40	3.80%	A+
Metal Articles (Miscellaneous)	Padlocks, base metal, of cylinder or pin tumbler construction, ov 3.8cm but n/o 6.4cm wide	8301.10.80	4.80%	A+
Metals and Products of Metals (Other than Steel and Iron)	Cobalt alloy, unwrought	8105.10.30	4.40%	A+
Metals and Products of Metals (Other than Steel and Iron)	Magnesium, raspings, turnings and granules graded according to size; magnesium powders	8104.30.00	4.40%	A+

Products Eligible for Duty-Free Treatment Under AGOA if Exported to the U.S. from an AGOA Beneficiary Country

Metals and Products of Metals (Other than Steel and Iron)	Magnesium, unwrought, nesoi	8104.19.00	6.50%	A+
Metals and Products of Metals (Other than Steel and Iron)	Molybdenum, powders	8102.10.00	9.1 cents/kg on molybdenum content + 1.2%	A+
Metals and Products of Metals (Other than Steel and Iron)	Molybdenum, unwrought (including bars and rods obtained simply by sintering)	8102.91.10	13.9 cents/kg on molybdenum content + 1.9%	A+
Metals and Products of Metals (Other than Steel and Iron)	Niobium (columbium), unwrought; niobium, powders	8112.91.40	4.90%	A+
Metals and Products of Metals (Other than Steel and Iron)	Thallium, unwrought; thallium, powders	8112.91.60	4%	A+
Metals and Products of Metals (Other than Steel and Iron)	Titanium, unwrought; titanium, powders	8108.10.50	15%	A+
Metals and Products of Metals (Other than Steel and Iron)	Tungsten, bars and rods (o/than those obtained simply by sintering), profiles, plates, sheets, strip and foil	8101.92.00	6.50%	A+
Metals and Products of Metals (Other than Steel and Iron)	Tungsten, powders	8101.10.00	7%	A+
Metals and Products of Metals (Other than Steel and Iron)	Tungsten, unwrought (including bars and rods obtained simply by sintering)	8101.91.50	6.60%	A+
Metals and Products of Metals (Other than Steel and Iron)	Tungsten, wire	8101.93.00	4.40%	A+
Metals and Products of Metals (Other than Steel and Iron)	Vanadium (o/than waste & scrap) and articles thereof	8112.40.60	2%	A+

Products Eligible for Duty-Free Treatment Under AGOA if Exported to the U.S. from an AGOA Beneficiary Country

Metals and Products of Metals (Other than Steel and Iron)	Zirconium, unwrought; zirconium, powders	8109.10.60	4.20%	A+
Musical Instruments and parts	Parts & access. for pianos (o/than tuning pins and strings) nesoi	9209.91.80	4.20%	A+
Nuts	Almonds, fresh or dried, in shell	0802.11.00	7.7 cents/kg	A+
Nuts	Almonds, fresh or dried, shelled	0802.12.00	24 cents/kg	A+
Nuts	Hazelnuts or filberts, fresh or dried, in shell	0802.21.00	7 cents/kg	A+
Nuts	Hazelnuts or filberts, fresh or dried, shelled	0802.22.00	14.1 cents/kg	A+
Nuts	Nuts nesi, fresh or dried, shelled	0802.90.98	5 cents/kg	A+
Nuts	Pecans, fresh or dried, in shell	0802.90.10	8.8 cents/kg	A+
Nuts	Walnuts, fresh or dried, shelled	0802.32.00	26.5 cents/kg	A+
Nuts (Preparations)	Almonds, otherwise prepared or preserved, nesi	2008.19.40	32.6 cents/kg	A+
Nuts (Preparations)	Blanched peanuts, subject to add. US note 2 to Ch. 12, not GN15	2008.11.25	6.6 cents/kg	A+
Nuts (Preparations)	Blanched peanuts, subject to gen. note 15 of the HTS	2008.11.22	6.6 cents/kg	A+
Nuts (Preparations)	Filberts, otherwise prepared or preserved, nesi	2008.19.20	11.3 cents/kg	A+
Nuts (Preparations)	Peanuts, otherwise prepared or preserved, nesoi, subject to add. US note 2 to chap. 12, not GN15	2008.11.45	6.6 cents/kg	A+
Nuts (Preparations)	Peanuts, otherwise prepared or preserved, nesoi, subject to gen. note 15 of the HTS	2008.11.42	6.6 cents/kg	A+
Ores	Molybdenum ores and concentrates, not roasted	2613.90.00	17.8 cents/kg on molybdenum content	A+
Ores	Molybdenum ores and concentrates, roasted	2613.10.00	12.8 cents/kg on molybdenum content + 1.8%	A+
Ores	Precious metal (other than silver) ores and concentrates	2616.90.00	1.7 cents/kg on lead content	A+
Ores	Silver ores and concentrates	2616.10.00	0.8 cents/kg on lead content	A+
Petroleum Oils and Products (Excluding Plastics)	Distillate and residual fuel oils (including blends) derived from bituminous minerals, testing 25 degrees A.P.I. or more	2710.00.10	10.5 cents/bbl	A+
Petroleum Oils and Products (Excluding Plastics)	Distillate and residual fuel oils (including blends) derived from bituminous minerals, testing under 25 degrees A.P.I.	2710.00.05	5.25 cents/bbl	A+

Products Eligible for Duty-Free Treatment Under AGOA if Exported to the U.S. from an AGOA Beneficiary Country

Petroleum Oils and Products (Excluding Plastics)	Kerosene (ex. motor fuel or mtr fuel blend. stock), fr. petro oils and bitumin. minrls. o/than crude. or preps. 70%+ by wt. fr. petro. oils	2710.00.20	10.5 cents/bbl	A+
Petroleum Oils and Products (Excluding Plastics)	Lubricating oils. w/or w/o additives. fr. petro oils and bitumin. minrls. o/than crude. or preps. 70%+ by wt. fr. petro. oils	2710.00.30	84 cents/bbl	A+
Petroleum Oils and Products (Excluding Plastics)	Mixt.ofhydrocarbons(fr.petro oils & bitum. min.. o/than crude. or preps.70%+ by wt. fr. petro. oils). nesoi. n/o 50% single hydrocarbon	2710.00.45	10.5 cents/bbl	A+
Petroleum Oils and Products (Excluding Plastics)	Motor fuel blending stock. from petro oils and bitumin. minrls. o/than crude. or preps. 70%+ by wt. from petro. oils	2710.00.18	52.5 cents/bbl	A+
Petroleum Oils and Products (Excluding Plastics)	Motor fuel. from petro oils and bitumin. minrls. o/than crude. or preps. 70%+ by wt. from petro. oils	2710.00.15	52.5 cents/bbl	A+
Petroleum Oils and Products (Excluding Plastics)	Naphthas (ex. motor fuel or mtr fuel blend. stock). fr. petro oils and bitumin. minrls. o/than crude. or preps. 70%+ by wt. fr. petro. oils	2710.00.25	10.5 cents/bbl	A+
Petroleum Oils and Products (Excluding Plastics)	Petroleum oils & oils from bitum. min. or preps nesoi 70+% by wt. from petro. oils or bitum. min., nesoi	2710.00.60	7%	A+
Petroleum Oils and Products (Excluding Plastics)	Petroleum oils and oils from bituminous minerals. crude. testing 25 degrees A.P.I. or more	2709.00.20	10.5 cents/bbl	A+
Petroleum Oils and Products (Excluding Plastics)	Petroleum oils and oils from bituminous minerals. crude. testing under 25 degrees A.P.I.	2709.00.10	5.25 cents/bbl	A+
Plants or Trees (Live)	Hyacinth bulbs. dormant	0601.10.30	38.4 cents/1000	A+
Plants or Trees (Live)	Hyacinth bulbs. without soil attached. in growth or in flower	0601.20.10	38.4 cents/1000	A+
Plants or Trees (Live)	Lily of the valley pips. dormant	0601.10.85	$1.44/1000	A+
Plants or Trees (Live)	Live mushroom spawn	0602.90.50	1.4 cents/kg	A+
Plants or Trees (Live)	Roses. fresh cut	0603.10.60	6.80%	
Plastics	Belting and belts (except V-belts) for machinery. of plastics. containing textile fibers nesoi	3926.90.59	2.40%	A+
Plastics	Cellulose nitrates (including collodions). in primary forms	3912.20.00	5.20%	A+
Plastics	Clothespins. spring type. of plastics	3926.90.65	4.20%	A+
Plastics	Fasteners. in clips suitable for use in a mechanical attaching device. of plastics	3926.90.85	8.30%	A+
Plastics	Fittings for furniture. coachwork or the like. other than handles and knobs. of plastics	3926.30.50	5.30%	A+
Plastics	Gloves. nesoi. of plastics	3926.20.40	9.50%	A+

Products Eligible for Duty-Free Treatment Under AGOA if Exported to the U.S. from an AGOA Beneficiary Country

Plastics	Monafilament nesoi, of plastics, excluding ethylene, vinyl chloride and acrylic polymers	3916.90.30	6.50%	A+
Plastics	Nonadhesive plates, sheets, film, foil and strip, cellular, of polyurethanes, combined with textile materials nesoi	3921.13.19	5.30%	A+
Plastics	Nonadhesive plates, sheets, film, foil and strip, of noncellular plastics combined with cotton, over 1.492 kg/sq m	3921.90.21	6.50%	A+
Plastics	Nonadhesive plates, sheets, film, foil and strip, of noncellular plastics combined with textile materials, nesoi, not over 1.492 kg/sq m	3921.90.19	5.30%	A+
Plastics	Nonadhesive plates, sheets, film, foil and strip, of noncellular plastics combined with textile materials, nesoi, over 1.492 kg/sq m	3921.90.29	4.40%	A+
Plastics	V-belts of plastics, containing textile fibers	3926.90.55	5.10%	A+
Plastics	Wall or ceiling coverings of plastics other than of polymers of vinyl chloride with a backing of textile fibers other than of manmade fiber	3918.90.30	5.30%	A+
Plastics	Wall or ceiling coverings of polymers of vinyl chloride with a backing of textile fibers other than of manmade fibers	3918.10.40	5.30%	A+
Plastics	Wall or ceiling coverings, with a backing of manmade fibers, less than or equal to 70% by weight of PVC	3918.10.32	6.50%	A+
Plastics	Wall or ceiling coverings, with a backing of manmade fibers, of plastics other than polymers of vinyl chloride	3918.90.20	6.50%	A+
Plastics	Waterbed mattresses and liners and parts of the foregoing, of plastics	3926.90.77	2.40%	A+
Radio Equipment	Radiobroadcast receiver combinations incorporating tape recorders, nesi	8527.31.50	2.50%	A+
Radio Equipment	Radiobroadcast receiver combined w/ sound recording or reproducing apparatus for connection to telegraphic/telephonic apparatus/network	8527.31.05	4.90%	A+
Radio Equipment	Radiobroadcast receivers, not operating w/o external power, for motor vehicles, w/o sound recording or reproducing apparatus, other	8527.29.80	4.40%	A+
Railway Parts	Parts of railway/tramway locomotives/rolling stock, parts of axles	8607.19.06	0.40%	A+
Rubber and Products of Rubber	Articles of apparel and clothing accessories, excluding gloves, of vulcanized rubber other than hard rubber	4015.90.00	4%	A+
Rubber and Products of Rubber	Conveyor belts or belting of vulcanized rubber reinforced only with textile materials, nesoi	4010.12.90	1.90%	A+
Rubber and Products of Rubber	Conveyor belts/belting of vulcanized rubber, nesoi, combined with textile materials nesoi	4010.19.80	1.90%	A+
Rubber and Products of Rubber	Endless synchronous transmission belt of vulcanized rubber, circumference 60 to 150 cm, combined with textile materials nesoi	4010.23.50	1.90%	A+
Rubber and Products of Rubber	Endless synchronous transmission belts of vulcanized rubber, circumference 150 to 198 cm, combined with textile materials nesoi	4010.24.50	1.90%	A+
Rubber and Products of Rubber	Nonseamless gloves of vulcanized rubber, other than surgical or medical gloves	4015.19.50	14%	A+
Rubber and Products of Rubber	Transmission belts or belting of vulcanized rubber, nesoi, combined with textile materials nesoi	4010.29.50	1.90%	A+
Rubber and Products of Rubber	Transmission V-belts and V-belting of vulcanized rubber, nesoi, combined with textile materials	4010.29.10	3.40%	A+
Rubber and Products of Rubber	Transmission V-belts of vulcanized rubber, circumference exceeding 180 cm but not exceeding 240 cm, combined with textile materials	4010.22.30	3.40%	A+

Products Eligible for Duty-Free Treatment Under AGOA if Exported to the U.S. from an AGOA Beneficiary Country

Rubber and Products of Rubber	Transmission V-belts of vulcanized rubber, circumference exceeding 60 cm but not exceeding 180 cm, combined with textile materials	4010.21.30	3.40%	A+
Seafood	Fillets of herrings, dried, salted or in brine, but not smoked, in immediate containers weighing with their contents 6.8 kg or less each	0305.30.20	4%	A+
Seafood	Fillets of mackerel, dried, salted or in brine, but not smoked, in immediate containers weighing with their contents 6.8 kg or less each	0305.30.40	5%	A+
Seafood	Herrings, in brine or salted but not dried or smoked, in immediate containers weighing with their contents 6.8 kg or less each	0305.61.20	4%	A+
Seafood	Mackerel, in brine or salted but not dried or smoked, in immediate containers weighing with their contents 6.8 kg or less each	0305.69.20	5%	A+
Seafood	Salmon, in brine or salted but not dried or smoked	0305.69.40	3%	A+
Seafood	Smoked Pacific, Atlantic and Danube salmon, including fillets	0305.41.00	5%	A+
Seafood (Prepared)	Bonito (Sarda spp.), in oil	1604.14.70	4.90%	A+
Seafood (Prepared)	Bonito (Sarda spp.), not in oil	1604.14.80	6%	A+
Seafood (Prepared)	Bonito, yellowtail and pollock, whole or in pieces, but not minced, in airtight containers, not in oil	1604.19.10	4%	A+
Seafood (Prepared)	Clam juice	1603.00.10	8.50%	A+
Seafood (Prepared)	Fish sticks and like products of any size or shape, fillets or other portions of fish, breaded, coated with batter, not cooked nor in oil	1604.19.40	10%	A+
Seafood (Prepared)	Fish sticks and like products of any size or shape, fillets or other portions of fish, if breaded, coated with batter, cooked or in oil	1604.19.50	10.50%	A+
Seafood (Prepared)	Fish sticks and similar products of any size or shape, if breaded, coated with batter or similarly prepared, cooked or in oil	1604.20.50	7.50%	A+
Seafood (Prepared)	Fish sticks and similar products of any size or shape, if breaded, coated with batter or similarly prepared, not cooked nor in oil	1604.20.40	10%	A+
Seafood (Prepared)	Oysters, prepared or preserved, but not smoked	1605.90.50	4.70%	A+
Seafood (Prepared)	Prepared or preserved herrings, whole or in pieces, but not minced, in oil, in airtight containers	1604.12.20	4%	A+
Seafood (Prepared)	Prepared or preserved salmon, whole or in pieces, but not minced, in oil, in airtight containers	1604.11.20	6%	A+
Seafood (Prepared)	Sardines, not smoked, sardinella, brisling or sprats, neither skinned nor boned, in oil, in airtight containers	1604.13.20	15%	A+
Seafood (Prepared)	Sardines, sardinella, brisling or sprats, skinned or boned, in oil, in airtight containers	1604.13.30	20%	A+
Seafood (Prepared)	Tunas and skipjack, not in airtight containers, not in oil, in bulk or in immediate containers weighing with contents over 6.8 kg each	1604.14.40	1.1 cents/kg	A+
Seafood (Prepared)	Tunas and skipjack, not in oil, in airtight cont., n/o 7 kg, not of U.S possessions, product within quota	1604.14.20	6%	A+
Seafood (Prepared)	Tunas and skipjack, not in oil, in airtight containers, n/o 7 kg, not of U.S. possessions, over quota	1604.14.30	12.50%	A+
Seafood (Prepared)	Tunas and skipjack, whole or in pieces, but not minced, in oil, in airtight containers	1604.14.10	35%	A+
Spices	Anaheim and ancho pepper, dried or crushed or ground	0904.20.40	5 cents/kg	A+
Spices	Bay leaves, other than crude or not manufactured	0910.40.40	3.20%	A+
Spirits	Effervescent wine, nesi	2206.00.60	13.9 cents/ liter	A+
Spirits	Ethyl alcohol and other spirits, denatured, of any strength	2207.20.00	1.90%	A+

Products Eligible for Duty-Free Treatment Under AGOA if Exported to the U.S. from an AGOA Beneficiary Country

Spirits	Prune wine	2206.00.30	3.1 cents/liter + 22.1 cents/pf. Liter on ethyl alcohol content	A+
Spirits	Rum and tafia, in containers each holding not over 4 liters, valued not over $3/proof liter	2208.40.20	23.7 cents/pf.liter	A+
Spirits	Rum and tafia, in containers each holding not over 4 liters, valued over $3/proof liter	2208.40.40	13 cents/pf.liter	A+
Spirits	Rum and tafia, in containers each holding over 4 liters, valued not over $0.69/proof liter	2208.40.60	23.7 cents/pf.liter	A+
Spirits	Rum and tafia, in containers each holding over 4 liters, valued over $0.69/proof liter	2208.40.80	13 cents/pf.liter	A+
Spirits	Undenatured ethyl alcohol of 80 percent vol. alcohol or higher, for nonbeverage purposes	2207.10.60	2.50%	A+
Spirits	Vermouth in containers each holding over 4 liters	2205.90.40	3.8 cents/liter	A+
Sports Equipment	Artificial baits and flies	9507.90.70	9%	A+
Sports Equipment	Badminton nets, of cotton	9506.99.08	2.80%	A+
Sports Equipment	Fishing reels, valued not over $2.70 each	9507.30.20	9.20%	A+
Sports Equipment	Fishing reels, valued over $2.70 but not over $8.45 each	9507.30.40	24 cents each	A+
Sports Equipment	Fishing rods and parts & accessories thereof	9507.10.00	6%	A+
Starch (Preparations)	Tapioca and substitutes, prepared from starch nesi, in the form of flakes, grains, pearls, siftings or in similar forms	1903.00.40	0.8 cents/kg	A+
Straw Products	Products nesi of plaiting materials, bound together in parallel strands or woven, in sheet form, nesi	4601.99.00	3.30%	A+
Sugars and Sugar Confectionery	Candied nuts, not containing cocoa	1704.90.10	4.50%	A+
Sugars and Sugar Confectionery	Chemically pure fructose	1702.50.00	9.60%	A+
Sugars and Sugar Confectionery	Lactose and lactose syrup containing by weight 99% or more lactose, calculated on the dry matter	1702.11.00	6.40%	A+
Sugars and Sugar Confectionery	Lactose and lactose syrup containing by weight less than 99% lactose, calculated on the dry matter	1702.19.00	6.40%	A+
Sugars and Sugar Confectionery	Sugar confectionery nesoi o/10% by dry wt. of sugar described in add. US note 3 to Ch. 17, w/o cocoa, subj. to add. US note 8 to Ch.17	1704.90.74	12.20%	A+
Sugars and Sugar Confectionery	Sugar confectionery nesoi, not containing cocoa, subject to gen. note 15 of the HTS	1704.90.52	12.20%	A+
Sugars and Sugar Confectionery	Sugar confectionery nesoi, w/o cocoa, dairy products subject to add. US note 1 to chap. 4: subject to add US note 10 to chapter 4	1704.90.54	12.20%	A+
Sugars and Sugar Confectionery	Sugar confectionery, w/o cocoa, nesoi	1704.90.90	10.40%	A+

Products Eligible for Duty-Free Treatment Under AGOA if Exported to the U.S. from an AGOA Beneficiary Country

Tableware (excluding Cutlery)	Base metal forks (o/than plated w/prec. metal, or w/handles of stain. steel, wood, rubber or plastics), nesoi	8215.99.26	0.2 cents each + 3.1%	
Tableware (excluding Cutlery)	Base metal forks, w/stainless steel handles cont. Ni or o/10% by wt of Mn, nesoi	8215.99.05	0.5 cents each + 8.5%	
Tableware (excluding Cutlery)	Base metal forks, w/stainless steel handles cont. Ni or o/10% by wt of Mn, w/overall length n/o 25.9cm, valued under 25cents ea	8215.99.01	0.9 cents each + 15.8%	
Tableware (excluding Cutlery)	Base metal forks, w/stainless steel handles, nesoi, valued at 25 cents each or more	8215.99.15	0.4 cents each + 4.8%	
Tableware (excluding Cutlery)	Base metal forks, w/stainless steel handles, nesoi, valued under 25 cents each	8215.99.10	0.5 cents each + 6.3%	
Tableware (excluding Cutlery)	Base metal spoons, w/stainless steel handles & valued at 25 cents and over, and base metal ladles w/stainless steel handles	8215.99.35	6.80%	
Tableware (excluding Cutlery)	Base metal spoons, w/stainless steel handles & valued under 25 cents each	8215.99.30	14%	
Tableware (excluding Cutlery)	Sets of assted. base metal spoons, forks, ladles, etc. & similar kitchen or tableware, w/at least one article plated w/prec. metal	8215.10.00	The rate of duty applicable to that article in the set subject to the highest rate of duty	
Tableware (excluding Cutlery)	Sets of assted. base metal spoons, forks, ladles, etc. & similar kitchen or tableware, w/no articles plated with precious metal	8215.20.00	The rate of duty applicable to that article in the set subject to the highest rate of duty	
Tableware (with Silver)	Sets of two or more knives or forks w/silver handles or spoons and ladles of silver, whether or not clad or plated w/prec.metal	7114.11.45	3%	A+
Tannings	Synthetic organic tanning substances, nonaromatic	3202.10.50	6.50%	A+
Television Equipment	Black and white or other monochrome television reception apparatus	8528.13.00	5%	A+
Television Equipment	Black and white or other monochrome video monitors	8528.22.00	5%	A+
Television Equipment	Black and white or other monochrome video projectors	8528.30.90	5%	A+
Television Equipment	Cathode-ray television camera tubes	8540.20.20	6%	A+
Television Equipment	Cathode-ray television picture tubes incl. video monitor, color, high definition, display diagonal > 35.56 cm	8540.11.30	15%	A+

Products Eligible for Duty-Free Treatment Under AGOA
if Exported to the U.S. from an AGOA Beneficiary Country

Television Equipment	Cathode-ray television picture tubes incl. video monitor, color, non-high definition, non-projection, display > 35.56 cm	8540.11.10	15%	A+
Television Equipment	Cathode-ray television picture tubes incl. video monitor, color, non-high definition, projection type	8540.11.50	15%	A+
Television Equipment	Cathode-ray television picture tubes incl. video monitor, monochrome, high definition, nesi	8540.12.70	3.30%	A+
Television Equipment	Cathode-ray television picture tubes incl. video monitor, monochrome, non-high definition, nesi	8540.12.50	3.30%	A+
Television Equipment	Cathode-ray tubes nesoi	8540.60.00	3%	A+
Television Equipment	Cathode-ray TV & video monitor tubes, color, high definition, having video display display diagonal <or= 34.29 cm	8540.11.44	7.50%	A+
Television Equipment	Cathode-ray TV & video monitor tubes, color, high definition, video display diagonal video display diagonal > 34.29 cm & <or= 35.56 cm	8540.11.48	15%	A+
Television Equipment	Cathode-ray TV & video monitor tubes, color, non-high definition, non-projection, video display diagonal <or= 34.29 cm	8540.11.24	7.50%	A+
Television Equipment	Cathode-ray TV & video monitor tubes, color, non-high definition, non-projection, video display diagonal > 34.29 cm & <or= 35.56 cm	8540.11.28	15%	A+
Television Equipment	Color television reception apparatus nesoi, video display diagonal over 34.29 cm, not incorporating a VCR or player, nesoi	8528.12.97	5%	A+
Television Equipment	Color television reception apparatus w/flat panel screen, video display diagonal over 34.29 cm, not incorporating a VCR or player	8528.12.72	5%	A+
Television Equipment	Color video monitors nesoi, with video display diagonal over 34.29 cm, not incorporating VCR or player	8528.21.90	5%	A+
Television Equipment	Color video monitors w/flat panel screen, video display diagonal over 34.29 cm, not incorporate VCR or player	8528.21.70	5%	A+
Television Equipment	Color video projectors nesoi, not incorporating a video recording or reproducing apparatus	8528.30.78	5%	A+
Television Equipment	Color video projectors w/flat panel screen, video display diagonal over 34.29 cm, not incorporating VCR or player	8528.30.68	5%	A+
Television Equipment	Combinations of parts of television receivers specified in U.S. note 10 to chapter 85, other than printed circuit assemblies, nesi	8529.90.49	2.90%	A+
Television Equipment	Data graphic cathode-ray display tubes, black and white or other monochrome	8540.50.00	3%	A+
Television Equipment	Data/graphic cathode-ray display tubes, color, with a phosphor dot screen pitch smaller than 0.4 mm	8540.40.00	3%	A+
Television Equipment	Flat panel screen assemblies for the apparatus of subheadings 8528.12.62, 8528.12.64, 8528.12.68, 8528.12.72, 8528.21.55 and 7 other HTS	8529.90.53	2.90%	A+
Television Equipment	Front panel assemblies for cathode-ray tubes	8540.91.15	5.40%	A+
Television Equipment	High definition color television reception apparatus, nonprojection, with cathode-ray tube, not incorporating a VCR or player	8528.12.48	5%	A+
Television Equipment	High definition color television reception apparatus, projection type, with cathode-ray tube, not incorporating a VCR or player	8528.12.56	5%	A+
Television Equipment	High definition color video monitors, nonprojection type, with cathode-ray tube, not incorporating VCR or player	8528.21.49	5%	A+
Television Equipment	High definition color video monitors, projection type, with cathode-ray tube, not incorporating VCR or player	8528.21.52	5%	A+
Television Equipment	High definition color video projectors, with a cathode-ray tube, not incorporating VCR or player	8528.30.60	5%	A+
Television Equipment	Klystron tubes	8540.72.00	3.30%	A+
Television Equipment	Magnetron tubes nesoi	8540.71.40	3.70%	A+

Products Eligible for Duty-Free Treatment Under AGOA if Exported to the U.S. from an AGOA Beneficiary Country

Television Equipment	Microwave tubes (other than magnetrons or klystrons) excluding grid-controlled tubes	8540.79.00	3.70%	A+
Television Equipment	Non-high def. color television reception app., nonprojection, w/CRT, display diag. ov 34.29 cm but n/ov 35.56 cm, n/incorp. VCR or player	8528.12.24	5%	A+
Television Equipment	Non-high definition color television reception apparatus, nonprojection, w/CRT, video display diag. ov 35.56 cm, not incorp. a VCR or player	8528.12.32	5%	A+
Television Equipment	Non-high definition color television reception apparatus, projection type, with a cathode-ray tube, not incorporating a VCR or player	8528.12.40	5%	A+
Television Equipment	Non-high definition color video monitors, nonprojection type, w/CRT, video display diagonal over 35.56 cm, not incorporating VCR or player	8528.21.39	5%	A+
Television Equipment	Non-high definition color video monitors, nonprojection, w/CRT, video display diag. ov 34.29 cm but n/ov 35.56 cm, not incorp. VCR or player	8528.21.29	5%	A+
Television Equipment	Non-high definition color video monitors, projection type, with cathode-ray tube, not incorporating VCR or player	8528.21.42	5%	A+
Television Equipment	Non-high definition color video projectors, with a cathode-ray tube, not incorporating VCR or player	8528.30.40	5%	A+
Television Equipment	Other parts of television apparatus (other than television cameras), nesi	8529.90.83	2.90%	A+
Television Equipment	Parts of cathode-ray tubes other than deflection coils or front panel assemblies	8540.91.50	5.40%	A+
Television Equipment	Parts of printed circuit assemblies (including face plates and lock latches) for television apparatus other than television cameras	8529.90.69	2.90%	A+
Television Equipment	Parts of television apparatus, nesi	8529.90.93	2.90%	A+
Television Equipment	Parts of television receivers specified in U.S. note 10 to chapter 85, other than printed circuit assemblies, nesi	8529.90.39	2.90%	A+
Television Equipment	Printed circuit assemblies for television apparatus, nesi	8529.90.13	2.90%	A+
Television Equipment	Printed circuit boards and ceramic substrates and subassemblies thereof for color TV, with components listed in add. U.S. note 4, chap. 85	8529.90.03	4%	A+
Television Equipment	Printed circuit boards and ceramic substrates and subassemblies thereof for color TV, with components listed in add. U.S. note 4, chap. 85	8529.90.33	4%	A+
Television Equipment	Printed circuit boards and ceramic substrates and subassemblies thereof for color TV, with components listed in add. U.S. note 4, chap. 85	8529.90.43	4%	A+
Television Equipment	Printed circuit boards and ceramic substrates and subassemblies thereof for color TV, with components listed in add. U.S. note 4, chap. 85	8529.90.88	4%	A+
Television Equipment	Receiver or amplifier tubes	8540.81.00	4.20%	A+
Television Equipment	Television antennas and antenna reflectors, and parts suitable for use therewith	8529.10.20	1.80%	A+
Television Equipment	Television camera tubes, image converters and intensifiers, and other photocathode tubes, other than cathode-ray tubes	8540.20.40	3.30%	A+
Television Equipment	Thermionic, cold cathode or photocathode tubes, nesi	8540.89.00	3.70%	A+
Television Equipment	Transmission apparatus for television, nesoi	8525.10.30	1.80%	A+
Textile Preparations	Preparations for the treatment of textile materials, containing 50 but not over 70 percent or more by weight of petroleum oils	3403.11.20	0.20%	A+

Products Eligible for Duty-Free Treatment Under AGOA if Exported to the U.S. from an AGOA Beneficiary Country

Tobacco	"Homogenized" or "reconstituted" tobacco, not suitable for use as wrapper tobacco, to be used in cigarettes, des. in addl US note 5 to chap	2403.91.45	19.9 cents/kg	A+
Tobacco	"Homogenized" or "reconstituted" tobacco, not suitable for use as wrapper tobacco, to be used in products other than cigarettes	2403.91.43	19.9 cents/kg	A+
Tobacco	Cigarettes containing tobacco but not containing clove, paper-wrapped	2402.20.80	$1.05/kg + 2.3%	A+
Tobacco	Cigars, cheroots and cigarillos and cigarettes of tobacco substitutes	2402.90.00	$1.05/kg + 2.3%	A+
Tobacco	Cigars, cheroots and cigarillos containing tobacco, each valued 15 cents or over but less than 23 cents	2402.10.60	57 cents/kg + 1.4%	A+
Tobacco	Cigars, cheroots and cigarillos containing tobacco, each valued less than 15 cents	2402.10.30	$1.89/kg + 4.7%	A+
Tobacco	Leaf tobacco, the product of two or more countries or dependencies, when mixed or packed together, partly or wholly stemmed, not threshed	2401.20.05	$5.48/kg	A+
Tobacco	Other manufactured tobacco, tobacco substitutes, tobacco extracts or essences, other, to be used in products other than cigarettes	2403.99.30	24.7 cents/kg	A+
Tobacco	Other manufactured tobacco, tobacco substitutes, tobacco extracts or essences, prepared for marketing directly to consumer as packaged	2403.99.20	24.7 cents/kg	A+
Tobacco	Other manufactured tobacco, tobacco substitutes, tobacco extracts or essences, to be used in cigarettes, described in addl US note 5 to chap	2403.99.60	24.7 cents/kg	A+
Tobacco	Smoking tobacco, whether or not containing tobacco substitutes, other, to be used in cigarettes, described in addl US note 5 to chap 24	2403.10.60	32.8 cents/kg	A+
Tobacco	Smoking tobacco, whether or not containing tobacco substitutes, other, to be used in products other than cigarettes	2403.10.30	32.8 cents/kg	A+
Tobacco	Smoking tobacco, whether or not containing tobacco substitutes, prepared for marketing directly to consumer as packaged	2403.10.20	32.8 cents/kg	A+
Tobacco	Tobacco refuse, from other tobacco, for cigarettes, described in addl US note 5 to chap 24, not tobacco stems	2401.30.37	28.4 cents/kg	A+
Tobacco	Tobacco refuse, from other tobacco, for cigarettes, described in addl US note 5 to chap 24, tobacco stems, cut, ground or pulverized	2401.30.35	97 cents/kg	A+
Tobacco	Tobacco refuse, from other tobacco, other than for cigarettes, tobacco stems, cut, ground or pulverized	2401.30.25	97 cents/kg	A+
Tobacco	Tobacco refuse, from other tobacco, other than for cigarettes,tother than tobacco stems	2401.30.27	28.4 cents/kg	A+
Tobacco	Tobacco, not stemmed or stripped, not or not over 35% wrapper tobacco, flue-cured burley etc. not for cigarettes	2401.10.61	23.9 cents/kg	A+
Tobacco	Tobacco, not stemmed or stripped, not or not over 35% wrapper tobacco, flue-cured burley, etc., described in addl US note 5 to chap 24	2401.10.63	23.9 cents/kg	A+
Tobacco	Tobacco, partly or wholly stemmed/stripped, n/threshed or similarly proc., not or n/over 35% wrapper, des. in addl US note 5 to ch. 24	2401.20.33	40.9 cents/kg	A+
Tobacco	Tobacco, partly or wholly stemmed/stripped, n/threshed or similarly proc., not or n/over 35% wrapper, flue-cured burley etc. not for cigaret	2401.20.31	40.9 cents/kg	A+
Tobacco	Tobacco, partly or wholly stemmed/stripped, threshed or similarly processed, not from cigar leaf , described in addl US note 5 to chap 24	2401.20.85	37.5 cents/kg	A+
Tobacco	Tobacco, partly or wholly stemmed/stripped, threshed or similarly processed, not from cigar leaf , not oriental or turkish, not for cigarett	2401.20.83	37.5 cents/kg	A+

Products Eligible for Duty-Free Treatment Under AGOA if Exported to the U.S. from an AGOA Beneficiary Country

Tools	Sets of articles (handtools and other specified tools) of two or more subheadings of heading 8205	8205.90.00	The rate of duty applicable to that article in the set subject to the highest rate of duty	A+
Tools	Slip joint pliers	8203.20.40	12%	A+
Tools	Tools of two or more of headings 8202 to 8205 put up in sets for retail sale	8206.00.00	The rate of duty applicable to that article in the set subject to the highest rate of duty	A+
Vegetable Fiber Products	Luggage, handbags and flat goods, whether or not lined, made from plaiting materials nesi	4602.10.29	5.30%	
Vegetable Fiber Products	Luggage, handbags and flat goods, whether or not lined, of bamboo	4602.10.21	6.20%	
Vegetable Fiber Products	Luggage, handbags and flat goods, whether or not lined, of rattan or of palm leaf, nesi	4602.10.25	18%	
Vegetable Fiber Products	Luggage, handbags and flat goods, whether or not lined, of willow	4602.10.22	5.80%	
Vegetable Preparations	Artichokes, prepared or preserved otherwise than by vinegar or acetic acid, not frozen	2005.90.80	14.90%	A+
Vegetable Preparations	Asparagus, prepared or preserved otherwise than by vinegar or acetic acid, not frozen	2005.60.00	14.90%	A+
Vegetable Preparations	Black-eye cowpeas, shelled, prepared or preserved otherwise than by vinegar or acetic acid, not frozen	2005.51.20	1.5 cents/kg on entire contents of container	A+
Vegetable Preparations	Capers, prepared or preserved by vinegar or acetic acid, nesi	2001.90.20	8%	A+
Vegetable Preparations	Mushrooms, prepared or preserved otherwise than by vinegar or acetic acid	2003.10.00	6 cents/kg drained weight + 8.5%	A+
Vegetable Preparations	Olives (not green), in a saline solution, canned, not pitted	2005.70.50	9.3 cents/kg on drained weight	A+
Vegetable Preparations	Olives (not green), in a saline solution, canned, pitted	2005.70.60	10.1 cents/kg on drained weight	A+
Vegetable Preparations	Olives (not green), in a saline solution, in airtight containers of glass or metal but not canned	2005.70.70	9.9 cents/kg on drained weight	A+
Vegetable Preparations	Olives, green, container less 13 kg, quota of 550 m tons/year, prepared or preserved otherwise than by vinegar/acetic acid, not in saline	2005.70.91	5.5 cents/kg on drained weight	A+
Vegetable Preparations	Olives, prepared or preserved otherwise than by vinegar, acetic acid or saline soln, not frozen, nesoi	2005.70.97	8.8 cents/kg on drained weight	A+
Vegetable Preparations	Pimientos, prepared or preserved by vinegar or acetic acid	2001.90.35	8.10%	A+

Products Eligible for Duty-Free Treatment Under AGOA if Exported to the U.S. from an AGOA Beneficiary Country

Vegetable Preparations	Pimientos, prepared or preserved otherwise than by vinegar or acetic acid, not frozen	2005.90.50	8.10%	A+
Vegetable Preparations	Potatoes (not Solano), prepared or preserved otherwise than by vinegar or acetic acid, frozen	2004.10.80	8%	A+
Vegetable Preparations	Sauerkraut, prepared or preserved otherwise than by vinegar or acetic acid, not frozen	2005.90.30	4.80%	A+
Vegetable Preparations	Tomatoes, other than whole or in pieces, prepared or preserved otherwise than by vinegar or acetic acid, nesoi	2002.90.80	11.60%	A+
Vegetable Preparations	Tomatoes, whole or in pieces, prepared or preserved otherwise than by vinegar or acetic acid	2002.10.00	12.50%	A+
Vegetable Preparations	Vegetables and mixtures of vegetables, nesoi, prepared or preserved other than by vinegar or acetic acid, frozen, not preserved by sugar	2004.90.90	11.20%	A+
Vegetable Products NESOI	Broomcorn of a kind used primarily in brooms or brushes	1403.10.00	$4.95/t	A+
Vegetable Products NESOI	Vegetable hair of a kind used primarily as stuffing or padding, whether or not supported	1402.90.10	0.5 cents/kg	A+
Vegetable Products NESOI	Willow (osier), of a kind used primarily for plaiting	1401.90.20	4.40%	A+
Vegetables	Asparagus, nesi, fresh or chilled	0709.20.90	21.30%	A+
Vegetables	Beans nesi, fresh or chilled, shelled or unshelled	0708.20.90	4.9 cents/kg	A+
Vegetables	Beans nesi, uncooked or cooked by steaming or boiling in water, frozen, reduced in size	0710.22.40	11.20%	A+
Vegetables	Brussels sprouts, uncooked or cooked by steaming or boiling in water, frozen, reduced in size	0710.80.85	14%	A+
Vegetables	Carrots, fresh or chilled, not reduced in size, 10 cm or over in length	0706.10.20	0.7 cents/kg	A+
Vegetables	Carrots, fresh or chilled, reduced in size	0706.10.05	14.90%	A+
Vegetables	Celery, other than celeriac, fresh or chilled, not reduced in size, if entered August 1 through the following April 14, inclusive	0709.40.60	1.9 cents/kg	
Vegetables	Celery, other than celeriac, fresh or chilled, reduced in size	0709.40.20	14.90%	
Vegetables	Cucumbers, including gherkins, fresh or chilled, if entered May 1 to June 30, inclusive, or Sept. 1 to Nov. 30, inclusive, in any year	0707.00.50	5.6 cents/kg	
Vegetables	Dried mushrooms nesi, whole, cut, sliced, broken or in powder, but not further prepared	0712.30.20	1.9 cents/kg + 2.6%	A+
Vegetables	Dried olives, ripe	0712.90.20	2.5 cents/kg	A+
Vegetables	Dried onion powder or flour	0712.20.20	29.80%	
Vegetables	Dried onions whole, cut, sliced or broken, but not further prepared	0712.20.40	21.30%	
Vegetables	Dried tomatoes, whole, cut, sliced or broken, but not in powder or further prepared	0712.90.78	8.70%	A+
Vegetables	Fiddlehead greens, fresh or chilled	0709.90.30	8%	A+
Vegetables	Fiddlehead greens, uncooked or cooked by steaming or boiling in water, frozen, not reduced in size	0710.80.60	8%	A+
Vegetables	Fresh or chilled arrowroot, salep, Jerusalem artichokes and similar roots and tubers nesoi, whether or not sliced or in the form of pellets	0714.90.40	16%	A+
Vegetables	Fresh potatoes, other than yellow (Solano) potatoes or seed potatoes	0701.90.50	0.5 cents/kg	A+
Vegetables	Frozen beans nesi, not reduced in size	0710.22.37	4.9 cents/kg	A+
Vegetables	Kohlrabi, kale and similar edible brassicas nesi, including sprouting broccoli, fresh or chilled	0704.90.40	20%	A+
Vegetables	Leeks and other alliaceous vegetables nesi, fresh or chilled	0703.90.00	20%	A+
Vegetables	Leguminous vegetables nesi, fresh or chilled, shelled or unshelled	0708.90.40	4.9 cents/kg	A+

Products Eligible for Duty-Free Treatment Under AGOA if Exported to the U.S. from an AGOA Beneficiary Country

Vegetables	Leguminous vegetables nesi, uncooked or cooked by steaming or boiling in water, frozen	0710.29.40	3.5 cents/kg	A+
Vegetables	Mixtures of vegetables nesi, uncooked or cooked by steaming or boiling in water, frozen	0710.90.90	14%	A+
Vegetables	Mushrooms, fresh or chilled	0709.51.00	8.8 cents/kg + 20%	A+
Vegetables	Mushrooms, provisionally preserved but unsuitable in that state for immediate consumption	0711.90.40	5.7 cents/kg on drained weight + 8%	A+
Vegetables	Mushrooms, uncooked or cooked by steaming or boiling in water, frozen	0710.80.20	5.7 cents/kg + 8%	A+
Vegetables	Olives, fresh or chilled	0709.90.35	8.8 cents/kg	A+
Vegetables	Olives, n/pitted, nesoi	0711.20.38	5.9 cents/kg on drained weight	A+
Vegetables	Olives, pitted or stuffed, provisionally preserved but unsuitable in that state for immediate consumption	0711.20.40	8.6 cents/kg on drained weight	A+
Vegetables	Potatoes, uncooked or cooked by steaming or boiling in water, frozen	0710.10.00	14%	A+
Vegetables	Salsify, celeriac, radishes and similar edible roots nesi, fresh or chilled	0706.90.40	10%	A+
Vegetables	Seed potatoes, fresh or chilled	0701.10.00	0.5 cents/kg	A+
Vegetables	Spinach, New Zealand spinach and orache spinach (garden spinach), fresh or chilled	0709.70.00	20%	A+
Vegetables	Spinach, New Zealand spinach and orache spinach (garden spinach), uncooked or cooked by steaming or boiling in water, frozen	0710.30.00	14%	A+
Vegetables	Sweet corn, fresh or chilled	0709.90.45	21.30%	
Vegetables	Sweet corn, uncooked or cooked by steaming or boiling in water, frozen	0710.40.00	14%	A+
Vegetables	Tomatoes, fresh or chilled, entered during July 15 to Aug.31 in any year	0702.00.40	2.8 cents/kg	
Vegetables	Tomatoes, fresh or chilled, entered during Mar.1 to July 14, or the period Sept.1 to Nov.14 in any year	0702.00.20	3.9 cents/kg	
Vegetables	Tomatoes, uncooked or cooked by steaming or boiling in water, frozen, if entered July 15 through August 31, inclusive, in any year	0710.80.45	2.1 cents/kg	A+
Vegetables	Tomatoes, uncooked or cooked by steaming or boiling in water, frozen, if entered Mar. 1 thru July 14, incl. or Sept. 1 thru Nov. 14, incl.	0710.80.40	2.9 cents/kg	
Vegetables	Vegetables nesi, uncooked or cooked by steaming or boiling in water, frozen, reduced in size	0710.80.97	14.90%	A+
Vegetables	Vegetables, nesoi, fresh or chilled	0709.90.90	20%	A+
Vehicles and Parts	Bicycles, n/motor., w/front wheel diam. o/55 cm but n/o 63.5 cm & rear wheel diam. o/63.5 cm in diam., & wt <16.3 kg w/o acces., value $200+	8712.00.44	5.50%	A+
Vehicles and Parts	Bicycles, n/motor., w/front wheel w/diameter different than rear wheel diam., nesoi	8712.00.48	11%	A+
Vehicles and Parts	Bicycles, not motorized, w/both wheels not over 63.5 cm in diameter	8712.00.15	11%	A+
Vehicles and Parts	Bicycles, not motorized, w/both wheels o/63.5 cm in diam., weighing 16.3 kg or more, and/or for use w/tires w/x-sect. diam. o/4.13 cm	8712.00.35	11%	A+
Vehicles and Parts	Bicycles, not motorized, w/both wheels o/63.5 cm in diam., weighing under 16.3 kg & not design. for tires w/x-sect. diam. o/4.13cm	8712.00.25	5.50%	A+
Vehicles and Parts	Bodies (including cabs), for mtr. vehicles (o/than tract. for agri. use) of headings 8701-8705 (except 8703)	8707.90.50	4%	A+

Products Eligible for Duty-Free Treatment Under AGOA if Exported to the U.S. from an AGOA Beneficiary Country

Vehicles and Parts	Bodies (including cabs), for mtr. vehicles for transport of persons of heading 8703	8707.10.00	2.50%	A+
Vehicles and Parts	Chassis fitted w/engines, for mtr. vehicles for transport of goods of 8704.21 or 8704.31	8706.00.03	4%	A+
Vehicles and Parts	Chassis fitted w/engines, for mtr. vehicles for transport of persons of 8703	8706.00.15	2.50%	A+
Vehicles and Parts	Chassis fitted w/engines, for mtr. vehicles of 8701.20, 8702, & 8704 (except 8704.21 or 8704.31)	8706.00.05	4%	A+
Vehicles and Parts	Chassis fitted w/engines, for mtr. vehicles of heading 8705	8706.00.25	1.60%	A+
Vehicles and Parts	Motor vehicles specially designed for traveling on snow	8703.10.10	2.50%	A+
Vehicles and Parts	Mtr cars & o/mtr. vehicles for transport of persons, w/compress-ign. int. combust. recip. piston engine w/cyl. cap. n/o 1500 cc	8703.31.00	2.50%	A+
Vehicles and Parts	Mtr cars & o/mtr. vehicles for transport of persons, w/compress-ign. int. combust. recip. piston engine w/cyl. cap. o/1500 cc n/o 2500 cc	8703.32.00	2.50%	A+
Vehicles and Parts	Mtr cars & o/mtr. vehicles for transport of persons, w/compress-ign. int. combust. recip. piston engine w/cyl. cap. o/2500 cc	8703.33.00	2.50%	A+
Vehicles and Parts	Mtr cars & o/mtr. vehicles for transport of persons, w/spark-ign. int. combust. recip. piston engine w/cyl. cap. n/o 1000 cc	8703.21.00	2.50%	A+
Vehicles and Parts	Mtr cars & o/mtr. vehicles for transport of persons, w/spark-ign. int. combust. recip. piston engine w/cyl. cap. o/ 3000 cc	8703.24.00	2.50%	A+
Vehicles and Parts	Mtr cars & o/mtr. vehicles for transport of persons, w/spark-ign. int. combust. recip. piston engine w/cyl. cap. o/1000 cc n/o 1500 cc	8703.22.00	2.50%	A+
Vehicles and Parts	Mtr cars & o/mtr. vehicles for transport of persons, w/spark-ign. int. combust. recip. piston engine w/cyl. cap. o/1500 cc n/o 3000 cc	8703.23.00	2.50%	A+
Vehicles and Parts	Mtr cars & other motor vehicles for transport of persons, o/than w/spark ign. or compress. ign. recip. piston engine, nesoi	8703.90.00	2.50%	A+
Vehicles and Parts	Mtr. vehicl. for transport of goods (o/than cab chassis), w/compress.-ign. int. combust. recip. piston engine, w/G.V.W. o/5 but n/o 20 mtons	8704.22.50	25%	A+
Vehicles and Parts	Mtr. vehicles for transport of goods, cab chassis, w/compress.-ign. int. combust. recip. piston engine, w/G.V.W. o/5 but n/o 20 metric tons	8704.22.10	4%	A+
Vehicles and Parts	Mtr. vehicles for transport of goods, o/than w/compress. ign. or spark ign. recip. piston engine, nesoi	8704.90.00	25%	A+
Vehicles and Parts	Mtr. vehicles for transport of goods, w/compress.-ign. int. combust. recip. piston engine, w/G.V.W. not over 5 metric tons	8704.21.00	25%	A+
Vehicles and Parts	Mtr. vehicles for transport of goods, w/compress.-ign. int. combust. recip. piston engine, w/G.V.W. over 20 metric tons	8704.23.00	25%	A+
Vehicles and Parts	Mtr. vehicles for transport of goods, w/spark-ign. int. combust. recip. piston engine, w/G.V.W. not over 5 metric tons	8704.31.00	25%	A+
Vehicles and Parts	Mtr. vehicles for transport of goods, w/spark-ign. int. combust. recip. piston engine, w/G.V.W. over 5 metric tons	8704.32.00	25%	A+
Vehicles and Parts	Pts. & access. for bicycles & o/cycles, brakes and parts thereof, nesoi	8714.94.90	10%	A+
Vehicles and Parts	Pts. & access. for bicycles & o/cycles, crank-gear nesoi and parts thereof	8714.96.90	10%	A+
Vehicles and Parts	Pts. & access. for bicycles & o/cycles, frames, valued at $600 or less each	8714.91.30	3.90%	A+
Vehicles and Parts	Pts. & access. for bicycles & o/cycles, non-variable speed hubs, nesoi	8714.93.35	10%	A+
Vehicles and Parts	Pts. & access. for bicycles & o/cycles, pedals and parts thereof	8714.96.10	8%	A+

Products Eligible for Duty-Free Treatment Under AGOA if Exported to the U.S. from an AGOA Beneficiary Country

Vehicles and Parts	Pts. & access. for bicycles & o/cycles, saddles	8714.95.00	8%	A+
Vehicles and Parts	Pts. & access. for bicycles & o/cycles, variable speed hubs, w/internal gear changing mechanisms, nesoi	8714.93.28	3%	A+
Vehicles and Parts	Pts. & access. for bicycles & o/cycles, wheel rims	8714.92.10	5%	A+
Vehicles and Parts	Pts. & access. for bicycles, sets of steel tubing cut to exact length for the assembly (w/other pts) into the frame & fork of one bicycle	8714.91.50	6%	A+
Vehicles and Parts	Pts. & access. nesoi, for bicycles and other cycles of heading 8712	8714.99.80	10%	A+
Vehicles and Parts	Pts. & access. of mtr. vehic. of 8701, nesoi, and 8702-8705, mufflers & exhaust pipes	8708.92.50	2.50%	A+
Vehicles and Parts	Road tractors for semi-trailers	8701.20.00	4%	A+
Watch Parts	Any plate, or set of plates, suitable for assembling thereon a clock movement	9114.40.40	10 cents each	A+
Watch Parts	Assemblies and subassemblies for watch movements consisting of 2 or more pieces or parts fastened or joined inseparably together	9114.90.15	7.20%	A+
Watch Parts	Bezels, backs and centers, of watch cases, not of precious metal or of metal clad with precious metal	9111.90.50	1.6 cents each + 6.8%	A+
Watch Parts	Complete clock movements, unassembled or partly assembled (movement sets)	9110.90.20	The rate applicable to the complete, assembled movement	A+
Watch Parts	Complete watch movements, unassembled or partly assembled (movement sets)	9110.11.00	The rate applicable to the complete, assembled movement	
Watch Parts	Incomplete clock movements consisting of 2 or more pieces or parts fastened or joined together	9110.90.40	4.3% + 1.7 cents/jewel + 0.2 cents for each other piece or part, but if consisting in part of a plate or a set of plates the total duty shall not exceed the duty for the complete movement	A+
Watch Parts	Incomplete clock movements, nesi	9110.90.60	4.20%	A+
Watch Parts	Incomplete watch movements, assembled	9110.12.00	9%	
Watch Parts	Parts of watch cases, of precious metal or of metal clad with precious metal	9111.90.40	6.40%	A+
Watch Parts	Parts of watch cases, other than bezels, backs and centers, not of precious metal or of metal clad with precious metal	9111.90.70	6.40%	A+
Watch Parts	Plates and bridges for watches, nesi	9114.40.60	7.30%	A+
Watch Parts	Rough watch movements	9110.19.00	9%	
Watch Parts	Springs, including hair-springs, for watches	9114.10.40	7.30%	A+

Products Eligible for Duty-Free Treatment Under AGOA if Exported to the U.S. from an AGOA Beneficiary Country

Watch Parts	Watch cases of base metal not gold- or silver-plated	9111.20.40	3.6 cents each + 7.6%	A+
Watch Parts	Watch cases of gold- or silver-plated base metal	9111.20.20	7 cents each + 5.4%	A+
Watch Parts	Watch cases of precious metal or of metal clad with precious metal	9111.10.00	12 cents each + 4.8%	A+
Watch Parts	Watch cases, not of precious metal, of metal clad with precious metal or of base metal	9111.80.00	3.6 cents each + 7.6%	A+
Watch Parts	Watch movement bottom or pillar plates or their equivalent	9114.40.20	12 cents each	A+
Watch Parts	Watch movements, complete and assembled, electrically operated, w/both optoelectronic & mechanical displays, having 0-1 jewels	9108.19.40	28 cents each + 4.2% on the battery	
Watch Parts	Watch movements, complete and assembled, electrically operated, w/both optoelectronic & mechanical displays, having over 1 jewel	9108.19.80	53 cents each + 3.9% on the battery	
Watch Parts	Watch movements, complete and assembled, electrically operated, with mechanical display or device to incorporate such display, 0-1 jewel	9108.11.40	36 cents each + 5.3% on the battery	
Watch Parts	Watch movements, complete and assembled, electrically operated, with mechanical display or device to incorporate such display, over 1 jewel	9108.11.80	72 cents each + 5.3% on the battery	
Watch Parts	Watch movements, complete and assembled, electrically operated, with opto-electronic display only	9108.12.00	3.1% on the movement + 4.2% on the battery	
Watch Parts	Watch movements, complete and assembled, nesi, measuring 33.8 mm or less, 0-1 jewel	9108.91.10	29 cents each	
Watch Parts	Watch movements, complete and assembled, nesi, measuring 33.8 mm or less, 2-7 jewels	9108.91.20	57 cents each	
Watch Parts	Watch movements, complete and assembled, nesi, measuring 33.8 mm or less, 8-17 jewels, valued over $15 each	9108.91.50	90 cents each	
Watch Parts	Watch movements, complete and assembled, nesi, measuring 33.8 mm or less, over 17 jewels	9108.91.60	$1.50 each	
Watch Parts	Watch movements, complete and assembled, nesi, measuring not over 15.2 mm, 8-17 jewels, valued not over $15 each	9108.91.30	$2.16 each	
Watch Parts	Watch movements, complete and assembled, nesi, measuring over 15.2 mm but not over 33.8 mm, 8-17 jewels, valued not over $15 each	9108.91.40	$1.80 each	
Watch Parts	Watch movements, complete and assembled, nesi, measuring over 33.8 mm, 0-7 jewels	9108.99.20	25 cents each	
Watch Parts	Watch movements, complete and assembled, nesi, measuring over 33.8 mm, 8-17 jewels, valued not over $15 each	9108.99.40	$1.44 each	
Watch Parts	Watch movements, complete and assembled, nesi, measuring over 33.8 mm, over 17 jewels	9108.99.80	$1.72 each	
Watch Parts	Watch parts, nesi	9114.90.40	8.80%	A+
Watch Parts	Watch straps, watch bands and watch bracelets of base metal, whether or not gold- or silver-plated, valued over $5 per dozen	9113.20.40	11.20%	
Watches	Straps/bands/bracelets of tex. mat. or base metal, whether or not gold- or silver-plated entered with wrist watches of subheading 9101.21.50	9101.21.10	3.10%	

Products Eligible for Duty-Free Treatment Under AGOA if Exported to the U.S. from an AGOA Beneficiary Country

Watches	Straps/bands/bracelets of tex. mat. or base metal, whether or not gold- or silver-plated entered with wrist watches of subheading 9101.29.90	9101.29.70	3.10%	
Watches	Straps/bands/bracelets of tex. mat. or base metal, whether or not gold- or silver-plated entered with wrist watches of subheading 9102.29.04	9102.29.02	14%	
Watches	Watches (excl. wrist watches) nesoi, electrically operated, with 0-1 jewel in the movement	9102.91.40	40 cents each + 6% on the case + 5.3% on the battery	
Watches	Watches (excl. wrist watches) nesoi, electrically operated, with over 1 jewel in the movement	9102.91.80	76 cents each + 6% on the case + 5.3% on the battery	
Watches	Wrist watches nesi, automatic winding, 0-1 jewel, watch band not of textile material or base metal	9102.21.25	75 cents each + 6% on the case + 2.8% on the strap, band or bracelet	
Watches	Wrist watches nesi, automatic winding, 0-1 jewel, watch band of textile material or base metal	9102.21.10	75 cents each + 6% on the case + 14% on the strap, band or bracelet	
Watches	Wrist watches nesi, automatic winding, 2-17 jewels, watch band not of textile material or base metal	9102.21.50	$1.75 each + 4.8% on the case + 2.2% on the strap, band or bracelet	
Watches	Wrist watches nesi, automatic winding, 2-17 jewels, watch band of textile material or base metal	9102.21.30	$1.75 each + 4.8% on the case + 11.2% on the strap, band or bracelet	
Watches	Wrist watches nesi, automatic winding, over 17 jewels, watch band not of textile material or base metal	9102.21.90	$1.53 each + 4.2% on the case + 2% on the strap, band or bracelet	
Watches	Wrist watches nesi, automatic winding, over 17 jewels, watch band of textile material or base metal	9102.21.70	$1.53 each + 4.2% on the case + 9.8% on the strap, band or bracelet	

Products Eligible for Duty-Free Treatment Under AGOA if Exported to the U.S. from an AGOA Beneficiary Country

Watches	Wrist watches nesoi, electrically operated, mechanical display only, 0-1 jewel, case nesoi, with band of material nesoi	9102.11.45	40 cents each + 8.5% on the case + 2.8% on the strap, band or bracelet + 5.3% on the battery	
Watches	Wrist watches nesoi, electrically operated, mechanical display only, 0-1 jewel, case nesoi, with band of textile material or base metal	9102.11.25	40 cents each + 8.5% on the case + 14% on the strap, band or bracelet + 5.3% on the battery	
Watches	Wrist watches nesoi, electrically operated, mechanical display only, 0-1 jewel, gold- or silver-plated case, with band of material nesoi	9102.11.30	44 cents each + 6% on the case + 2.8% on the strap, band or bracelet + 5.3% on the battery	
Watches	Wrist watches nesoi, electrically operated, mechanical display only, 0-1 jewel, gold/silver-plated case, band of textile mat. or base metal	9102.11.10	44 cents each + 6% on the case + 14% on the strap, band or bracelet + 5.3% on the battery	
Watches	Wrist watches nesoi, electrically operated, mechanical display only, over 1 jewel, case nesoi, with band of material nesoi	9102.11.95	76 cents each + 8.5% on the case + 2.8% on the strap, band or bracelet + 5.3% on the battery	
Watches	Wrist watches nesoi, electrically operated, mechanical display only, over 1 jewel, case nesoi, with band of textile material or base metal	9102.11.65	76 cents each + 8.5% on the case + 14% on the strap, band or bracelet + 5.3% on the battery	
Watches	Wrist watches nesoi, electrically operated, mechanical display only, over 1 jewel, gold- or silver-case, with band of material nesoi	9102.11.70	80 cents each + 6% on the case + 2.8% on the strap, band or bracelet + 5.3% on the battery	

Products Eligible for Duty-Free Treatment Under AGOA if Exported to the U.S. from an AGOA Beneficiary Country

Watches	Wrist watches nesoi, electrically operated, mechanical display only, over 1 jewel, gold/silver-plated case, band of textile or base metal	9102.11.50	80 cents each + 6% on the case + 14% on the strap, band or bracelet + 5.3% on the battery	
Watches	Wrist watches nesoi, electrically operated, w/both optoelectronic & mechanical displays, 0-1 jewel, band of material nesoi	9102.19.40	32 cents each + 4.8% on the case + 2.2% on the strap, band or bracelet + 4.2% on the battery	
Watches	Wrist watches nesoi, electrically operated, w/both optoelectronic & mechanical displays, 0-1 jewel, band of textile material or base metal	9102.19.20	32 cents each + 4.8% on the case + 11% on the strap, band or bracelet + 4.2% on the battery	
Watches	Wrist watches nesoi, electrically operated, w/both optoelectronic & mechanical displays, over 1 jewel, band of material nesoi	9102.19.80	57 cents each + 4.5% on the case + 2.1% on the strap, band or bracelet + 4% on the battery	
Watches	Wrist watches nesoi, electrically operated, w/both optoelectronic & mechanical displays, over 1 jewel, band of textile mat. or base metal	9102.19.60	57 cents each + 4.5% on the case + 10.6% on the strap, band or bracelet + 4% on the battery	
Watches	Wrist watches nesoi, not electrically operated, n/autowind, 8-17 jewels, mvmt n/o $15 & n/o 15.2 mm, band of textile material or base metal	9102.29.25	$2.19 each + 4.8% on the case + 11.2% on the strap, band or bracelet	
Watches	Wrist watches nesoi, not electrically operated, n/autowinding, 8-17 jewel, mvmt n/o $15 & ov 15.2 mm, band of textile material or base metal	9102.29.35	$1.61 each + 4.2% on the case + 9.8% on the strap, band or bracelet	

Products Eligible for Duty-Free Treatment Under AGOA if Exported to the U.S. from an AGOA Beneficiary Country

Watches	Wrist watches nesoi, not electrically operated, n/autowinding, 8-17 jewel, mvmt n/o $15 & over 15.2 mm, with band of material nesoi	9102.29.40	$1.83 each + 4.8% on the case + 2.2% on the strap, band or bracelet	
Watches	Wrist watches nesoi, not electrically operated, not auto winding, 8-17 jewels, movement over $15 each, with band of textiles or base metal	9102.29.45	93 cents each + 4.8% on the case + 11.2% on the strap, band or bracelet	
Watches	Wrist watches nesoi, not electrically operated, not auto winding, 8-17 jewels, mvmt over $15 each, with band of material nesoi	9102.29.50	93 cents each + 4.8% on the case + 2.2% on the strap, band or bracelet	
Watches	Wrist watches nesoi, not electrically operated, not automatic winding, 2-7 jewels, with strap/band of textile material or base metal	9102.29.15	58 cents each + 4.6% on the case + 10.6% on the strap, band or bracelet	
Watches	Wrist watches nesoi, not electrically operated, not automatic winding, 2-7 jewels, with strap/band/bracelet of material nesoi	9102.29.20	56 cents each + 4 4% on the case + 2% on the strap, band or bracelet	
Watches	Wrist watches nesoi, not electrically operated, not automatic winding, 8-17 jewels, movement n/o $15 & n/o 15.2 mm, band of material nesoi	9102.29.30	$2.19 each + 4.8% on the case + 2.2% on the strap, band or bracelet	
Watches	Wrist watches nesoi, not electrically operated, not automatic winding, over 17 jewels in the movement, with band of material nesoi	9102.29.60	$1.75 each + 4.8% on the case + 2.2% on the strap, band or bracelet	
Watches	Wrist watches nesoi, not electrically operated, not automatic winding, over 17 jewels in the mvmt, with band of textiles or base metal	9102.29.55	$1.55 each + 4.2% on the case + 9.9% on the strap, band or bracelet	

Products Eligible for Duty-Free Treatment Under AGOA if Exported to the U.S. from an AGOA Beneficiary Country

Watches	Wrist watches with cases of or clad with precious metal, electrically operated, w/both opto-electronic & mechanical displays, over 1 jewel	9101.19.80	61 cents each + 4.4% on case and strap, band or bracelet + 3.7% on the battery	
Watches	Wrist watches with cases of or clad with precious metal, electrically operated, with both opto-electronic and mechanical displays, 0-1 jewel	9101.19.40	41 cents each + 5% on the case and strap, band bracelet + 4.2% on battery	
Watches	Wrist watches with cases of or clad with precious metal, electrically operated, with mechanical display only, w/more than 1 jewel in mvmt	9101.11.80	87 cents each + 6.25% on the case and strap, band or bracelet + 5.3% on the battery	
Watches	Wrist watches with cases of or clad with precious metal, electrically operated, with mechanical display only, with 0-1 jewel in mvmt	9101.11.40	51 cents each + 6.25% on the case and strap, band or bracelet + 5.3% on the battery	
Watches	Wrist watches with cases of or clad with precious metal, not electrically operated, n/auto winding, 8-17 jewels, mvmt n/o $15 & n/o 15.2 mm	9101.29.30	$2.28 each + 5% on the case and strap, band or bracelet	
Watches	Wrist watches with cases of or clad with precious metal, not electrically operated, n/auto winding, 8-17 jewels, mvmt n/o $15 & ov 15.2 mm	9101.29.40	$1.92 each + 5% on the case and strap, band or bracelet	
Watches	Wrist watches with cases of or clad with precious metal, not electrically operated, not automatic winding, 8-17 jewels, movement over $15	9101.29.50	90 cents each + 4.4% on the case and strap, band or bracelet	
Watches	Wrist watches with cases of or clad with precious metal, not electrically operated, not automatic winding, with 0-1 jewel in mvmt	9101.29.10	40 cents each + 5% on the case and strap, band or bracelet	
Watches	Wrist watches with cases of or clad with precious metal, not electrically operated, not automatic winding, with 2-7 jewels in mvmt	9101.29.20	61 cents each + 4.4% on the case and strap, band or bracelet	

Products Eligible for Duty-Free Treatment Under AGOA if Exported to the U.S. from an AGOA Beneficiary Country

Watches	Wrist watches with cases of or clad with precious metal, not electrically operated, with automatic winding, w/17 jewels or less in mvmt	9101.21.80	$1.61 each + 4.4% on the case and strap, band or bracelet	
Wines	Effervescent grape wine, in containers holding 2 liters or less	2204.21.20	19.8 cents/liter	A+
Wines	Grape must, nesi, in fermentation or with fermentation arrested otherwise than by addition of alcohol	2204.30.00	4.4 cents/liter + + 31.4 cents/pf. Liter	A+
Wines	Grape wine, other than sparkling, not over 14% vol. alcohol, in containers holding over 2 but not over 4 liters	2204.29.20	8.4 cents/liter	A+
Wines	Grape wine, other than sparkling, not over 14% vol. alcohol, in containers holding over 4 liters	2204.29.60	14 cents/liter	A+
Wines	Grape wine, other than sparkling, over 14% vol. alcohol, in containers holding over 2 but not over 4 liters	2204.29.40	22.4 cents/liter	A+
Wines	Grape wine, other than sparkling, over 14% vol. alcohol, in containers holding over 4 liters	2204.29.80	22.4 cents/liter	A+
Wines	Wine other than Tokay (not carbonated), not over 14% alcohol, in containers not over 2 liters	2204.21.50	6.3 cents/liter	A+
Wood and Articles of Wood	Clothespins made of wood, other than the spring-type	4421.90.85	4.80%	A+
Wood and Articles of Wood	Coniferous wood dowel rods, continuously shaped along any of its edges or faces, sanded, grooved or otherwise advanced in condition	4409.10.65	4.90%	A+
Wood and Articles of Wood	Nonconiferous wood dowel rods, continuously shaped along any of its edges or faces, sanded, grooved or otherwise advanced in condition	4409.20.65	4.90%	A+
Wood and Articles of Wood	Plywood of wood sheets, n/o 6 mm thick each, with outer plies of coniferous wood, nesi, surface covered, nesi	4412.19.50	5.10%	A+
Wood and Articles of Wood	Spring-type clothespins made of wood	4421.90.80	6.5 cents/gross	A+
Wood and Articles of Wood	Wood blinds, shutters, screens and shades, not consisting of wooden frames in the center of which are fixed louver boards or slats	4421.90.40	5.10%	A+
Wood and Articles of Wood	Wood dowel pins, sanded, grooved or otherwise advanced in condition	4421.90.20	4.90%	A+
Wood and Articles of Wood	Wood wool (excelsior); wood flour	4405.00.00	3.20%	A+
Wood and Articles of Wood	Wooden clothes hangers	4421.10.00	3.20%	A+
Zinc and Zinc Articles	Zinc (o/than alloy), unwrought, casting-grade zinc, containing at least 97.5% but less than 99.99% by weight of zinc	7901.12.10	3%	A+

Annex 3

List of Fabrics Currently Deemed to Be in Short Supply in the U.S.

Short Supply Fabrics

Apparel goods of Chapter 62 may use the following fabrics for the outer shell of the apparel, provided the outer shell, exclusive of collars or cuffs, is wholly of one or more of the following:

(A) Velveteen fabrics of subheading 5801.23, containing 85 per cent or more by weight of cotton;

(B) Corduroy fabrics of subheading 5801.22, containing 85 per cent or more weight of cotton and containing more than 7.5 wales per centimeter;

(C) Fabrics of subheadings 5111.11 or 5111.19, if hand-woven, with a loom width of less than 76 cm, woven in the United Kingdom in accordance with the rules and regulations of the Harris Tweed Association, Ltd., and so certified by the Association;

(D) Fabrics of subheading 5112.30, weighing not more than 340 grams per square meter, containing wool, not less than 20 per cent by weight of fine animal hair and not less than 15 per cent by weight of man-made staple fibers; or

(E) Batiste fabrics of subheadings 5513.11 or 5513.21, of square construction, of single yarns exceeding 76 metric count, containing between 60 and 70 warp ends and filling picks per square centimeter, of a weight not exceeding 110 grams per square meter.

Men's or boys' shirts of cotton (subheading 6205.20) or of man-made fibers (subheading 6205.30) may use the following fabrics for the outer shell of the shirts, exclusive of collars or cuffs, provided the outer shell is wholly of one or more of the following:

(a) Fabrics of subheadings 5208.21, 5208.22, 5208.29, 5208.31, 5208.32, 5208.39, 5208.41, 5208.42, 5208.49, 5208.51, 5208.52 or 5208.59, of average yarn number exceeding 135 metric;

(b) Fabrics of subheadings 5513.11 or 5513.21, not of square construction, containing more than 70 warp ends and filling picks per square centimeter, of average yarn number exceeding 70 metric;
(c) Fabrics of subheadings 5210.21 or 5210.31, not of square construction, containing more than 70 warp ends and filling picks per square centimeter, of average yarn number exceeding 70 metric;
(d) Fabrics of subheadings 5208.22 or 5208.32, not of square construction, containing more than 75 warp ends and filling picks per square centimeter, of average yarn number exceeding 65 metric;
(e) Fabrics of subheadings 5407.81, 5407.82 or 5407.83, weighing less than 170 grams per square meter, having a dobby weave created by a dobby attachment;
(f) Fabrics of subheadings 5208.42 or 5208.49, not of square construction, containing more than 85 warp ends and filling picks per square centimeter, of average yarn number exceeding 85 metric;
(g) Fabrics of subheading 5208.51, of square construction, containing more than 75 warp ends and filling picks per square centimeter, made with single yarns, of average yarn number 95 or greater metric;
(h) Fabrics of subheading 5208.41, of square construction, with a gingham pattern, containing more than 85 warp ends and filling picks per square centimeter, made with single yarns, of average yarn number 95 or greater metric, and characterized by a check effect produced by the variation in color of the yarns in the warp and filling; or
(i) Fabrics of subheading 5208.41, with the warp colored with vegetable dyes, and the filling yarns white or colored with vegetable dyes, of average yarn number greater than 65 metric.

Men's and boys' nightshirts and pajamas, and women's and girls' briefs, panties, nightdresses and pajamas (exclusive of collar, cuffs, waistband or elastic or lace, respectively), wholly of circular knit fabric, wholly of cotton yarns exceeding 100 metric number per single yarn

For all apparel, the following may be used:

Woven silk fabric
Silk yarn
Woven linen fabric
Flax yarn
Quilted textile products in the piece of heading 5811.00, HTSUS

Annex 4

AFRICAN GROWTH AND OPPORTUNITY ACT TEXTILE CERTIFICATE OF ORIGIN

The following is the African Growth and Opportunity Act Textile Certificate of Origin. An exporter of apparel/textiles wishing to obtain the preferential treatment available under AGOA (i.e. duty-free treatment) for specific apparel/textile products must complete the Certificate and provide it to the importer, which is importing the apparel/textiles to the United States. The Certificate must be available to U.S. Customs on request but does not accompany the actual shipment.

1. Exporter Name & Address		2. Producer Name & Address
3. Importer Name & Address		6. U.S./ African Fabric Producer Name & Address
4. Description of Article	5. preference group	7. U.S./ African Yarn Producer Name & Address
		8. U.S. Thread Producer Name & Address
		9.Name of handloomed, handmade or folklore Article
10. Name of Preference Group H Fabric or Yarn:		

Preference Groups:

A: Apparel assembled from U.S.-formed and cut fabric from U.S. yarn. [19 CFR 10.213(a)(1)]

B: Apparel assembled and further processed from U.S.-formed and cut fabric from U.S. yarn. [19 CFR 10.213(a)(2)]

C: Apparel cut and assembled from U.S. fabric from U.S. yarn and thread. [19 CFR 10.2 13(a)(3)]

D: Apparel assembled from regional fabric from yarn originating in the U.S. or one or more beneficiary countries. [19 CFR 10.213(a)(4)]

E: Apparel assembled in one or more lesser developed beneficiary countries. [19 CFR 10.2 13(a)(5)].

F: Sweaters knit to shape in chief weight of cashmere. [19 CFR 10.21 3(a)(6)]

G: Sweaters knit to shape with 50 percent or more by weight of fine wool. [19 CFR 10.21 3(a)(7)]

H: Apparel cut and assembled in one or more beneficiary countries from fabrics or yarn not formed in the United States or beneficiary country (as identified in NAFTA) or as designated not available in commercial quantities in the United States. [19 CFR 10.2 13(a)(8) or (a)(9)]

I: Handloomed, handmade or folklore articles.[19 CFR 10.213(a)(10)]

I certify that the information on this document is complete and accurate and I assume the responsibility for proving such representations. I understand that I am liable for any false statements or material omissions made on or in connection with this document.

I agree to maintain and present upon request, documentation necessary to support this certificate.

1 2.Authorized Signature		13. Company
14. Name (Print or Type)		15. Title
16a.Date(DD/MM/YY)	16b.Blanket Period From:	17. Telephone Number Facsimile Number

<u>Preparation of Certificate.</u> The following rules will apply for purposes of completing the Certificate of Origin:

(1) Blocks 1 through 5 pertain only to the final article exported to the United States for which preferential treatment may be claimed;

(2) Block 1 should state the legal name and address (including country) of the exporter;

(3) Block 2 should state the legal name and address (including country) of the producer. If there is more than one producer, attach a list stating the legal name and address (including country) of all additional producers. If this information is confidential, it is acceptable to state "available to Customs upon request" in block 2. If the producer and the exporter are the same, state "same" in block 2;

(4) Block 3 should state the legal name and address (including country) of the importer;

(5) Block 4 should provide a full description of each article. The description should be sufficient to relate it to the invoice description and to the description of the article in the international Harmonized System. Include the invoice number as shown on the commercial invoice or, if the invoice number is not known, include another unique reference number such as the shipping order number;

(6) In block 5, insert the letter that designates the preference group which applies to the article according to the description contained in the CFR provision cited on the Certificate for that group;

(7) Blocks 6 through 10 must be completed only when the block in question calls for information that is relevant to the preference group identified in block 5;

(8) Block 6 should state the legal name and address (including country) of the fabric producer;

(9) Block 7 should state the legal name and address (including country) of the yarn producer;

(10) Block 8 should state the legal name and address (including country) of the thread producer;

(11) Block 9 should state the name of the folklore article or should state that the article is handloomed or handmade;

(12) Block 10, which should be completed only when preference group "H" is inserted in block 5, should state the name of the fabric or yarn that is not formed in the United States or a beneficiary country or that is not available in commercial quantities in the United States;

(13) Block 16a should reflect the date on which the Certificate was completed and signed;

(14) Block 16b should be completed if the Certificate is intended to cover multiple shipments of identical articles as described in block 4 that are imported into the United States during a specified period of up to one year (see § 10.2 16(b)(4)(ii)). The "from" date is the date on which the Certificate became applicable to the article covered by the blanket Certificate (this date may be prior to the date reflected in block 16a). The "to" date is the date on which the blanket period expires; and

(15) The Certificate may be printed and reproduced locally. If more space is needed to complete the Certificate, attach a continuation sheet.

INDEX

I

J

K

L

M

N

O

P

Q

R

S

T

U

V

W

Y

Z